# HUSSERL'S "INTRODUCTIONS TO PHENOMENOLOGY"

# PHAENOMENOLOGICA

89

WILLIAM R. McKENNA

# HUSSERL'S "INTRODUCTIONS TO PHENOMENOLOGY "

*Interpretation and Critique*

WILLIAM R. McKENNA

HUSSERL'S "INTRODUCTIONS
TO PHENOMENOLOGY"
*Interpretation and Critique*

1982

MARTINUS NIJHOFF PUBLISHERS
THE HAGUE/BOSTON/LONDON

IV

*Distributors:*

*for the United States and Canada*

Kluwer Boston, Inc.
190 Old Derby Street
Hingham, MA 02043
USA

*for all other countries*

Kluwer Academic Publishers Group
Distribution Center
P.O. Box 322
3300 AH Dordrecht
The Netherlands

**Library of Congress Cataloging in Publication Data**

B
3279
.H94
M34
1983

ISBN 90-247-2665-4 (this volume)
ISBN 90-247-2339-6 (series)

PRINTED IN THE NETHERLANDS

# CONTENTS

# ACKNOWLEDGEMENTS

For the inspiration and knowledge which made it possible for me to begin this work, I owe my gratitude to my great teacher Aron Gurwitsch.

To Wendy McKenna goes my deepest appreciation for helping me with the language of this text and for the sustaining faith and encouragement which allowed me to complete this project.

I am most grateful to Richard Zaner and J.N. Mohanty for their support and for their helpful suggestions concerning the content of this work.

Finally, I thank The Graduate Faculty of Political and Social Science, of the New School for Social Research, where an earlier version of this work was submitted as my doctoral dissertation, for making available to me a faculty of truly remarkable philosophers whose teaching and writing presented a model of scholarship I must continually strive to emulate.

# ABBREVIATIONS

The following abbreviations of some of Husserl's works are used in the notes and, in some cases, also in the text. For the full references, see the bibliography.

| | |
|---|---|
| *APS* | *Analysen zur passiven Synthesis.* |
| *CM* | *Cartesian Meditations.* |
| *Crisis* | *The Crisis of European Sciences and Transcendental Phenomenology.* |
| *EJ* | *Experience and Judgment.* |
| *EP* II | *Erste Philosophie,* second part. |
| *FTL* | *Formal and Transcendental Logic.* |
| *Ideas* | *Ideas: A General Introduction to Pure Phenomenology.* |
| *Ideen* I | *Ideen zu einer reinen Phänomenologie und phänomenologischen Philosophie,* first book, Biemel edition (unless otherwise specified). |
| *Ideen II* | *Ideen zu einer reinen Phänomenologie und phänomenologischen Philosophie.* |
| *IP* | *The Idea of Phenomenology.* |
| *Krisis* | *Die Krisis der europäischen Wissenschaften und die transzendentale Phänomenologie.* |
| *LI* | *Logical Investigations* |
| *LU* | *Logische Untersuchungen.* |
| *PBE* | *Phantasie, Bildbewusstsein, Erinnerung: zur Phänomenologie der anschaulichen Vergegenwärtigungen.* |
| *PITC* | *The Phenomenology of Internal Time-Consciousness.* |
| *PP* | *Phänomenologische Psychologie.* |
| *ZB* | *Zur Phänomenologie des innern Zeitbewusstseins.* |

# 1. INTRODUCTION

There is a remarkable unity to the work of Edmund Husserl, but there are also many difficulties in it. The unity is the result of a single personal and philosophical quest working itself out in concrete phenomenological analyses; the difficulties are due to the inadequacy of initial conceptions which becomes felt as those analyses become progressively deeper and more extensive.[1] Anyone who has followed the course of Husserl's work is struck by the constant reemergence of the same problems and by the insightfulness of the inquiries which press toward their solution. However one also becomes aware of Husserl's own dissatisfaction with his work, once so movingly expressed in a personal note.[2] It is the purpose of the present work to examine and revive one of the issues which gave Husserl difficulty, namely, the problem of an introduction to phenomenology.

Several of Husserl's writings published after *Logical Investigations* were either subtitled or referred to by him as "introductions to phenomenology."[3] These works serve to acquaint the reader with the specific character of Husserl's transcendental phenomenology and with the problems to which it is to provide the solution. They include discussions and analyses which pertain to what has come to be known as "ways" into transcendental phenomenology.[4] The issue here is the proper access to transcendental phenomenology. This problem occupied Husserl a great deal, not only because of the misunderstandings of his work which the earliest of these "introductions," *Ideas,* occasioned in the philosophical community, but also, and more importantly, because of his effort to achieve clarity for himself and overcome his own naiveté with respect to some of the central concepts and methods of his philosophy.

The discussions of the "ways" into transcendental phenomenology both by Husserl and by his commentators tend to emphasize the differences between the "introductions." This approach, although valid and important, tends to overlook a line of thought which runs through all these "introductions" and which makes them in a certain respect similar and complementary. I wish to draw attention to this line of thought, because I believe there is a difficulty in it which seems not to have been commented upon in the literature on Husserl's philosophy, but which has serious consequences for the success of his "introductions," particularly for the way in which some of the central concepts and methods that are "introduced" in them are to be understood. In order to expose this line of thought I will construct one introduction to transcendental phenomenology from the many Husserl has left us, supplementing this material with material from some of his other writings, and with some thoughts of my own. The intention is to form a composite which, from a certain perspective, is more logically complete than any one of Husserl's "introductions." No claims will be made that this "one" introduction is what Husserl should have written. Rather, it is put forth as an interpretation which allows us to see the unity of Husserl's thought from a certain point of view.

The construction of the "one" introduction will be based on what I will call the "schema" of Husserl's "introductions." This schema has three main parts: 1) the motivating problem, 2) the acquisition of the idea of pure transcendental consciousness, and 3) the entry into the transcendental realm. These parts, as well as some of their subdivisions, correspond to certain continuous sections of Husserl's "introductions," and thus it can be said that they articulate a plan which, in one respect at least, underlies them. This is not to say that it is the plan upon which *each* of the "introductions" is based; rather, it is an ordering of themes which can be discerned in them when they are taken together. The schema, then, like the "one" introduction which it outlines, is an interpretive device; it gives structure to a line of thought which runs *through* Husserl's "introductions."

My construction of the "one" introduction to transcendental phenomenology aims to show how Husserl develops and responds to what I take to be the dominent concern of his transcendental phenomenology, the question of how knowledge of the world, or, as he often expresses it, of "transcendent objects" is possible. Husserl attempts to answer this question with the theory that consciousness "constitutes" the world. Each of his "introductions to phenomenology" begins with a discussion which serves to generate the problem for which turning to consciousness as world-constitutive is indicated as the solution. The elaboration of the first part of the schema of Husserl's "introductions," in Chapter 3 below, shows how the different "introductions" contribute to the development of this "motivating problem."

The title of the second part of the schema is derived from a way in which Husserl characterizes what corresponds to this part in *Ideas*.[5] The issue here, to be dealt with in Chapter 4, is the transition from the "natural attitude" to the "transcendental attitude," i.e., the passage from our usual way of regarding ourselves and the world to the radically new standpoint required for the ultimate clarification and treatment of the problems which have motivated the turn to subjectivity. In the portions of his texts which correspond to this part of the schema, Husserl puts forth the thesis that consciousness constitutes the world and explains in a general way what that means. This aspect of Husserl's "introductions" will be examined most extensively, for it is here that he advances what I will call a "general argument" to prove that consciousness is world-constitutive and it is this argument which is of central concern to me.

The first and second parts of the schema are pre-transcendental, i.e., the discussions and analyses in them, although phenomenological, are not transcendental; rather, they are intended to prepare the way for and to justify the specifically transcendental phenomenological methods. As such, they are not intended to presuppose these methods or any result obtained by using them. The third part of the schema concerns the transcendental methods. In the sections of Husserl's "introductions" which correspond to this part, Husserl explains these methods and presents some of the results he has obtained from using them, sometimes also including the concrete analyses which produced the results. The methods are the transcendental phenomenological "reduction" and "epoche," and the method of "constitutive intentional analysis." My discussion of these methods in Chapter 5 will show that, as Husserl presents them, they derive a significant part of their meaning from the presupposition that his "general argument" that consiousness is world-constitutive is successful and, in the case of the latter two methods, from a thesis which constitutes one of the premises of the argument which I shall call the "coherence-thesis."

The coherence-thesis is asserted by Husserl in many places in his writings. It states that our perceptual consciousness of any worldly object contains a belief in the object's "actuality," a belief which is motivated and sustained by the harmoniousness of the course of our perceptual experience of the object. In principle, however, this harmoniousness could break down, with the consequence that the belief would be cancelled and the object would be revealed to have been an illusion. I will show that the kind of illusion which Husserl has in mind when he presents the coherence-thesis as part of his argument that consciousness is world-constitutive is what he calls "transcendental illusion." My discussion of the argument will show that its success depends upon the soundness of the coherence-thesis, which in turn rests on a successful demonstration of the existence of the possibility of transcendental illusion.

Chapter 6 will be devoted to a discussion of transcendental illusion. I will present an interpretation of what Husserl means by "transcendental illusion" which shows how it is a fundamentally different kind of illusion than "empirical illusion," the latter being the type of illusion with which we are familiar. This interpretation will define the nature of the "belief" in the "actuality" of worldly objects and of the world in general in a way which, it seems to me, has not been done before in the literature on Husserl's philosophy. In this respect my discussion of Husserl's concept of transcendental illusion will serve to lift it from the marginal status which it usually enjoys in discussions of Husserl's phenomenology to the place of central importance which I think it deserves. It is often taken for granted that our consciousness does contain the "belief" which Husserl says it does, and that a suspension of this belief, for the purpose of philosophical analysis, through the method of the epoche, is possible. I will claim that the existence of this belief, once its nature is understood, is not at all obvious, but needs to be shown, and that to show it is to demonstrate the existence of the possibility of transcendental illusion. Husserl's attempt to demonstrate the existence of the possibility of transcendental illusion will be presented, interpreted, and critically discussed in Chapter 6. The interpretation employs an understanding of "possibility" as "imaginability" which I develop in a parallel discussion of the possibility of empirical illusion in Chapter 4. The critical examination of Husserl's demonstration will show it to be inconclusive.

In Chapter 7, the implications of the inconclusiveness of Husserl's demonstration of the existence of the possibility of transcendental illusion are drawn. In particular, both the thesis that consciousness is world-constitutive and the coherence-thesis will emerge as items yet to be demonstrated. This demonstration, I will claim, is the task of transcendental phenomenology itself. In accordance with this, the concepts and methods which received much of their sense from the presupposition that those two theses were established will be reinterpreted as components which structure the task of what I will call the "concrete" demonstration that consciousness constitutes the world.

The interpretation and critique of Husserl's "introductions to phenomenology" offered here centers on the thesis that consciousness "constitutes" the world. The overall intention is not to question the validity of this thesis, but to examine the motive for putting it forth and the manner in which it is to be proved. The effect which this work is meant to have is to revive interest in the problem of an "introduction to phenomenology," not only as a scholarly interest in the nature of the difficulty which it posed for Husserl, but as a vital issue for the present-day practice of phenomenology. We will begin by clarifying the meaning of Husserl's thesis and the idea of its demonstration.

NOTES

1.  See Edmund Husserl, *The Crisis of European Sciences and Transcendental Phenomenology: An Introduction to Phenomenological Philosophy,* trans. David Carr (Evanston: North-

western University Press, 1970), p. 181 (hereafter cited as *Crisis*). See also Edmund Husserl, *Ideas: A General Introduction to Pure Phenomenology,* trans. W.R. Boyce Gibson (London: George Allen & Unwin, 1931), section 84, p. 244 (hereafter cited as *Ideas*).

2. "Nur eins erfüllt mich: ich muss Klarheit gewinnen, ich kann sonst nicht leben, ich kann nicht das Leben ertragen, wenn ich nicht glauben kann, dass ich es erringe, dass ich ins gelobte Land wirklich und selbst und mit klaren Augen hineinschauen kann" (Edmund Husserl, "Persönliche Aufzeichningen," ed. Walter Biemel, *Philosophy and Phenomenological Research* XVI [1956]: 297).

3. *Ideas* and *Crisis* are subtitled "introductions," as is *Cartesian Meditations: An Introduction ot Phenomenology,* trans. Dorion Cairns (The Hague: Martinus Nijhoff, 1960) (hereafter cited as *CM*). The work referred to by Husserl as an "introduction" is *Formal and Transcendental Logic,* trans. Dorion Cairns (The Hague: Martinus Nijhoff, 1969) (hereafter cited as *FTL*). See Carr's introduction to *Crisis,* p. xv, n.l.

4. For discussions of these "ways," see the editor's introduction to Husserl's *Erste Philosophie,* second part, *Husserliana* VIII, ed. Rudolf Boehm (The Hague: Martinus Nijhoff, 1959) (hereafter cited as *EP* II); the "Preface" of *Ideas,* p. 17; Iso Kern, *Husserl und Kant* (The Hague: Martinus Nijhoff, 1964), pp. 195-239; R. Elveton, ed., The *Phenomenology of Husserl* (Chicago: Quadrangle Books, 1970), editor's "Introduction."

5. See *Ideas*, section 55, pp. 169-70.

## 2. HUSSERL'S THESIS THAT CONSCIOUSNESS IS WORLD-CONSTITUTIVE AND ITS DEMONSTRATION

### A. HUSSERL'S THESIS

The thesis that consciousness constitutes the world is the thesis that the being there *(Dasein)* for us of the world and of anything that is in it is an achievement *(Leistung)* of consciousness. This thesis is not the seemingly obvious one that I must "be conscious," that is, be awake, for the world to be given to me.[1] Such a thesis would consider consciousness to be a state or condition which I must be in so that what is there all along and on its own can become manifest *to me*. Becoming conscious in this sense is like experiencing the lighting of a dark room, and like the phenomenon of light, consciousness can be thought to be a transparent and homogeneous medium which allows the existence as well as the true structures and qualities of objects to be revealed to me — but precisely by being itself unstructured and without qualities.

In contrast to this, the thesis to be discussed here holds that this very being there of the world "all along" and "on its own" is an achievement of consciousness, and that the world cannot exist for me in its multiplicity and with the structures and qualities it has except through a consciousness at least as articulated and as possessed of qualities as the world. This does not mean that the structures and qualities of consciousness and of the world are of the same sort, but just that there is a certain correlation between consciousness and world such that there is no moment on the side of the world for which there is not a moment on the side of consciousness which corresponds to its (the world's) particularity.[2] Thus if the object before me is a pair of scissors, there are *particular* processes of consciousness at play whose achievement is to present that thing *as scissors*.[3] The presence before me of *scissors* is due to an experience *(Erlebnis)* now going on in my mental life which has particular features different from the features it would have if the object in question were a pencil.

Likewise, this object's being actually before me points to another feature of this experience, its intuitive character, which of course it would share with the experience of a pencil actually before me. The presence to me of an object, according to this thesis, is not brought about simply through an awareness which is in itself indifferent to the peculiarities of that object and which merely serves as a medium of encounter with it, the object on its part being simply there with all its peculiarities.

Nor is this thesis simply maintaining that it is through my consciousness that objects come to be noticed by me. Understood in this way, to be "conscious" of something is to be attentive to something, something which, before I turn attentively to it, is already there for me, only not through my being conscious of it. In contrast to this, Husserl's thesis holds that if I become attentive to something that was there for me all along in my surroundings, then there was some sort of consciousness of it prior to my turning explicitly to it which made it to be there for me as an unnoticed part of my surroundings. Thus, according to the thesis, "being there for me" has a sense which goes beyond merely being an object of focal awareness, and includes the horizon of what is explicitly before me. My surroundings are also there for me, and that too is an achievement of consciousness. Furthermore, the "being there of a world," in the sense of the thesis, means that there are objects, events, etc., not just in my immediate surroundings but beyond them. These too are there for me, and this thereness points to certain potentialities of consciousness linked to the actual consciousness I am now living through.[4]

One might ask at this point whether the expression "an object is there for me" simply means "I am (somehow) conscious of the object," and if this is the case, whether Husserl's thesis merely states that whatever *of* the world I am conscious of is there for me through by being conscious of it — surely not a very bold contention to say the least. One might go on to ask, "Isn't this thesis just maintaining that we have, as that of which we are conscious, a certain *idea* of the world, a partially individual and partially common *representation* of it which of course is an achievement of consciousness? But that is not the world itself, not the 'transcendent objects' referred to in Husserl's leading question 'How is cognition of transcendent objects possible?' " To raise this issue is the first step toward understanding the problem to which Husserl's thesis is the solution. The second step begins with the awareness that this interpretation cannot be Husserl's thesis, and passes on through wondering what "the world is there for me" can mean other than "I am conscious of the world" to a concrete phenomenological analysis of what "consciousness" and "world" are for us *at first,* most fundamentally, and ultimately, always. In other words, the very setting up of the problem is the first task of phenomenology. The goal of

8

this pre-transcendental analysis is to descriptively capture what "the being there of the world to me" means as that phrase is used in my statement of Husserl's thesis. This analysis would show that there is a sense of "being there for me" that is not a being there through consciousness, when "consciousness" is understood in a certain fundamental way. Once this becomes clear, and I shall attempt to make it so later, the boldness of Husserl's thesis becomes manifest. Husserl's demonstration of the thesis is an attempt to establish a concept of consciousness which far exceeds that fundamental understanding of it, and which has the being there of the world for me as its achievement.

In the literature on Husserl's philosophy there has been considerable discussion of what it is that consciousness achieves when it is said by him to "constitute" the world. All responsible interpreters are in agreement about what this achievement is not. It is not a creating of the world in the sense of "causing" it to be.[5] But there seems to be less agreement on what this achievement *is*. For Sokolowski, "consciousness constitutes the world" means that it is *a* necessary condition for the world to become real,[6] it "allows [objects] to emerge as real."[7] Carr denies that this is what Husserl means.[8] In his interpretation, consciousness is constitutive of the world in the sense that it is responsible for the givenness of objects, for the being of objects for me. Consciousness renders objects present.[9] For Mohanty, constitution in Husserl means constitution of the *sense* of objects.[10]

The interpretation offered here is closest to Carr's, but adds a certain provisio which he does not express. Consciousness is responsible for the being there of the world for me, but this is not to be understood as saying that consciousness performs some kind of subjectivizing transformation of the world into a (subjectively understood) "thereness for me," which would be some kind of *representation* of the world. Rather, this "being there for me," although it contains a reference to me, is *not* something subjective. As expressing that which is to be accounted *for* by *establishing* a reference to subjectivity, this phrase must first of all be understood as referring to a state of affairs which is entirely *un*-subjective.[11] It is this understanding which the preliminary phenomenological analysis to which I have already referred brings about. This analysis would reveal just what the nature of this "transcendence" which appears in the problem of cognition is, and make salient the profound enigma attending that problem. It is an analysis which shows what "world" is for us most fundamentally. Such an analysis, I believe, is the real intent of what Husserl refers to as an "ontology of the life-world."[12] Its task is made especially formidable because we are heirs to a certain philosophical and cultural tradition that makes it almost impossible for us to understand "being there for me" in other than subjective terms.[13] The preliminary analysis is not preliminary in a temporal sense; it is not an analyis which is to be completed before the next phase of phenomenology can commence. Rather, it proceeds hand in hand with the transcendental phenomenological analysis for which it provides *what* the latter is to account for, both in general terms and in particular for each new set of constitutional problems. As envisioned here, Husserlian phenomenology moves constantly between two realms of discouse: one provides a conception of the problem and forges a language for it; the other, in a different language, formulates the constitutive response to the problem. With these two languages the talk of a "correlation" between consciousness and world takes on an added dimension. There is also a third realm of discourse here, and one which Husserl also developed, that of phenomenological psychology. The status of that discipline with respect to its contribution to both the problem and its solution will be taken up later.

The thesis whose demonstration is to be discussed here has thus far been described in a highly general way. The problem which it is put forth to solve has been discussed. Husserl attempts to demonstrate that consciousness constitutes the world. But the sense and import of this demonstration cannot be understood until one more thought, which may have occurred to the reader, is dispelled. It might be asked: "In saying that 'it is through consciousness that a world is there for us,' don't you simply mean that consciousness is *intentional*? Isn't that Husserl's response to the problem of cognition? But the intentionality of consciousness is not something that Husserl sets out to demonstrate through an argument; it is simply a descriptive finding." The following discussion will show that the world-constituting function of consciousness is not the same as its intentionality, although the latter is a fundamental aspect of the former. Through this discussion two criteria will emerge which Husserl's demonstration must fulfill, criteria which will further help to define the meaning of Husserl's thesis.

The sphere of "transcendence" that the problem of cognition concerns includes first and foremost the world which we encounter in our everyday lives. We have seen that a knowledge of the particular sense of the world's transcendence is not furnished to us by our everyday encounters, but requires a special phenomenological analysis. One of the results of that analysis is to produce in us a profound sense of wonder as to how there can be a world for us at all. As Husserl so cogently put it in a passage that I would interpret as an example of such an analysis: "I see and grasp the thing itself in its bodily reality....Here perceiving...appears as something in itself essenceless, an empty looking of an empty 'Ego' towards the object itself which comes in contact with it in some astonishing way."[14] Once this wonder is aroused, one begins to grasp the problem of cognition in its most elementary form: How is it that we come into contact with the world; how are things, persons and events there for us in the first place? As the passage from Husserl shows, this wonder has its origin as much in a certain conception of consciousness as it does in an understanding of the sense of the transcendence of the world. It is a theoretical wonder conditioned by a certain concept of consciousness, one which is developed on the basis of and in accordance with our natural apprehension of ourselves and our mental life, a fundamental apprehension that no theory will ever replace. The relationship of mind and world has given, and perhaps always will give, rise to many theories which seek to solve the mystery contained in it. Husserl's phenomenology represents one way that modern philosophy has responded to this problem — through a theory of consciousness. At the core of Husserl's theory is the concept of intentionality. But we must now see that intentionality is only the beginning of a response to the problem.

Intentionality is "the unique peculiarity of experiences 'to be the consciousness *of* something'."[15] By means of a certain kind of reflective and descriptive study of mental life, one can find as an essential feature of a mental process not only temporality, the fact that it arises, endures and passes away in time, but also the feature that it is a consciousness of this or that particular item. At a given moment one is not seeing or hearing in general, but seeing a particular house, hearing a certain voice. This reference to that "of which" one is conscious is as essential as temporality for the individuation and qualitative particularity of a mental process, for its being the very mental process that it is. As we shall see in more detail later, the reference of a mental process to an item outside itself is achieved through certain content within the mental process, content whose specificity is in accordance with the particularity of the reference. Thus the descriptive study of mental life discloses as "consciousness" highly articulated correlates of what is there for us in the world through them, and from the idea of "intentional contents," we learn what "through" means when it is said that something is there for us "through consciousness."

However, it does not follow from the fact that we have intentional experiences that everything or every aspect of everything that is there for us as world is there for us through intentional experiences. It could be that some parts or aspects of the world are there for us through them and others are not, these latter being there for us without there being any corresponding contents within consciousness. It could be that the intentional contents of consciousness "fall short" of corresponding to the world in the particularity with which it is there for us. This is precisely what Husserl's thesis denies: "there is no conceivable place where the life of consciousness is broken through, or could be broken through, an we might come upon a transcendency that possibly had any sense other than that of an intentional unity making its appearance in the subjectivity itself of consciousness."[16] What is required for a demonstration of the thesis, then, is that any seeming gaps on the side of consciousness be filled, but in such a way that the theory does not have us so enclosed within our own contents of consciousness such that it becomes even more mysterious how we "come into contact" with a world, or such that we are led to wonder even *whether* we do. From these considerations two criteria for the success of Husserl's demonstration can be derived.

The thesis to be examined here can be expressed in this way: consciousness includes within itself intentional subjective processes of such scope, complexity, and joint functional efficacy so as to make the world, with its "whole content and ontic validity"[17] there for me. Demonstrating this thesis, then, involves showing: 1) that consciousness has such a *scope* that its intentional content is wide enough to be coextensive with the world, and 2) that the transcendent reality of the world can be accounted for in terms of consciousness. The first criterion expresses the minimal requirement that consciousness be as "rich" as the world, so that when its intentional content is declared to be the correlate of the world, there will be no excess on the side of the world whose being there has been left unaccounted for. I will call this the "scope criterion." It is the world as it is there for us in our daily lives which is the measure of the success of the world-constitutive theory of consciousness. The problem is to develop a conception of consciousness such that it becomes plausible that it is *consciousness* by virtue of which we have *such* a world. The criterion of scope requires that the theory to justice to the richness of the world. This criterion is set up to insure that some impoverished version of the world is not substituted in place of the actual world.

"Scope" does not only refer to the "spread" of consciousness, but just as importantly to its "depth." The theory must not only account for the being there of the world in its sheer numerical multiciplicity, but as well for its qualitative features. For instance, it must not only show that both the objects in front of me as well as those somehow present to me behind by back are there for me, albeit in different ways, by virtue of mental processes, it must also account, in terms of consciousness, for *what* these objects are for me as well as for such features as their being for me objects which others can also experience. It must not merely show how I have some object before me, but how I have, for example, a *man* before me. Meeting the criterion of scope involves, among other things, the identification of the major dimensions and regions of worldly being so that their being there can be accounted for. The danger here is that some crucial aspect will be overlooked, or, if seen, its importance for the very structuring of consciousness will not be realized. This happened a number of times in Husserl's writings, for instance once with intersubjectivity and another time with the historical nature of the life-world. Once he saw the importance of such dimensions, old grounds were gone over again with revisions made to accomodate the new dimension.[18]

It must not be thought that the criterion of scope is imposed merely for the sake of completeness and that rigid adherence to it is not necessary for the demonstration of Husserl's thesis. For the thesis is not simply that consciousness *can* make the world to be there and does so for the most part, rather it is that consciousness *must* be involved if there is to be a world there at all. It is a thesis about being-there (period), which seeks to establish that being-there equals being-there to consciousness. Should there be any moments on the side of the world whose being there is left unaccounted for, then the possibility would remain open that there is thereness which is not thereness to consciousness, as possibility which endangers the whole theory. Something whose being there is not correlated with a suitably articulated consciousness, a "sheer" thereness, something simply-there, could be regarded not as an enrichment beyond what consciousness provides, indicating that Husserl's theory concerning the being there of the world yields an incomplete account that needs to be supplemented, but rather as the basis for the charge that Husserl is not really demonstrating that consciousness is world-constitutive, but that it is world-representational, i.e., that it constitutes a representation of the world and not the world itself.

Meeting the criterion of scope, however, is not enough to establish that consciousness constitutes the world, for even if a complete correspondence between consciousness and world is established in terms of *content* moments, the *ontic* moment of the world, its status for us as transcendent reality, still must be accounted for. We normally think of consciousness as our "inward" side and as a part of the world because we are in the world. From the point of view of this inwardness (or immanence), the rest of the world is external, transcendent, not a part of consciousness at all. But the intentional content of consciousness is immanent content with respect to which the external world is totally transcendent. How, then, could we ever understand the transcendence of the world in terms of such content? Yet this must be done if consciousness is to be shown to constitute the world. As Husserl remarks, "transcendence is both the initial and central problem of the critique of cognition."[19] "All cognition of the natural sort, the prescientific and indeed the scientific is transcendently objectivating cognition. Its posits objects as existing, claims to reach matters of fact which are not 'strictly given to it,' are not 'immanent' to it."[20]

Moreover, the world is not just any transcendency, it is, as Husserl expresses it, actuality (*Wirklichkeit*).[21] In this regard Husserl asks: "how in the spirit of phenomenological science are we to describe...all the connections of consciousness which render necessary a plain object (and this in common speech always means an *actual* object) precisely in its character as actual?''[22] ''What does this 'actual' mean for objects which are indeed given to consciousness, yet only through meanings and positions?''[23]

Although there seem to be two problems here, transcendency and actuality, we shall see later that Husserl views them as intimately connected. For that reason, as well as for historical reasons, I will call the problem and the criterion to which it gives rise by one name, the ''problem of reality'' and the ''reality criterion'' respectively. The name ''problem of reality'' is used to call to mind the traditional philosophical problem of the objective reference of consciousness or the problem of the reality of phenomena.[24] But it is only analogous to this problem, since unlike many of its traditional formulations,[25] it is not the problem of *deciding* whether the world we live in is actual or is some sort of illusion. Husserl's demonstration is not aimed at convincing the skeptic or doubter *that* the world of everyday life is actual. Rather, it is aimed at those who unquestionably take it to be so and seeks to make it clear to them *how* they have such a world. The account wishes to preserve the natural understanding of the world while at the same time broadening and deepening the understanding of consciousness to the point where one can see how, through consciousness, there comes to be contituted a world which is a transcendent actuality in precisely the sense it is naturally taken to be. Husserl's approach is to show what such a person's natural apprehension of the world as transcendent actuality, i.e., the ''natural attitude,'' consists of and how it is a formation (*Gebilde*) of consciousness.[26] For Husserl, this is part of the broader task of accounting for the world as it is understood in scientific endeavors. It is the first part of that task since, according to him, scientific modes of cognitive endeavor have their roots and very possibility in the natural world-view and its correlative world of everyday life.[27] This world is ''world'' in its most original sense and all other ''worlds,'' for example the conception of the world arrived at in mathematical physics, are constructed starting out from it. The demonstration that consciousness is world-constitutive shows how consciousness ''reaches'' the world in the world's most original sense. The rest of the task is accomplished by showing how consciousness ''reaches'' these other ''worlds.'' Meeting the reality criterion insures that it is the world of everyday life that consciousness ''reaches.''

Husserl's theory of perceptual coherence, to be referred to as the ''coherence-thesis,'' is central to his attempt to meet the reality criterion. According to this thesis, it is from the harmonious development of the process of world-perception that our experience of its actuality arises and is sustained. However, this harmonious process is always open to dissolution, so that ''every experience, however far it extends, leaves open the possibility that what is given,

14

despite the persistent consciousness of its bodily self-presence, does *not* exist."[28] This applies not just to individual objects in the world, but to the world as a whole.[29]

B. THE IDEA OF A DEMONSTRATION OF THE THESIS

Now that Husserl's thesis that consciousness constitutes the world has been explained (at least in a preliminary way to be deepened later), the question of what is meant by the "demonstration" of that thesis must be addressed. Husserl states the thesis in many places, both in sections of his writings that are designed to lead up to transcendental phenomenology,[30] and in sections that come after entering into it.[31] When reading these sections one gets the distinct impression that Husserl believes the thesis to have been demonstrated by a general argument he has advanced in its support. It is a major contention of the present work that this general argument does not and cannot succeed in proving the thesis, and that consequently only Husserl's attempts at a "concrete" demonstration should be regarded as his real demonstration of the thesis. However, this concrete demonstration was never completed by Husserl. Since this is so, all statements of the thesis in Husserl's works must be regarded as anticipatory of its complete demonstration. We will see later that interpreting occurrences of statements of the thesis as anticipatory of its complete demonstration is of major import for the understanding of some of the key methods of Husserl's phenomenology, especially the methods of epoche, reduction and intentional analysis.

What I call the "concrete demonstration" that consciousness constitutes the world is the actual exhibiting of the "world-constituting intentionalities," the "equivalents of consciousness,"[32] of the major dimensions of the world. One example of a part of Husserl's concrete demonstration is his attempt in the fifth "Cartesian Meditation" to show the constitution of the intersubjective sense of the world. Husserl refers to this aspect of his work as part of a more encompassing demonstration of his "transcendental Idealism."[33] In this Idealism, "every sort of existent, real or ideal, would become understandable as a 'product' of transcendental subjectivity by a science which would carry out a 'sense explication' as regards every type of existent ever conceivable by me." The part of this which corresponds to the demonstration that consciousness is world-constitutive I identify with the one dealing with "the transcendency actually given to me beforehand through experience: nature, culture, the world as a whole." Of this overall task Husserl says: "This idealism is not a product of sportative argumentations....It is...achieved by actual work...[by] systematic uncovering of the constituting intentionality itself."

A "concrete" demonstration can be contrasted with a "general argument." By the latter I mean an argument which seeks to secure a thesis "in one sweep," as it were, through reasoning whose premises are certain general considerations. It would be an argument which seeks to show *that* something is the case without showing *how* it is the case. The contrast I have in mind is illustrated by the objective versus the subjective sides of Kant's "transcendental deduction."[34] Whereas the "objective deduction" seeks to establish *that* the categories of the understanding have objective validity, the "subjective deduction" concerns the question of *how* the understanding can have a cognitive relation to objects.[35] As Norman Kemp Smith puts it, "the subjective deduction seeks to determine...the generative processes to whose agency human knowledge is due."[36] Kant evidently thought that the objective deduction (a "general argument") was sufficient for his purposes, for in the first edition of the *Critique of Pure Reason* he says that the subjective deduction does not form an essential part of his overall deduction.[37] Later I will critically examine Husserl's attempt to argue *that* consciousness constitutes the world. First, however, we must examine the nature of the problem which motivates Husserl's thesis.

## NOTES

1. Unless otherwise specified, the expression "the world" will serve as an abbreviation for "the world, and all the objects, persons, events, etc. in it."
2. *FTL*, p. 244. See also Husserl's *Analysen zur passiven Synthesis, Husserliana* XI, ed. Margot Fleischer (The Hague: Martinus Nijhoff, 1966), p. 19 (hereafter cited as *APS*); and Husserl's *The Idea of Phenomenology*, trans. William Alston and George Nakhnikian (The Hague: Martinus Nijhoff, 1964), pp. 9-10 (hereafter cited as *IP*).
3. *CM*, p. 111.
4. *Ideas*, section 45, p. 142.
5. See, for instance, David Carr, *Phenomenology and the Problem of History* (Evanston: Northwestern University Press 1974), p. 15; J.N. Mohanty, *The Concept of Intentionality* (St. Louis: W.H. Green, 1972), pp. 115-16; and Robert Sokolowski, *The Formation of Husserl's Concept of Constitution* (The Hague: Martinus Nijhoff, 1964), pp. 136-39, 159.
6. Sokolowski, *The Formation of Husserl's Concept of Constitution*, pp. 137, 217.
7. Ibid., p. 138.
8. Carr, *Phenomenology and the Problem of History*, p. 15, n. 37.
9. Ibid., p. 15.
10. J.N. Mohanty, "Consciousness and Life-World," *Social Research* 42 (1975): 160.
11. See Eugen Fink, "Das Problem der Phänomenologie Edmund Husserls," *Revue internationale de Philosophie* 1 (1938-39, 246-47.
12. *Crisis*, p. 142.
13. Fink, "Das Problem der Phänomenologie Edmund Husserls," p. 242.

16

14.  *Ideas,* section 39, p. 127. See also *IP*, p. 9, and *APS*, p. 19.
15.  *Ideas,* section 84, p. 242. See also section 36.
16.  *FTL*, p. 236.
17.  *Crisis*, p. 153.
18.  See *Crisis,* p. 181 and section 55.
19.  *IP*, p. 28.
20.  Edmund Husserl, *Die Idee der Phänomenologie, Husserliana* II, ed. Walter Biemel (The Hague: Martinus Nijhoff, 1973), p. 35 − translation mine (English text, *IP*, p. 27).
21.  Following Dorion Cairns, I have translated *"Wirklichkeit"* and *"wirklich"* as "actuality" and "actual" respectively. See Dorion Cairns, *Guide for Translating Husserl* (The Hague: Martinus Nijhoff, 1973), pp. 139-40.
22.  *Ideas*, section 135, p. 377 − translation slightly altered, see Edmund Husserl, *Ideen zu einer reinen Phänomenologie und phänomenologischen Philosophie,* first book, *Husserliana* III, ed. Walter Biemel (The Hague: Martinus Nijhoff, 1950), p. 220 (hereafter cited as *Ideen* I). This edition of Husserl's *Ideen* I has been superseded by one edited by Karl Schuhmann and published in 1976 by Martinus Nijhoff in two volumes (see bibliography). Unlike the Biemel edition, Schuhmann's edition reproduces Husserl's text as Husserl published it, and places Husserl's corrections and additions to the text in a separate volume rather than incorporating them into the text. In my references to *Ideen* I, I will cite the page numbers of the Biemel edition, since many scholars perhaps still only own that edition. As my references also include the section numbers, which correspond in all editions (English and German) of *Ideen*, and since the sections are short, the passages referred to or quoted should not be difficult to find in the other editions.
23.  Ibid.
24.  See Aron Gurwitsch, "Husserl's Theory of the Intentionality of Consciousness in Historical Perspective," in this Phenomenology and the Theory of Science (Evanston: Northwestern University Press, 1974), pp. 210-40. See also Gurwitsch's article "Towards a Theory of Intentionality," *Philosophy and Phenomenological Research* 30 (1970): 354-67.
25.  See, for instance, Descartes' *Meditations,* especially the first meditation and the last paragraph of the sixth meditation. See also Leibnitz, *New Essays concerning the Human Understanding,* trans. A. Langley (Chicago: Open Court, 1916), pp. 421-22, 512-13.
26.  *EP* II, Beilage XIX, p. 418. See also Eugen Fink, "The Phenomenological Philosophy of Edmund Husserl and Contemporary Criticism," in *The Phenomenology of Husserl,* ed. Elveton, pp. 106-110.
27.  Edmund Husserl, *Ding und Raum, Husserliana* XVI, ed. Ulrich Claesges (The Hague: Martinus Nijhoff, 1973), pp. 6-7; *Crisis*, p. 128.
28.  *Ideas*, section 46, p. 144.
29.  Ibid., p. 145 and section 49, pp. 50-51. See also *EP* II, Beilage XIII, p. 406.
30.  For example, in sections 34 to 49 of *Ideas* (pp. 114-53), the thesis is stated repeatedly. See section 42, p. 135 for one example.
31.  For example, *CM*, p. 62; *Ideas,* section 76, p. 212; *Ideas,* section 135, p. 374.
32.  *Ideas,* section 152, p. 442; Gurwitsch, *Phenomenology and the Theory of Science,* p. 214.
33.  *CM*, pp. 85-86. The following quotes are all from these pages.
34.  Immanuel Kant, *Critique of Pure Reason,* trans. Norman Kemp Smith (London: Macmillan, 1929), p. 12 (Axvi).
35.  H.J. Paton, *Kant's Metaphysics of Experience,* 2 vols. (London: Allen & Unwin, 1936), 1: 352, 529; Norman Kemp Smith, *A Commentary to Kant's "Critique of Pure Reason"* (New York: Humanities Press, 1962), pp. 234-36.

36. Smith, *A Commentary to Kant's "Critique of Pure Reason,"* p. 236.
37. Ibid. Kant seems to equivocate on this in the second edition − see Paton, *Kant's Metaphysics of Experience,* 1: 527, 529.

## 3. THE MOTIVATING PROBLEM

Each of Husserl's "introductions" begins with the development of a set of problems whose ultimate treatment requires transcendental phenomenology. Despite whatever differences there may be between the "introductions" in this regard, there is one problem which emerges in all of them, namely, the problem of cognition of the world. This problem is only partially developed in each of the "introductions," each adding components lacking in the others or concentrating on aspects only alluded to in them. The complete elaboration of this problem fills out the first part of the schema of the "introductions." My treatment of this part of Husserl's "introductions" will be relatively brief. It is only intended to serve the following functions: 1) to provide a general view of the larger philosophical context within which the theory of consciousness as world-constitutive appears; 2) to indicate how each of the "introductions" contributes to the development of the problem of cognition; 3) to yield the idea of the correlation between subjective apriori on the one hand, and objective eidos and objective kind on the other.

In *Ideas*, Husserl tells us that his interest there is to found a "new eidetic science" whose field is a "new region of being," " 'pure consciousness' with its pure "correlates of consciousness'" and its " 'pure ego'."[1] This science is transcendental phenomenology. Why is this science sought? In the first section of *Ideas*, entitled "Fact and Essence," the nature of eidetic sciences and their relations to one another and to sciences of fact are delineated. For every region of being, formal or material, to which an eidetic science (a formal or material ontology) pertains, there are fundamental and *a priori* truths which express what must belong *a priori* to an individual object of the region. It is the task of the pertinent eidetic science to formulate these truths.[2] Developed independently from the sciences of fact, these eidetic sciences nonetheless furnish essential laws which are binding for any possible concrete objects of the factual sciences.[3] What Husserl has in mind here is exemplified by the relation of the eidetic science of space and spatial form, geometry, to the factual science of objects in space, physics. Husserl's major concern is the relations between the regions of being and correspondingly between their respective sciences. He tells us that phenomenology is needed for a radical "classification" of the sciences and for the separating of the regions of being. As an example of this he mentions the two regions "material thing" and "soul."[4] Here, as elsewhere, phenomenology would clarify the intrinsic essence of each region and the manner in which they relate to one another, and in this case shed some light on the age old "mind-body" problem.[5]

Some of the ontologies Husserl has in mind are already developed, as in the case of geometry, whereas others are perhaps in nascent form, for example, the eidetics of the soul as a result of Brentano's work. Still others are only possible ontologies. Whatever the case, Husserl implies that a radical criticism is required before their development or redevelopment. Thus Husserl tells us, in a remark which pertains as well to the factual sciences, that "phenomenology supplies the definitive criticism of every fundamentally distinct science, and in particular therewith the final determination of the sense in which their objects can be said 'to be'. It also clarifies their methodology in the light of first principles."[6] The sciences themselves are incapable of supplying this self-criticism in principle, while phenomenology can criticize itself.[7] Modern philosophy (since Descartes) has sought to provide this criticism of the sciences, but has thus far failed. In this sense, phenomenology is the "secret longing" of modern philosophy.[8]

How phenomenology can perform this service becomes clearer in the last chapter of *Ideas*, where Husserl explicitly takes up the topic of the connection between phenomenology and the formal and material ontologies.[9] In the sections of the book between "Fact and Essence" and the last chapter, the main structures of consciousness are delimited. The last chapter begins with an outline of the phenomenological inquiries into formal logic and formal ontology which are extensively elaborated in *Formal and Transcendental Logic*. These formal problems lead to material problems, which in turn refer to the phenomenological problem of the constitution of objects in consciousness.[10] It is these constitutional inquiries that will clarify the basic concepts of the regional sciences. Finally, we are told that the basic concepts and truths pertaining to formal or material regions of being indicate strata and lawfulness in a more fundamental being, transcendental consciousness.[11]

It is often wondered why Husserl included the "Fact and Essence" chapter in *Ideas*. The lack of continuity between it and the chapters that follow is no doubt the initial source of that puzzlement. Ricoeur, in his introduction to his

French translation of *Ideas*, even remarks that "the reader can temporarily omit [it] in order to understand the spiritual movement of the whole book."[12] He adds that the chapter must, however, be integrated along the way. In fact, this advice is sound, although in principle it is like recommending that the reader begin reading *Formal and Transcendental Logic* with Part II. It is sound, in *fact,* because it is not until page 404 of *Ideas* that Husserl connects the themes discussed in "Fact and Essence" with the rest of the book. There it becomes clear that the problem of a philosophical grounding of the sciences, or, more generally expreseed, the critique of reason and cognition, is for Husserl what motivates the turn to transcendental subjectivity. This is not only true historically, i.e., with regard to Husserl's personal biography,[13] but more importantly, it is also true in terms of the systematic position of this problem in his whole philosophy. In so far as the "way" into transcendental phenomenology means "motivating problem," the problem of cognition provides the only "way" in Husserl's thought. A discussion of parallel sections of some of his other works, to which I shall now turn, strengthens this point.

The corresponding schematic parts of *Cartesian Meditations* and *Formal and Transcendental Logic* also point to the need for transcendental phenomenology to provide a foundation for the sciences. In the former work, the nature of this need, only hinted at in *Ideas*, is elaborated, and in the latter the development of the problems culminating in this need takes up more than half of the volume. Two factors crucial for an understanding of the need for transcendental phenomenology, intentionally omitted from *Ideas*,[14] are dealt with in these works: 1) an explanation of why the "positive" sciences themselves cannot perform the role assigned to phenomenology, and 2) why there is a *need* to clarify the fundamentals of the sciences in the first place. *Cartesian Meditations* develops the first point by attempting to show that any positive science,[15] including practically all of previous philosophy, is incapable of a radical self-criticism.[16] The reason for this is that their objects are given in a "naive" experiencing and the concepts pertaining to these objects are generated in "naive" producings, i.e., experiencings and producings which contain hidden, "anonymous" functions. As a result of this, these sciences deal with objects and concepts with undisclosed horizons which form "presuppositions" they cannot clarify.[17] The ultimate presuppotition of these sciences is the world.[18] Transcendental phenomenology, which has developed a method for disclosing these intentional functions and horizons, can illuminate these presuppositions and, at the same time, its own presuppositions by the same method. It can thus provide the ultimate foundation for all sciences, including itself.[19]

But why do the sciences need this clarification of their fundamental concepts? The answer to this is only hinted at in *Cartesian Meditations*. Because concepts like "world," "nature," "space" and "social community," which pervade a given science and determine the sense of its objects and theories, originate naively, such a science has "problems of fundamentals, paradoxes, unintelligibilities."[20] What are these problems? Husserl provides examples of these problems in *Formal and Transcendental Logic* from the sphere of logic. Although it has become a special science, for Husserl logic occupies a unique position among the sciences due to its "historical vocation." It is the science of science, i.e., a science which prescribes norms for *genuine* science.[21]

The sense of this "genuineness" is given in the "Introduction" to *Formal and Transcendental Logic,* where Husserl refers in a general way to the "problems" of the (European) sciences. The sciences, in their present condition, "have lost their great belief in themselves, in their absolute significance. The modern man of today, unlike the 'modern' man of the Enlightenment, does not behold in science and in the new culture formed by means of science, the self-objectivation of human reason or the universal activity mankind has devised for itself in order to make possible a truly satisfying life, an individual and social life of practical reason. The belief that science leads to wisdom...this great belief, once the substitute for religious belief, has (at least in wide circles) lost its force. Thus men live entirely in a world that has become unintelligible, in which they ask in vain for the wherefore, the sense, which was once so doubtless and accepted by the understanding, as well as by the will."[22] The blame for this condition rests primarily on logic, which, understood as a philosophical discipline, embracing both the theory of judgements (apophantics) and the theory of objects (ontology), has strayed from its task of providing the proper guidance. Thus we see that the "genuineness" of science does not refer, in its deepest import, to technical proficiency, practical usefulness, or even explanatory efficacy; rather, it refers to the ethical ideal of a genuine human life, a rational life.[23] Only a "transcendental logic," according to Husserl, can guide cognition to such genuineness.[24]

But, although profound, this critical statement does not yet tell us how this condition manifests itself in the sciences themselves, or in logic. How does it show up in the form of "problems of fundamentals, paradoxes, unintelligibilities" *within* the sciences? Husserl provides an example of this in a discussion of what later logicians refer to as the problem of the relation of syntactics and semantics. In an analysis of the law of excluded middle (p or not p), he uncovers a presupposiion underlying this law which necessitates a consideration of its possible material content (i.e., actual judgements), content which is usually left emptily indeterminate due to the alleged universality of the law. But if this law is to range over all judgements universally, as logic seems to claim, then it would be untenable, for it is not true of the judgement "the sum of the angles of a triangle is equal to the color red" that it is either true or false. This judgement cannot be brought to evidential verification in a possible experience. Furthermore, no purely syntactical subdiscipline of logic, such as the pure logical grammar which Husserl has outlined, can prescribe laws to eliminate such judgements from the range of the laws of formal logic. The problem is essentially a material or semantic one. Today, a similar problem besets the fundamental notion of "logically true" (and therewith "consequence" and "consistency") in first order predicate logic. There, a sentence formulatable under the formation rules of a logical system (a "well-formed formula"), is said to be logically true if and only it is true under every interpretation of that system.[26] The concept of "interpretation" is a semantic and not a syntactic one. It is resorted to because no one has yet been able to provide a syntactical definition of "logically true" as has been done with its counterpart "tautologous" in sentential calculus (via truth tables). But the notion of "interpretation" is not without its problems. Involved is the idea of a "universe of discourse," or a domain of objects about which judgements can be made. Any sentence of the form p or not p, for example, is alleged to be logically true, i.e., true in every universe of discourse. With this we come back to Husserl's discussion, and in a way which shows that it pertains to "consequence logic" just as much to the "logic of truth," once one goes beyond sentential calculus, which cannot even formalize syllogistic arguments.[27]

The discussion of such issues explores the interface between judgement and experience and, for Husserl, involves an analysis of the genesis of judgements in the context of the experiences that motivate them, as well as an analysis of the coherence of that experience which provides the ultimate basis for the coherence of the material content of judgements.[28] Thus, an understanding of the proper sense of the principles of logic requires a critique of experience.[29] Although logic is an *a priori* science and, as such, must not assert facts or posit a de facto world, Husserl points out that it does presuppose *possible* worldly being, a notion that logicians have acquired as a possibility-variant of the actual world which is, then, also presupposed.[30] For a radical grounding of logic, the whole real world must be called into question, "not to show its actuality, but to bring out its possible and genuine sense and the range of this sense, the range with which this sense can enter into the fundamental concepts of logic.... If the anything-whatever of formal logic [for instance, any judgement whatever], taken as Objective logic, ultimately involves the sense, worldly being, then this sense is precisely *one of logic's fundamental concepts,* one of those determining the whole sense of logic."[31] In this manner, and as the title of the section immediately following the above quote tells us, "The grounding of logic leads into the all-embracing problem of transcendental phenomenology."[32]

The transition to transcendental phenomenology is mediated by a new discipline, a material ontology which "ties together all separate material-apriori provinces in one totality," an ontology which deals with possible universes of being, i.e., worlds.[33] This ontology, which forms the beginning phase of phenomenology,[34] would have at its first level a discipline called "transcendental aesthetics" which deals with "the eidetic problem of any possible world *as a world given in 'pure experience'*."[35] Among the central problems of this discipline would be those pertaining to space and time. "Pure experience" refers to an experience of objects and of a world prior to categorial activities such as judging and counting.[36] As "transcendental aesthetics" is also said by Husserl to pertain to the "primordial world,"[37] i.e., a world which is not yet an intersubjective world, "pure experience" must also refer to a type of experience prior to "empathy," i.e., prior to the experience of someone else. This primordial world becomes accessible to the phenomenologist by starting from the "concrete world,"[38] the full intersubjective world in which phenomenologists find themselves along with others. This latter world, Husserl says, must be submitted to a constitutional clarification before the questions concerning the constitution of a theoretical world can be asked, for a theoretical world, that is, one to which the various formal and regional ontologies pertain, is constructed on the basis of the concrete world, a process which involves "idealizations."[39] "Transcendental aesthetics," then, would be one aspect of this whole constitutional clarification.

With the problem of the constitution of the "concrete world," the transition from these *ontic* considerations to transcendental phenomenology as a study of consciousness can be made, since *"any straight-forwardly constituted objectivity* (for example: an object belonging to Nature) *points back,* according to its essential sort (for example: physical thing *in specie*), to a *correlative essential form of* manifold, actual and possible, *intentionality...which is constitutive for that objectivity."*[40] This quotation expresses the correlation between subjective apriori on the one hand and objective eidos and objective kind on the other which was mentioned in the beginning of this chapter. Husserl explains the correlation as follows: "The multiplicity of possible perceptions, memories and, indeed, intentional processes of whatever sort, that relate, or can relate, 'harmoniously' to one and the same physical thing has (in all its tremendous complication) a quite definite *essential style,* which is identical in the case of any physical thing whatever and is particularized only according to the different individual things constituted in different cases."[41] It should be pointed out that the word "harmoniously" points to the "coherence-thesis" which has been mentioned earlier.

Before proceeding further with this outline of the motivating problem, I will show how some of the preceeding themes relate to one another by using Husserl's example, the "straightforwardly constituted objectivity": "object belonging to nature." We might think of a tree. Such an object points back, "according to its essential sort," to a correlative form of intentionality. This "essential sort" refers to an eidos, one of many which pertain to the object in question. Taking one of these eide, "physical thing" (we could have chosen "organic thing," for example, instead), which we make intuitively present to ourselves through "free variation,"[42] we can proceed in two directions. On the one hand, since we now have a "fundamental concept" of a regional ontology, let us say some completely theoretical form of physics, we can proceed to elaborate that ontology in "positive naiveté." On the other hand, we can use the eidos as a "transcendental clue,"[43] as something which is a clue to one stratum of the intentionality correlative to our objectivity (object belonging to nature, a tree), a stratum which has an "essential form," an "essential style," and which constitutes that object for us *as* a physical thing. Now we can pursue phenomenological, constitutional investigations which will clarify the *sense* of "physical thing" by showing the complex processes of consciousness by virtue of which physical things can be there for us and can be experienced as physical things. In this way, we will have shown the most fundamental sense in which such an object of a factual science can be said "to be."

The all-embracing material ontology which Husserl envisions seems not to proceed in either of these two directions. Rather, it investigates eidetically that which forms the starting point for both of these procedures, namely the concrete life-world. Let us continue or example to show how this ontology relates to the two proceeding procedures and thus to the regional ontologies and to transcendental phenomenology as the study of consciousness. In our daily lives we encounter objects, trees for example. One constituent of the make-up of such objects, as they are there for us in our encounter of them, is "something" (and I am deliberately vague here) which, on the one hand, can be isolated and conceptualized by the various abstractive, idealizing and eidetic procedures of some theoretical activity. These procedures give rise to an eidos, which then becomes a fundamental concept of some regional ontology and provides a certain theoretical perspective within which some factual science can study concrete objects. On the other hand, this "something" points back to processes of consciousness which constitute it. The all-embracing material ontology discloses these "somethings," these strata of individual objects and of the life-world as a whole. What are these "somethings?" "Physicality" is one, but what is meant by this is not that feature *as* it is conceptualized by either a regional ontology or a factual science. Rather, it is some givenness which provides the foundation for the concept "physical thing." Precisely one problem encountered in the attempt to disclose such "somethings" is that they are cloaked by the conceptualizations which have resulted from a tradition of theoretical activity. Nonetheless, the conceptualizations can serve as a clue to the "somethings," and it is in this way that the "essential sorts" provide a clue to constitutive processes.

This all-embracing material ontology, then, is the same science that Husserl, in *Crisis,* refers to as an "ontology of the life-world."[44] The life-world theme is not new to *Crisis.* Husserl has already, in *Ideas,* spoken of the study of the life-world (although not naming it such) as a task of "extraordinary importance," characterizing it as a study of "what is given to us in the natural attitude."[45] Husserl devoted several sections of *Ideas* to this task,[46] but only went so far as to yield "a few features of a quite general character."[47] The theme was taken up again in *Phänomenologische Psychologie.* There, a science of the life-world and of the experience of the life-world was indicated as crucial for laying the foundations of a psychology which would be able to provide, in turn, the foundations for the human sciences (*Geisteswissenschaften*).[48]

*Crisis* contributes to the development of the motivating problem in two ways: it shows how the crisis of the sciences, whose symptoms show up as the problems disclosed in *Formal and Transcendental Logic,* relates to the more general theme, only briefly dealt with in the latter work, of the crisis of Western civilization; and it emphasizes and elaborates upon the role of a study of the life-world for transcendental phenomenology. The first point is developed chiefly in Parts I and II of *Crisis.* I will not elaborate on this aspect any further here. The second point is developed chiefly in Part IIIA of *Crisis.* It is there that the task of an ontology of the life-world is posed. Before discussing this second point, it will be helpful to summarize the motivation part of the schema of Husserl's "introductions" as we have it thus far, including the place which the life-world issue occupies.

Husserl wants to establish a science which will provide the foundation for all sciences, including itself, i.e., a foundation for all cognitive endeavors. Such a science is needed, to express it most generally, because modern humanity has lost faith in reason as a means toward a truly satisfying life. This loss of faith is occasioned by certain developments in the sciences, which have not only made them unsuitable for this grander purpose, but which have also produced problems internal to them. To every actual or conceivable empirical explanatory science there corresponds an eidetic science, a regional or material ontology which formulates the *a priori* truths valid for the specific region of being.[49] There are also purely formal eidetic sciences. For instance, formal ontology deals with the concept "anything whatever" in formal universality, and apophantic logic concerns propositions and systems of propositions in their formal aspect. These two sciences form branches of an all-embracing formal science which Husserl designates "pure formal logic." This one science would be the science of science. Husserl is primarily concerned with providing a foundation for all these eidetic sciences, and only through them is he concerned with having an effect on empirical sciences. His predominant concern is with "pure formal logic," understood as a discipline which formulates the formal conditions of possible truth and possible existing being, that is, with reason, which, as he says, is a "form concept,"[50] but with reason in the service of cognition.

Given such an interest, one cannot study the forms of thought without considering the possible material content which may appear within the forms. This is the province of the regional or material ontologies. But the formal region is *one*, and its science is unified, whereas on the material side there are *many* regions and sciences. Thus Husserl poses a new science as the material counterpart of "pure formal logic," an ontology of possible life-worlds. Pure formal logic deals with the determinations of "anything whatever," for example any judgement whatever, any object whatever. If an investigation of the possible material content of these forms is required for the determination of the sense and scope of pure formal logic, this investigation must also deal with the material content with a certain universality, i.e., not with this or that region of being, but with some all encompassing region, or with regionality as such.[51] In Husserl's words, this means dealing with a "synthetic Apriori," a "universal material Apriori," one "that predelineates the apriori of the eidos *world*.[53]

But this life-world ontology is to be quite different in kind from the regional ontologies. It is not to be a super-ontology, one developed in the same style as the regional ontologies, only of higher generality. Although it is to be developed in the natural attitude, as are the regional ontologies, it is not to be "guided by a constructive concepts of a world which is true in itself."[54] On the contrary, our very access to the life-world requires an epoche of the objective sciences, including all objective *a priori* sciences.[55] In particular, it requires an abstaining from participating in their style.[56]

We might pause to wonder why Husserl does not pose an objectivistically constructed all-embracing material ontology as the counterpart of pure formal logic, instead of advancing the idea of a descriptive science oriented toward the (relatively) "subjective-relative" life-world.[57] I suspect that Husserl thought that there could not be an all-embracing material ontology which would be developed by the procedures that give rise to the regional ontologies. There are two related reasons which, should the supposition be correct, may have led to think this. First, there is no all-embracing region of being except a life-world. Second, because of the nature of the objectivistic-constructive procedures which are followed in formulating regional ontologies, there necessarily results only "worlds" and not "a world" as the constructed product. This is not the place for an extensive discussion of these points.[58] However, it is important to note that an all-embracing region would have to be composed of the summa genera of some "concretum" which "contains" *all* summa genera, i.e., which contains eidetic singularities which are the lowest differentiations of every genus. This, in turn, would require a "this there" (*tóde ti*), in this case an "individual," corresponding to such a concretum.[59] Such an individual seems unimaginable. This would seem to rule out the idea of an all-embracing region *so conceived*, i.e., as a unity of highest genera. However, transcendental subjectivity is thought of by Husserl as that region of being on which all others depend. It is the ultimate concretum.[60] The life-world apriori is said to be a stratum of this subjectivity.[61] But the manner in which the other regions of being are contained in transcendental subjectivity is not through the genus-species relationship, rather it is through what is expressed by the words "constitution" and "foundation."[62] Husserl seeks the unity of being in this direction.

Having completed this summary of the motivational aspect of Husserl's "introductions," it is now possible to discuss the second contribution of *Crisis* to the development of the motivating problem, i.e., its elaboration of the role which a study of the life-world plays for transcendental phenomenological investigations into constitutions. We have seen that, for Husserl, the ultimate clarification of the fundatmental concepts of the sciences can only be achieved by an investigation of transcendental subjectivity. This is because there is a correlation between the subjective apriori and objective eide, a correlation which is such that the constitutive achievements of the former are what the latter conceptualize. It is now clear that the constitutive achievements referred to here are the life-world "kinds," i.e., the *sorts* of things that there are for us in the life-world as they are for us in our everyday lives, and not as they are conceptualized by the sciences. It is these "kinds" which are the most proximal clues to the constructive intentionalities. We can now understand why Husserl said in *Ideas* that the study of the life-world is a task of "extraordinary importance." Its importance is that it sets up the first-level problems for the constitutive investigations. The study of the life-world discloses those determinations of the experienced world whose constitution is to be sought. Each life-world kind points back to a multiplicity of intentional processes having a definite "essential style," to a constitutive apriori, to an intentional structure that is governed by a rule.[63] Such a rule prescribes those intentional processes that can unite harmoniously to form the experience of one and the same thing with regard to its being-so (*Sosein*).

There is one more way in which *Crisis* contributes to the development of the motivating problem, and this is perhaps the most significant way of all. Pure formal logic deals with the problem of the formal conditions under which objects can be thought. For the ultimate clarification of pure formal logic we are led to the phenomenological problem of how the kinds of objects conceptualized by the material ontologies can be there for us. This problem does not only concern the being-so, but also the very being-there (*Dasein*) of objects and of the world. Earlier, Husserl's motivating problem was stated in terms of the question: "How is cognition of transcendent objects possible?" How is one to understand this question? What is the nature of the "transcendence" spoken of and to what as "immanence" is it opposed? In *The Idea of Phenomenology,* Husserl expresses the problem in this way: "How can cognition posit something as existing that is not directly and truly given in it?"[64] This formulation of the question, as well as similar formulations elsewhere, focusses on the problem of the *actuality* of the world, and as we shall see later, presupposes a rather refined, theoretical conception of consciousness. But if we focus on the issue of the actuality of the world, are we addressing the problem of cognition in its most original form? If the problem of cognition involves the very being there of the life-world, should not immanence and transcendence in the first instance be understood as they manifest themselves in the life-world?

I believe that Husserl has already formulated a more original understanding of immanence and transcendence, one which, curiously, also appears in texts where the more theoretical formulations appear. This occurs, for example, in *The Idea of Phenomenology,* where Husserl says: "At the lowest level of reflection, the naive level, at first it seems as if evidence were a matter of simple 'seeing,' a mental inspection without a character of its own, always one and the same and in itself undifferentiated: the 'seeing' just 'sees' the things, the things are simply there....All difference is thus in the things that exist in themselves and have their differences through themselves."[65] This characterless "seeing," as an understanding of what is immanent, is far from the highly structured conception that, as we shall see, is involved in the issue of the actuality of the world. Likewise, the "simply-thereness" of things is a different understanding of transcendence than is actuality. In *Ideas* Husserl almost repeats the above characterization word for word in another "naive" reflection,[66] and further develops the idea of things being "simply-there" (*einfach da*), a character which he also terms "on hand" (*vorhanden*).[67] This character, as I will later discuss, turns out to be one aspect of the correlate of the belief which forms the core of the natural attitude.[68] But it is in *Crisis* where this idea of transcendence, there termed "pregivenness" (*Vorgegebenheit*), becomes emphasized as a theme in its own right. In this respect, I believe *Crisis* signals the emergence of a new way of setting up the problem of transcendence and of meeting the reality criterion. This way is different from the one pursued by following the "clue" of actuality, an ontic character which is also said by Husserl to be the correlate of the belief at the core of the natural attitude. I believe that the "new" way of formulating the problem is deeper and more original, whereas the other formulation has its roots in more traditional philosophical considerations.

This elaboration of the motivating problem has ended in a discussion of how the life-world theme provides clues to the subjective intentionalities which constitute the life-world. What it does not show us, but rather presupposes, is *that* consciousness constitutes the world. It is to this aspect of Husserl's "introductions" that we now turn.

## NOTES

1. *Ideas,* section 33, p. 112. See section 16, p. 77 for the definition of "region."
2. Ibid., section 16, pp. 77-78.
3. Ibid., section 8, pp. 63-69.
4. Ibid., section 17, p. 79.
5. See Ludwig Landgrebe, "Seinesregionen und regionale Ontologien in Husserls Phänomenologie," in his *Der Weg der Phänomenologie* (Gutersloh: Gerd Mohn, 1963) for a discussion of Husserl's treatment of the relationship between these two regions of being.
6. *Ideas*, sections 62, p. 183.
7. Ibid., p. 182.
8. Ibid., p. 183.
9. Ibid., sections 146-53, pp. 404-27.
10. Ibid., section 149, pp. 411-15; section 150.
11. Ibid., section 153, p. 426.
12. Paul Ricoeur, *Husserl: An Analysis of His Phenomenology,* trans. Edward G. Ballard and Lester E. Embree (Evanston: Northwestern University Press, 1967), p. 15. For the original French version, see Edmund Husserl, *Idées directrices pour une phénoménologie,* trans. Paul Ricoeur (Paris: Gallimard, 1950), p. xiv.
13. For Husserl's testimony in this regard, see *IP,* pp. VII-VIII, or Husserl, "Persönliche Aufzeichnungen," p. 297.
14. *Ideas,* "Introduction," p. 45. Here Husserl says that the second book of *Ideas* will explain the relation of phenomenology to the other sciences. On this, see the editor's introduction to Edmund Husserl, *Ideen zu einer reinen Phänomenologie und phänomenologischen Philosophie,* second book, *Husserliana* IV, ed. Marly Biemel (The Hague: Martinus Nijhoff, 1952), pp. XIV-XVI (hereafter cited as *Ideen* II).
15. A "positive" science is a science that presupposes the world (*Crisis,* p. 261). This seems to be the same as what Husserl calls a "dogmatic" (versus a "critical") sciece in *Ideas,* section 26.
16. Strasser's comment, in his introduction to the *Husserliana* edition of *Cartesian Meditations,* that the "way" to phenomenology represented by that work is not through logic, can be misleading, as can be the whole discussion of "ways" into transcendental phenomenology. Once one sees Husserl's "introductions" to transcendental phenomenology in their

systematic relatedness, as I am attempting to do here, one sees that they all pertain to logic, in the all-encompassing sense in which Husserl understood it, i.e., as the theory of science. There are indeed differences between these "introductions," and these differences no doubt have to do with different "ways." But exactly what these differences are cannot be seen until the common themes are separated out. In so far as "way" refers to "motivating problem," there are no differences between the "introductions." See Edmond Husserl, *Cartesianische Meditationen und Pariser Vorträge, Husserliana* I, 2d ed., ed. S. Strasser (The Hague: Martinus Nijhoff, 1963), p. XXIII.

17. *CM,* pp. 152-53. See also *FTL,* pp. 13, 226.

18. *FTL,* pp. 223-31.

19. *CM,* pp. 151-57.

20. Ibid., p. 153.

21. *FTL,* pp. 1-4, 26-29.

22. Ibid., p. 5.

23. This theme is taken up again in *Crisis* and was already present in the 1911 work "Phenomenology as Rigorous Science" (in Edmund Husserl, *Phenomenology and the Crisis of Philosophy,* trans. Quentin Lauer [New York: Harper & Row, 1965]).

24. *FTL,* p. 16.

25. Ibid., pp. 220-21. See Gurwitsch, *Phenomenology and the Theory of Science,* pp. 71-74 for an excellent discussion of this whole problem.

26. See Benson Mates, *Elementary Logic,* 2d ed. (New York: Oxford University Press, 1972), pp. 54-64.

27. See *FTL,* p. 54 for Husserl's separation of "consequence logic" from "truth logic."

28. *FTL,* pp. 218-19, 221.

29. Ibid., p. 211.

30. Ibid., p. 224.

31. Ibid., p. 229.

32. Ibid.

33. Ibid., p. 150.

34. *CM,* p. 138.

35. *FTL,* p. 243.

36. Ibid. See also, Suzanne Bachelard, *A Study of Husserl's "Formal and Transcendental Logic",* trans. Lester E. Embree (Evanston: Northwestern University Press, 1968), pp. 140-43, 218-19.

37. *CM,* p. 146.

38. Ibid., p. 142.

39. *FTL,* p. 243.

40. Ibid., p. 246.

41. Ibid.

42. See ibid., pp. 247-49.

43. See ibid., p. 245.

44. *Crisis,* pp. 142-43; 173-74. See also Bachelard, *A Study of Husserl's "Formal and Transcendental Logic",* pp. 140-43 and Aron Gurwitsch, "Problems of the Life-World," in *Phenomenology and Social Reality,* ed. Maurice Natanson (The Hague: Martinus Nijhoff, 1970), pp. 58-59 for this identification. I disagree, however, with what seems to be Gurwitsch's equation of this ontology with "Transcendental aesthetics." Transcendental aesthetics would only be one part of this discipline.

45. *Ideas,* section 30, pp. 105-6 — translation modified, see *Ideen* I, p. 62. See also Gurwitsch, "Problems of the Life-World," p. 35.

46. *Ideas,* sections 27-30.
47. Ibid., section 30, p. 106.
48. Edmund Husserl, *Phänomenologische Psychologie, Husserliana* IX, ed. Walter Biemel (The Hague: Martinus Nijhoff, 1962), pp. 55-56, 93 (hereafter cited as *PP*). See Aron Gurwitsch, "Edmund Husserl's Conception of Phenomenological Psychology," in his *Phenomenology and the Theory of Science,* pp. 78-79, 83, 85-87.
49. Edmund Husserl, *Ideen zu einer reinen Phänomenologie und phänomenologischen Philosophie,* third book, *Husserliana* V, ed. Marly Biemel (The Hague: Martinus Nijhoff, 1971), p. 25. See also Aron Gurwitsch, *The Field of Consciousness* (Pittsburgh: Duquesne University Press, 1964), p. 190.
50. *FTL,* p. 29.
51. What is meant here is regionality in its material and not formal aspect. Formal ontology deals with the "formal region," i.e., with the (empty) form of a region in general — see *Ideas*, section 10, p. 67.
52. *FTL,* p. 150.
53. Ibid., p. 291.
54. *Crisis,* p. 173.
55. Ibid., section 35 and p. 140.
56. Ibid., pp. 135, 140.
57. Ibid., p. 131.
58. The reader is referred to Appendix VII of the English translation of *Crisis* (pp. 379-83) for some clues to Husserl's thoughts on the second point. As for the first, one should consult his definition of a region in *Ideas,* section 16, p. 77.
59. See *Ideas,* section 14, p. 74, for the concept of "this there" and section 15, p. 76, for the concepts of "concretum" and "individual."
60. See Robert Sokolowski, *Husserlian Meditations* (Evanston: Northwestern University Press, 1974), p. 10.
61. *Crisis,* p. 174. See also the third book of Husserl's *Ideen,* pp. 77-78.
62. See Ricoeur, *Husserl: An Analysis of His Phenomenology,* p. 15.
63. *CM,* p. 53.
64. *IP,* p. 28.
65. Ibid., p. 9.
66. *Ideas,* section 39, p. 127.
67. Ibid., section 27; *Ideen* I, p. 57.
68. *Ideas,* section 31, p. 107; *Ideen* I, p. 64.

## 4. ACQUIRING THE IDEA OF PURE TRANSCENDENTAL CONSCIOUSNESS

When Husserl's various "introductions to phenomenology" are looked at together in order to discern the structure (or what I have called the "schema") of
the line of thought which runs through them all, one finds after a discussion of
the motivating problem an attempt by Husserl to demonstrate that consciousness constitutes the world, i.e., that the being there for us of the world and of
what is in it is an achievement of consciousness. This demonstration is a
general argument whose premises are supplied by non-transcendental, phenomenological analyses, phenomenological analyses carried out in the natural
attitude. This aspect of the "one" introduction to phenomenology which I am
constructing from Husserl's texts has two main sections. In the first, the
"natural attitude" is descriptively analyzed in order to disclose its "general
thesis," the belief in the being "on hand" (*Vorhandenheit*) and in the "actuality" (*Wirklichkeit*) of the world. Once this is achieved, the possibility of
suspending this belief is raised, a procedure which is called the "transcendental
phenomenological epoche." This is followed by the second main section,
which is a psychological investigation of consciousness. The purpose of this
investigation is to yield those premises needed for the conclusion that
consciousness constitutes the world.

The "purest" version of this aspect of Husserl's "introductions" is found in
*Ideas*, which contains twenty-two continuous sections devoted to it.[1] It is the
"purest" version in the sense that Husserl makes it explicit there that the
analyses are carried out in the natural attitude and in the sense that there is no
(at least intentional) inclusion of statements deriving from the transcendental
attitude. This version is to be compared with parallel sections of other texts,
such as *Cartesian Meditations* and *Crisis*,[2] where the two attitudes alternate,
and where it is often unclear from which attitude statements are being made. It
is also in *Ideas* that Husserl explicity characterizes the general form of his dis-

cussion as an argument.[3] Because *Ideas* contains the purest version of this aspect of his "introductions," I will use it as the basis of the following exposition, supplementing it, where necessary to clarify what Husserl is saying, with material from other texts and with some analyses of my own.

Since Husserl's argument will be critically examined later, his statement of his goal should be kept in mind during the following exposition: "But we must note that our aim has not been to present a detailed theory of such [previously mentioned] transcendental constituing, and therewith to sketch a new 'theory of knowledge' in respect of the spheres of reality, but only to make evident certain general thoughts which may help us in acquiring the idea of pure transcendental consciousness. What is essential for our purpose is to see upon evidence that the phenomenological reduction, as a means of disconnecting us from the natural attitude and its general thesis is possible, and that, when carried out, the absolute or pure transcendental consciousness is left over as a residuum to which it is then absurd to ascribe reality."[4] The residuum referred to includes the world as a "being-for-consciousness," i.e., as its intentional correlate. For us, the import of Husserl's statement is two-fold: 1) It implies that something quite short of a detailed theory of world-constitution, hence short of a "concrete demonstration," can assure us that the world is a being-for-consciousness. Certain "general thoughts," i.e., a "general argument," can provide this assurance. 2) This assurance can be gained by evidence available to us in the natural attitude. It will be precisely these two points on which my critique will focus.

## A. THE THESIS OF THE NATURAL ATTITUDE

### 1. The Thesis as Belief

Husserl begins section 27 of *Ideas* with the following statement: "We begin our considerations here as human beings who are living naturally, imagining, judging, feeling, willing, 'in the natural attitude'."[5] He then proposes that we reflect along with him to discover what this means. The investigation which follows, extending through section 30, attemps to characterize the general features of the natural attitude from the standpoint of that attitude itself.[6] The features Husserl uncovers are these: 1) When I am awake,[7] the world is continually on hand (*vorhanden*);[8] 2) I belong to this world, as do others to whom, I know, the world is also continually on hand;[9] 3) Anything of the world of which I am aware through experience and prior to any thinking, bears in its totality and in all its articulated saliencies the character: "there" (*da*), on hand.[10] These features form what Husserl calls the "general thesis" (*General-thesis*) of the natural attitude.[11] Husserl sums up the general thesis in this way: "I find continually on hand and standing over against me the one spatio-temporal actuality [*Wirklichkeit*] to which I myself belong, as do all other human beings found in it and related in the same way to it. The 'actuality', as the word already tells us, I find to be an actuality that is there [*daseiende*], and also *take it just as it gives itself* to me, as being-there."[12]

This thesis or positing is not, as Husserl explains, a particular or explicit act of consciousness; it is someting which pervades, and is implicit in, all mental processes which are directed toward the world.[13] This means, for example, that it is not solely a component of a theoretical attitude, although Husserl's text sometimes misleads us on this point.[14] Nor is this thesis one which only pertains to the world in some general sense, to an all-embracing structure or the like; it pertains to what is in the world as well.[15] Husserl does not tell us what sort of thesis the thesis of the natural attitude is in sections 27 through 30 of *Ideas*. In what follows I will elucidate the nature of the thesis.

An intentional experience can be characterized in a number of ways. One way is to refer to the kind of experience which it is, whether it is, for instance, a perceiving, a thinking, or a remembering. Another way is to describe it as "actual" (*aktuell*) or "potential," according to whether it is being lived through attentively or merely running its course in the background of consciousness. A third way refers to its "positionality," or to whether it is or is not positional, i.e., whether it does or does not posit something, and if it does, in what mode. It is this last descriptive character that concerns us here.

The different modes of positing something are called "thetic" modes by Husserl. A mere imagining of a fifteen-legged crab does not posit that object as actually existing, whereas my imagining of what my friend is now doing does posit my friend as actually existing. In this regard, Husserl distinguishes between positing and non-positing (or "neutral") presentations (*Vorstel-lungen*).[16] The thetic characters most often discussed by him are the modes of belief, although he does mention other modes of positing. In this connection, simple certainty of belief along with the modifications of belief, such as doubt, question and disbelief, form the doxically thetic modalities of positing, while acts of valuing, willing, feeling and taking pleasure in also posit something, according to Husserl, and do so "quite apart from the doxic positionality which 'lies in them'."[17]

According to Husserl, there is a moment of belief, in the form of simple certainty, in our normal perception of the world.[18] This moment is not only in our attentive perceivings, but also in our non-attentive consciousness of the world.

For instance, the environment which appears along with every sensuously perceived object also has correlative to it a consciousness which is doxically thetic.[19] Indeed, as we shall see in more detail later, an unmodalized form of doxic consciousness pervades our entire consciousness of the world. Since the general thesis of the natural attitude is also all-pervasive, we are led to ask whether this thesis is a *doxic* thesis. Of course it is quite clear from many of Husserl's writings that it is. But it is interesting that there seems to be no *direct* statement to this effect in *Ideas.* For reasons which will soon become clear, the way that Husserl does express this in *Ideas* is of significance to us here.

In *Ideas* Husserl indirectly conveys the idea that the thesis of the natural attitude is a belief. The objective correlate of belief, the character "actually existing," sometimes expressed as "certain being,"[20] is identified with the objective correlate of the thesis of the natural attitude, the character of being "on hand." This identification is made for the first time in section 31, where Husserl discusses the epoche. He writes: "It is further clear that we cannot doubt a being and in the same consciousness (under the unitary form of simultaneity) confer on the substrate of this being the thesis, and so have it consciously in the character of 'on hand' [*vorhanden*]. Equivalently expressed: we cannot at once doubt and hold for certain [*gewiss*] one and the same material of being [*Seinsmaterie*]."[21] In section 50, the identification is made again: "In the natural attitude we simply *carry out* all the acts through which the world is there [*da*] for us. We live naively in our perceiving and experiencing, in those thetic acts in which thing-unities appear, and not only appear, but are given with the character of "on hand" [*vorhanden*], actual [*wirklich*]."[22]

It seems from this that the thesis of the natural attitude is the same as the moment of belief which is in our consciousness of the world. Why, it might be asked, have I bothered to show what is obvious from many of Husserl's writings?[23] Before I answer, let us consider the significance of the thesis of the natural attitude for Husserl's demonstration that consciousness is world-constitutive. We recall that the demonstration involves showing that there is a correlation between consciousness and world, such that for every moment on the side of the world, there is a moment on the side of consciousness that corresponds to its particularity.[24] In this connection two criteria which the demonstration must meet, scope and reality, were discussed.[25] The reality criterion was set up to insure that the demonstration accounted for the world as transcendent actuality. The thesis of the natural attitude relates directly to this criterion, since the thesis is the correlate on the side of consciousness to the world's character as transcendent actuality. In saying that this thesis is doxic, then, Husserl is claiming that the subjective correlate of the world's ontic status is a belief. Above I showed that, in *Ideas,* Husserl conveys the idea that the thesis of the natural attitude is a belief by identifying the correlate of the thesis, "on hand," with the correlate of belief, "actual." The reason I have emphasized this was precisely to highlight this identification. Although it is plausible that "actual" is the correlate of a belief, it is not at all evident that "on hand" is. Yet Husserl seems to use the terms "*wirklich*" and "*vorhanden*" as equivalents in *Ideas*. Later we shall see that in his argument to show that consciousness constitutes the world Husserl tries to demonstrate that the correlate of the being-on-hand and the actuality of the world is a belief. We will also see that this aspect of his argument is the most problematic.

It was said before that the moments on the side of the world for which subjective correlates are to be sought are explicated in a pre-transcendental phenomenological analysis.[26] Sections 27 through 30 of *Ideas* represent just this sort of analysis. Throughout this "life-world" portion of the text, the term "*vorhanden*" is used constantly to express that most fundamental ontic feature which the world has for us. But in the more "Cartesian" sections of the pre-transcendental portions of the text, to be discussed later, where the theory of perceptual coherence plays a significant role, the term "*wirklich*" predominates in expressing this feature. In *Cartesian Meditations*, where, as the title of that work indicates, Husserl is once again concerned with the being of the world from a more traditional perspective, "*wirklich*" is used almost to the exclusion of "*vorhanden*." But in *Crisis,* where Husserl's novel "life-world" theme again emerges, "*vorhanden*" or terms expressing a similar idea predominates. The predominance of one or the other of these two terms in different contexts suggests that there may be two different features expressed by them, despite Husserl's apparent use of them at times as synonyms, and that a different type of phenomenological analysis is involved in the disclosure of each feature. I shall argue below that this is indeed the case.

## 2. The Correlate of the Thesis

The objective correlate of the doxic thesis of the natural attitude is sometimes referred to by Husserl as the "being-on-hand" of the world and at other times as its "actuality." These two terms, together with expressions related to them, designate what I shall refer to as the "on-hand idea" and the "actuality idea." These terms, in turn, conceptualize two features of the world. When terms expressing these two concepts are employed in the same context in Husserl's writings, there is often the impression that they have the same referent, or even that they are synonymous, i.e., that they express the same feature and perhaps in the same way. This impression is further reinforced by Husserl's designation of the same subjective correlate for both, namely belief. But it is of crucial importance for a proper understanding of Husserl to see that these are separate concepts and point to different features of the world, for then Husserl's relating them to the same subjective correlate becomes a noteworthy fact.

In the German language there is a close connection between *"vorhanden"* and *"wirklich."* One of the meanings of *"vorhanden"* is "existing," which comes close to the meaning of *"wirklich"* (real, actual). But *"vorhanden"* has other meanings, different from those of "wirklich," which specify more closely the way in which something "is." For instance, it can mean "present," or it can mean "available." These last two meanings can be expressed by the one English phrase "on hand," which I have used to translate *"vorhanden."* "On hand," then, means "present or available." It is this meaning which I believe Husserl develops when he discusses the way objects are for us in the natural attitude.

*"On hand,"* like *"vorhanden"* also has a connection with "real." For example, if merchandise is "on hand" in the warehouse, it would not have to be pointed out to a customer in a store that it is real, or exists in actuality. On the other hand, if a customer who has heard talk of a product with unusual properties asks if it really exists, or whether it is someone's mere fantasy, the salesman who affirms its existence does give the customer additional information if he says that he has some on hand. Thus, whereas *"wirklich"* merely states the existential status of something, *"vorhanden"* expresses that something is in a certain relation *to someone.* Being "on hand" implies someone *to whom* something is present or available, while being real (or actual) does not ordinarily have this reference to someone.

Husserl incorporates the ordinary understanding of these terms in his development of the on-hand and actuality ideas. I will discuss the on-hand idea first. Husserl often uses terms for it which express the reference to "someone for whom," expressions such as *"für mich einfach da"* (simply there *for me*),[27] and *"für mich da"* (there *for me*).[28] Husserl has also remarked that the world in on hand to someone who is awake.[29] Thus, it is not on hand in some absolute sense, nor even to someone at all times, but to someone who is in a certain state. When I am asleep, the world is not on hand to me, although it may be for others, if they are awake. Thus, in its general sense, the relation to someone implied in the on-hand idea is not to be understood to be a mere physical relationship, like that of spatial proximity, for example. Rather, it concerns the being there of something for someone within the context of a project or interest, a being there for someone who has a certain *"Einstellung,"* who is *"eingestellt,"* i.e., mentally "set into" a certain context so as to be oriented towards, and perhaps busied with, the objects of that "province of meaning.''[30] Someone who is "arithmetically *eingestellt*," for instance, and who is engaged in arithmetical calculations, has the natural numbers on hand to him, and not just the ones being dealt with at the moment. In a certain sense, all the natural numbers are on hand, forming the context within which he operates and being available to be present to him, in the special sense of intuitive presence, by means of the various ways (operations) that they can be reached. That this is so can be made evident by recalling those times when we all, in moments of "foggy-mindedness," seem to be unable to perform a simple arithmetical operation. We want the product of 8 times 6, for example, but the product does not "come to us." It is there, somewhere, but we cannot reach it. We try 5 times 8 plus 8, and there it is — 48. It was there and available all along, and we have finally found a way to it.

Being awake is the most fundamental way in which we can be *"eingestellt,"* for it is then that we are mentally "set into" the world, set into that context which we never leave when we are awake even though we may become *"einge-stellt"* in special ways, for instance, arithmetically.[31] When I am awake, the world is on hand. How is this to be explicated in terms of "presence" and "availability?" The world is present to me, but not in the sense that its whole content is spread out before me in all its clarity and distinctness. Nor does the world's "presence" mean that I somehow "know" all that is in the world. Rather, as Husserl describes it, this "presence" has varying degrees of vagueness and indeterminacy as it extends spatially and temporally from the here and now.[32] Furthermore, as Husserl's discussion indicates,[33] the being-on-hand of something vague and indeterminate is essentially connected with what I have called its "availability," i.e., to the possibility of its being clearly and distinctly before me and in that sense "known." Thus it can be said that whatever is on hand in the mode of vague and indistinct presence, is present *as being available* for me to be intuitively aware of it and to grasp it through that mode of consciousness in which I continually live when I am awake, attentional consciousness,[34] Thus we see that in this case being-on-hand in the mode of presence refers to availability, and that availability in turn refers to (the possibility of) presence. But this mutual reference is involved in all cases of being-on-hand. When something is "fully" present, as when it is before me and I am attending to it, the sense of its being-on-hand essentially refers to its being available for my continued attention and to its being available to be turned to again, should I turn away from it. Likewise, the "being-on-hand of the world" indicates aspects of "sheer" availability where there is zero presence. That there are events of which I have not the slightest knowledge happening in places beyond my immediate surroundings, for example, forms part of the sense of the being-on-hand of the world for me. The being-on-hand of such things means that there are events, etc., out there which if I were to (or could) move in the appropriate direction I could make them present and experience them intuitively, grasp them in an attentive consciousness.[35] Presence and availability, then, although distinct characters, refer in some way to one another and are thus *both* involved whenever something is on hand.

It should also be mentioned that the "being-on-hand of the world," besides referring to what is *in the world*, points to the fact that there is *always* an empty "out-thereness" of availability which is ever reinstated as it is penetrated and made present. It is this which gives the world the character of a "horizon." We shall also see later that the variation from "full" presence to "sheer" availability discussed above holds for individual objects, which also have their zones of vagueness and indeterminacy and their horizons of possibility.

There is another aspect of the on-hand idea that has not yet been discussed. It is stressed when Husserl uses the expressions *"einfach da"* or *"schlechthin da"* (both: simply there),[36] and *"schlicht daseiendes"* (simply being there)[37] to denote how the world is there for us in the natural attitude. These phrases emphasize that what is on hand is so *independently* of our consciousness. The way in which Husserl discloses this aspect of the sense of the world's being-on-hand in the "life-world" part of *Ideas* (sections 27-30) is of interest to us here, not only for what it tells us about this "independence," but also for what it reveals about the conception of consciousness which is implicit in the type of reflection that discloses the on-hand character of the world. In these sections he shows, through a kind of imaginative variation (performed in the natural attitude), that the world is continually on hand for us no matter what spontaneities of consciousness (cogitata) we may be momentarily experiencing and no matter how much of the world, if anything of it, these spontaneities may be intuitively apprehending. Thus, things, persons, etc., including their values or functional characteristics (their being books, friends, etc.) are simply there (*einfach da*) for me whether I *attend* to them or not. Even if I am thoroughly engrossed in proving some mathematical theorem, and am not attending to anything in the world at all, the world is still there for me. The being-on-hand of the world proves to be a constant over against the diverse and changing ways I have of actively averting to it, i.e., of being "conscious" of it in the specific sense of active attentional consciousness.

The type of reflection involved here, which, following Husserl,[38] I will call "naive reflection," seems to recognize only attention as "consciousness" (of the world), and in so far as it does, the being-on-hand of the world is disclosed to be independent of consciousness *per se*. Husserl often uses the term *"vorgegeben"* (pregiven),[39] as well as the expressions *"immer schon da"* (always already there), and *"im voraus für uns seiend"* (existing for us in advance),[40] to express the idea of something being on hand independently of consciousness. That objects in the world can be "pregiven" or "given beforehand" means, for naive reflection, that they can be there for me before I actively avert to them and busy myself with them, and that even when I do attend to them, they are pregiven to this active attending to them. Such an object is called an "*Ansich*" (In-itself) or a "*Selbst*" (Itself) by Husserl: "An Itself [*Selbst*] is an object...which is there only with respect to the active Ego, which is on hand for it as something permanently available and capable of being identified again and again."[41]

We recall that Husserl's theory of world-constitutive consciousness was developed in response to the problem of cognition. The key terms in Husserl's formulation of the problem are "immanence" and "transcendence," and the relationship of what they denote, mind or consciousness, and world, is the enigma. But how are these terms, and consequently how is the problem, to be understood? I believe that the most fundamental understanding of the problem of cognition to be found in Husserl's writings is expressed when he reports the results of his reflections on what he calls "naive reflection." In one such report he says that the knowing performance itself (evidence) seems to be "a matter of simple 'seeing', a mental inspection without a character of its own, always one and the same and in itself undifferentiated: the 'seeing' just 'sees' the things... All difference is thus in the things that exist in themselves and have their differences through themselves."[42] From the point of view of naive reflection, acts of consciousness (immanence), especially the most primative form of cognitive consciousness, acts of attending to and grasping an object, seem to be almost characterless, undifferientiated functions in comparison with the transcendent world. This contrast is captured in the on-hand idea: the world is pregiven to cognitive acts, it is there for us and there for us as what it is prior to our cognizing it. When something of the world is attended to and grasped, it presents itself to the mind through what seems to be a transparent act of consciousness. Compared to the fullness of the pregiven world, consciousness seems nearly empty. Likewise, the very basic meaning of "transcendence" which is expressed in the above quote by the phrases "in themselves" and "through themselves," phrases which seem to capture what Husserl calls the "naive" concept of transcendence,[43] is expressed in the on-hand idea. What is transcendent is that which is there for us, is present and available, yet not because of our consciousness of it.

A *problem* of cognition emerges from this understanding of consciousness and world when the "simple seeing" and the correlative "in-itselfness" and "through-itselfness" of the world lose their obviousness and become enigmatic. This can happen, it seems to me, if one engages in naive reflection, but in such a way as to distance oneself sufficiently from a total immersion in it so as to be able to make this obviousness thematic. Then, one permits oneself to be taken accross the thin line from acceptance to wonder such that it becomes astonishing that we can know things by just "looking" at them through a "look" that seems to do nothing more than clear the way between ourselves and them for our contact with them.

Husserls's response to the mystery of this "contact" is his theory that consciousness constitutes the world. In opposition to the naive view he says: "it is apparent that it really makes no sense at all to talk about things which are 'simply there' and just need to be 'seen'. On the contrary, this 'simply being there' consists of certain mental processes of specific and changing structure, such as perception, imagination, memory, predication, etc., and in them the things are not contained as in a hull or vessel. Instead, the things come to be constituted in these mental processes...."[44] "As in everyday life, so too in science...experience is the consciousness of being with the matters themselves, of seizing upon and having them quite directly. But experience is not an opening through which the world, existing prior to all experience, shines into a room of consciousness...."[45] "Experience is the performance in which for me, the experiencer, experienced being 'is there', and is there *as what* it is, with the whole content and the mode of being that experience itself, by the performance going on in its intentionality, attributes to it. If what is experienced has the sense of *'transcendent' being*, then it is the experiencing that constitutes this sense, and does so either by itself or in the whole motivational nexus pertaining to it and helping to make up its intentionality."[46]

The above passages reflect Husserl's reformulation of the problem. Husserl expresses this version of the problem in this way: "Is not the problem how, in the immanence of the ego, this outside [i.e., the transcendent world] can take on and confirm that sense of transcendence which we have, and use, naively-straightforwardly?"[47] As this quotation indicates, Husserl's approach will be to expand the notion of immanence and to show how the naive sense of transcendence is constituted in this enlarged immanence, i.e., in a constituting transcendental life, and to show how immanence in the naive sense is one of the forms that this life can assume.[48] In this connection Husserl remarks that "daily practical living is naive. It is immersion in the already-given [*vorgegeben*] world....Meanwhile all those productive intentional functions of experiencing, because of which physical things are simply there, go on anonymously. The experiencer knows nothing about them...,"[49] and cannot while remaining in the natural attitude.[50] It would appear from this that an important aspect of Husserl's overall account would be an account of the naiveté of the natural attitude, a naiveté which seems to consist of an ignorance or lack of cognizance of these productive intentional functions.

We turn now to a discussion of the actuality-idea, which, as we shall see later, provides the basis for another version of the problem of cognition. Husserl writes that in perception "that which appears stands there as something that exists [als Seiendes], it is taken to be actual [wirklich],"[51] it offers itself "as simply existing [seiend schlechthin], as an actuality that is there [daseiende Wirklichkeit]."[52] Going beyond perception in the narrow sense of thematic consciousness of something, he says that "natural life...is life within a universal unthematic horizon. This horizon is, in the natural attitude, precisely the world always pregiven as that which exists [Das Seiende].[53] In Ideas Husserl sums up his discussion of the natural attitude in this way: "I find continually on hand and standing over against me the one spatio-temporal actuality....'The' world is as actuality always there; at most it is here or there 'other' than I supposed, this or that under such names as 'illusion', 'hallucination' and the like, must be struck out of it...."[54]

In some of the above passages both the on-hand and actuality ideas are present, the latter seeming to express that, beyond being simply on hand in the sense so far explicated, the world is on hand as that which exists or is actual. Husserl opposes actuality to "illusion," i.e., to whatever might present itself as actual, but which lacks some essential determination of what is actual, a lack which can become disclosed in the course of experience. He uses various terms to express the opposite of actuality, including "illusion" (Schein), by which he means inactuality (Unwirklichkeit),[55] "what does not exist" (nicht Seiend),[56] and "pure nothing" (pures Nichts), by which he means pure illusion (blosser Schein).[57] In the following I will explicate the concept of actuality and also explain Husserl's apparent use of "vorhanden" and "wirklich" as synonyms in some of his texts.

To ask if a feature something is experienced to have is an "actual" feature of it is to ask if the feature pertains to the thing as it is in itself. Such questioning presupposes an awareness that things are not always as they appear to be. Likewise, to ask if something experenced is an "actual" thing at all, acknowledges that what appears is not always something which is. Thus the concept of actuality is essentially connected with the concept of appearance. For our purposes, two kinds of appearances must be distinguished.

Within the context of daily practical life, where our cognitive interest does not have as its goal the obtaining of scientific knowledge, an object as it is in actuality is the object as it is given under certain optimal conditions. This would be, for instance, a thing seen from just the "right" distance, under the "correct" illumination or in a "certain" orientation. A moment's reflection on what we do when it is really important for us to find out how something "really looks" makes this clear. We step closer or back from it, provide light where it is lacking, or diminish it where it is too bright; we turn the thing in our hands or orient ourselves so as to view it in a certain way. What is given to us under such optimal conditions, Husserl says, counts for us as an "Itself" *(Selbst)* in our practical lives.[58] Part of what he seems to mean is that under these conditions we believe we grasp the object as it is *in itself*. When we reflect on how something is given to us under non-optimal conditions, although we feel we are then still in the presence of the thing itself, we may observe that it has an appearance which we might understand to have arisen due to conditions which affect our correct apprehension of the thing. Thus objects appear "darkened" and "grayed" in dim illumination because we cannot see colors in the dark, and rough-textured objects appear "smoothed" from a distance because we cannot see their details. Because the appearances objects have under such conditions are thought by us to arise from the way these conditions affect *us* and not the objects, we relegate these appearances to the realm of the "subjective," as opposed to what is "objective," that is, the way the thing is in itself and hence the way it remains despite the changes of the conditions affecting us.

In addition to subjective appearances of this sort there are what can be called, in a general sense, "illusory" appearances. Included among these are hallucinations (when not known to be such), illusions in the narrow sense, such as those often used in psychological experiments (when they *do* deceive us), and mistakenly apprehended objects. An example of the last is the case of seeing an acquaintance approaching who turns out to be someone else. Although these phenomena are very different from one another, they form a class of subjective appearances distinct from the previous class in the following sense: whereas the non-optimal subjective appearances are appearances *of* an aspect of an object, an aspect which is there and which actually pertains to the object, an illusory subjective appearance is not an appearance *of* anything at all which is there and which actually pertains to something. Thus the acquaintance that I see is not an appearance *of* the stranger, even though the stranger is certainly there. Furthermore, illusory subjective appearances, unlike the former kind, are taken by us to be something which is actual, and it is this which constitutes their illusory or deceptive character. When the deception is uncovered, the phenomenon which was present (or perhaps still is) would be regarded as something inactual. We think that these illusory appearances also arise because of conditions affecting our perceptual processes, although perhaps in different ways than in the case of the former class of appearances. It is perhaps because of their deceptive nature that Husserl says that they must be "*struck* out of" the world.[59]

When we subtract all these subjective appearances from the world, we are left with the world as it is in itself. Thus we have here a new concept of "Itself" or "In-itself" (*Ansich*). Before, an "Itself" was conceived as something which is on hand with respect to attentional consciousness, and as part of that, was something whose being-there was independent of attentional consciousness.[60] In the new concept, an "Itself" is an *actuality*, i.e., something whose being-there is independent of consciousness *also* in the sense of consciousness which is somehow responsible for appearances, and not only attentional consciousness. Here, an object as it is given in optimal conditions, provided that it is not itself an illusory appearance, qualifies as an "Itself."

Since they are dependent on consciousness, subjective appearances are not on hand. But to understand the sense in which they are not on hand requires a further discussion of the on-hand idea. This discussion will allow us to understand Husserl's frequent identification of "on hand" with "actual."

Up to now the being-on-hand of something referred in part to its being available to the *attentional* functions of consciousness and being there independently of these functions. In this sense, even subjective appearances can be on hand. That this is so is apparent in the case of non-illusory subjective appearances. For instance, if I sufficiently distance myself from something, an appearance of it is given to me in which some of its details are blurred, yet I do not attribute this appearance to my active attending to the object *per se*. The appearance is independent of my consciousness *qua* attentive. We understand these appearances, as well as illusory subjective appearances, as arising and being there because we are conscious of them, but not because we are specifically *attentively* conscious of them. Thus in the dark, *all* the object in my surroundings appear "darkened," not just those I am attending to. Those "darkened" appearances are on hand to my attentional functions, yet in another sense they are not on hand at all. They are only on hand to my attentional functions because of some non-attentional pregiving functions of consciousness to which, in turn, they are not on hand, but rather whose "achievement" they are. This also holds for illusory subjective appearances; they are *there* only when these functions are operating.

When it is said that subjective appearances are not on hand, this does not imply that the concept of "on hand" now has a different meaning than before. Rather, "on hand" is a relative concept—relative to one's conception of consciousness. "On hand" always means present and/or available to consciousness independently of consciousness. Naive reflection specifies this general meaning further: "consciousness" in the definition becomes "attentional consciousness," a form of consciousness that Husserl has called "consciousness in the pregnant sense that *offers itself first*."[61] But when another type of reflection is involved in which one recognizes and focuses upon subjective appearances, the concept of consciousness (of the world) is broadened to include consciousness of these appearances. I will call this form of consciousness "appearential" consciousness and the type of reflection which recognizes it "psychological" reflection. It is in this type of reflection where the distinction between subjective appearance and actuality is first made.

The relativity of the on-hand concept is due to the aspect of independence contained in its meaning. Thus, while subjective appearances are pregiven to attentional consciousness in all cases, once appearential functions of consciousness are acknowledged, subjective appearances are not considered to be pregiven to consciousness *in general*; they are understood to be pregiven *by* appearential functions but not *to* them. For psychological reflection, subjective appearances are "available" to attentional consciousness since the "ray" of attention can always be directed through the otherwise inactual (*inaktuell*) pregiving modes of consciousness to the appearances which they make to be there.

When consciousness is viewed psychologically, it is only actualities which are on hand in the sense of being pregiven to, yet pregiven independently of, consciousness in general. In this sense, the extension of the on-hand concept is identical with the extension of the actuality concept, although the meanings of these two concepts are different. It is perhaps for this reason that Husserl sometimes uses the terms "*vorhanden*" and "*wirklich*" as synonyms.

It should be emphasized that, as discussed here, what is given to us under optimal conditions, provided that this is not itself an illusion, is *not* a subjective appearance of an object. Rather, it is the givenness of an object or of some aspect of an object *directly,* i.e., "clearly and distinctly," without the "beclouding" that "stands in the way" whenever conditions are such as to give rise to subjective appearances Thus consciousness, as we have understood it thus far, is not our only "medium of access" to the world,[62] and subjective appearances do not, as it were, "enclose" us completely such that the world is only given to us through them. Rather, consciousness has "holes" through which the world "shines" directly in on us and through which the world is given to us as it is in itself. This being the case, the problem of cognition is the same as formulated above: How can we know things just by looking at them through a look that seems to do nothing more than clear the way between ourselves and them for out contact with them. But what I have reported on here from what I have called "psychological reflection" only prepares us for the deeper analyses which Husserl has given us under the same title. These analyses, to which we now turn, lead to a different formulation of the problem.

B. THE PSYCHOLOGICAL INVESTIGATION OF CONSCIOUSNESS AND
THE ARGUMENT THAT CONSCIOUSNESS CONSTITUTES THE WORLD

In section 34 of *Ideas* Husserl begins a series of observations "within which we are not troubled with any phenomenological epoche. We are directed to an 'outer world', and, without forsaking the natural attitude, reflect psychologically on our ego and its experiences."[63] This psychological reflection forms part of a wider investigation whose purpose is to disclose what is left over when the whole world is "bracketed," i.e., what remains as the "phenomenological residuum," as the field of study of the new science of phenomenology, after the phenomenological epoche has been performed.[64] This wider investigation, in turn, is designed to fulfill one of the aims of *Ideas* as a whole, namely, to lead the reader to a new scientific domain and to do so in a way which sharply distinguishes it from all other scientific domains and its science from all other sciences. Of special concern in this regard is distinguishing the domain of phenomenology form mundane domains and its science from mundane sciences (especially from psychology).[65]

The phenomenological epoche is introduced in sections 31 and 32 as the method for revealing this new domain. This method of access is in keeping with the just-mentioned aim of *Ideas,* specifically the aim of distinguishing phenomenology from the "positive" sciences of the world. These latter sciences are rooted in the natural attitude in the sense that they take their respective domains to be aspects of that actuality which is unquestionably on hand to all of us, and take them to be available to whatever special intuitions their methodologies prescribe. Their striving toward truth is a striving to bring to *knowledge* what is taken to be already there in itself. But in performing the phenomenological epoche one deprives oneself of this basis of acceptance, one brackets the world by putting the general thesis of the natural attitude "out of action."[66] This means that although the thesis remains a moment in our experiencing of the world, we render it inoperative in our phenomenological intuitions and judgements so that the world is no longer simply accepted by us as the thesis posits it and as it continues to present itself despite our new theoretical attitude. With this new scientific attitude in effect, the question naturally arises of what domain of objects is left which we may take for granted, on whose basis we may generate judgments and to which we may return with these judgements yielding to its dictates in their ultimate verification. "Is not 'the world' the name for the universe of whatever exists?"[67]

This privative characterization of the method of epoche determines the ostensible movement of thought in sections 33-55 of *Ideas* as the search for a residuum, for something to fill the void that seems to be left. This void is to be filled by " 'pure consciousness' with its pure 'correlates of consciousness', and...its 'pure Ego'...."[68] Although the imagery which Husserl employs in these sections often lends the impression that the world is excluded from the field of phenomenological research, nothing could be further from the truth.[69] Not only do these psychological reflections attempt to establish consciousness as an essentially independent realm of being despite its factual status as a reality in the world, but as well they try to show that the world in a certain sense is "contained" within this realm as a "pure correlate of consciousness." As Husserl states it, just after the end of the psychological investigations, "although we have 'suspended' the whole world...(w)e have literally lost nothing, but have won the whole of absolute Being, which, properly understood, conceals in itself all transcendencies, 'constituting' them within itself."[70]

Thus what on the surface appears to be a single movement of thought, guided by the image of the search for a residuum, is actually a two-fold movement. On the one hand there is the *separating* of consciousness and world as distinct realms of being, a movement which includes the development of the idea of consciousness, through a descriptive disclosure of its various forms, and the determination that consciousness so disclosed is a realm of being independent from the world, through an investigation of its essence. On the other hand there is the *relating* of consciousness and world through descriptive analyses and through the argument they support which attempt to show that the world is a dependent realm of being, i.e., is a being *for* consciousness. The former "separating" movement seems to be the dominant concern, its development being continuous, apparent and essentially complete. The latter "relating" movement is quite different. Although its conclusions are emphatically stated, the developments leading to them are not clearly identified (in fact, they often also form parts of the former movement) and certain aspects which would seem to be essential for this movement's completion must be supplied. It is this second movement of thought which will be our concern here.

### 1. Husserl's Argument

Before beginning the exposition of the psychological part of Husserl's "introductions to phenomenology," let us recall what I have said Husserl's argument seeks to establish, list its central points, and relate these points to Husserl's specific way of expressing them in *Ideas*. The argument seeks to show that the being there for me (i.e., for each of us) of the world and of anything that is in it is an achievement of consciousness. This formulation of Husserl's thesis can now be refined as a result of our recent discussion of the on-hand and actuality ideas. The thesis is that *consciousness constitutes the world,* and this means that *the being-on-hand of the world or actuality is an achievement of consciousness.*

Referring to the discussion of the meaning of the world-constitutive thesis in Chapter two, its main points can be summarized as follows: 1) there is a correlation between the world and consciousness such that there is no moment on the side of the world for which there is not a moment on the side of consciousness which corresponds to the world's particularity;[71] 2) to experience (*erleben*) the just-mentioned moments of consciousness *is* to have the world on hand. With regard to the first point, we should note that its successful demonstration would have to satisfy the "scope criterion" discussed in Chapter two.[72] The scond point incorporates the idea that consciousness "achieves" the being-on-hand of the world by being intentional, or, to express it more strongly, it implies an identification of the notion of achieving with that of intentionality. This identification was only suggested in the previous discussion of intentionality,[73] and will now be made explicit through a quotation from Husserl: "In displaying these [intentionalities], we must say to ourselves again and again that without them objects and the world would not be there for us and that they are for us only with the meaning and mode of being that they constantly derive or have derived from these subjective achievements."[74] Intentional mental processes (intentionalities) are "achievements" in the sense that only in experiencing them are we related to objects, confronted with a world; in short, only then do we have a world on hand.

Husserl states what I have called the world-constitutive thesis in many ways and in many places throughout his works. The above quote from *Crisis* is one example. In *Ideas,* one of Husserl's statements of the thesis emphasizes the first point above, the correlation between consciousness and world: "...whatever is phenomenologically disconnected [by the epoche] remains still, with a certain change of signature, within the framework of phenomenology. The real and ideal actualities, which come under the suspending clause, are represented in the phenomenological sphere by the whole nexus of corresponding senses and positions [*Sinnen und Sätzen*]."[75] The next quote, also from *Ideas,* comes at the culmination of Husserl's psychological discussion of consciousness as one of its results. "(T)he whole spatio-temporal world to which man and the human ego attribute themselves as subordinate singular realities, is *according to its sense mere intentional being*, a being, therefore, which has the merely secondary, relative sense of a being *for* a consciousness. It is a being which consciousness in its experiences posits, and which, in principle, is intuitable and determinable only as something identical in the harmoniously motivated appearance-manifolds, but *over and beyond* this, is just nothing at all.'"[76] This expression of the thesis relates closely to the second point above, and in addition, in its last sentence, contains a reference to the coherence-thesis which is the crux of Husserl's argument.[77] One final quote from *Cartesian Meditations* links the way objects are "contained" in consciousness to the idea of intentionality which in turn is related to the notion of achievement: "The existence of a world and, accordingly, the existence of this die [an example Husserl is using] are 'parenthesized' in consequence of my epoche; but the one identical die (as appearing) is continuously 'immanent' in the flowing consciousness, *descriptively 'in' it;* as is likewise the attribute 'one identical'. This being-in-consciousness is a *being in of a completely unique kind*: not a being-in-consciousness as a really intrinsic component part, but rather a being-in-it 'ideally' as something *identical*, something appearing—or, equivalently stated, a being-in-it as its immanent *'objective sense'*. The 'object' of consciousness, the object as having identity 'with itself' during the flowing subjective processes, does not come into the process from the outside; on the contrary, it is included as a sense in the subjective process itself—and thus as an *'intentional effect' produced by* the synthesis of consciousness.'"[78] Having reviewed what Husserl's argument seeks to establish, we now turn to the argument itself.

Husserl's argument concerns sensory perception, for, as he says, sensory perception furnishes to sensory experience the power which allows it to serve as the ultimate source of the nourishment for the thesis of the natural attitude "thereby enabling me as a conscious being to discover over against me an existing world of things, to ascribe to myself in this world a body, and to find for myself within this world a proper place'"[79] Moreover, the argument concerns sensory perception of *things*, for "it is sufficient for us to treat the perception of things as representing all other perceptions (of properties, processes, and the like.''[80]

I will now present five statements which concisely formulate what I take to be Husserl's argument. After that, I will discuss the meaning of each of the statements in turn, and wherever possible also some of the considerations Husserl advances in support of them. In addition, I will present analyses of my own to elucidate some of Husserl's points. Later I will criticize the argument from the point of view of its role in "introducing" the reader to transcendental phenomenology. We shall see later that the argument as formulated below admits of two radically different interpretations. The statements of the argument are:

1. The perception of a thing is necessarily inadequate, since it is percep-

tion through adumbrations or appearances.

2. Because of this inadequacy, any perceived thing could be inactual, which means that the perception of a thing is a believing or doxic consciousness.

3. Whatever *could* be inactual and is on hand, is on hand through consciousness.

4. Therefore, any perceived thing is on hand through consciousness, and

5. The world is on hand through consciousness.

## 2. The Inadequacy of Perception

Husserl affirms part of the first statement in section 43 of *Ideas*. As he expresses it, it belongs to the essence of the perception of things "to be adumbrating perception; and correlatively, it belongs to the sense of its intentional object, of the thing as given within it, to be perceivable, in principle, only through perceptions of such a kind, thus through adumbrating perceptions."[81] This finding is one result of a lengthly descriptive analysis of experience which culminates in a comparison between "transcendent" and "immanent" perception, i.e., between straight-forward perceivings of things and reflective perceptions of those perceivings.

Husserl's analysis begins by uncovering what can be found in the flow of mental life of an awake subject. His purpose is to develop the concept of "process of consciousness" (*Bewusstseinserlebnis*).[82] He first discloses what I have called "attentional consciousness," mental processes (*Erlebnisse*), such as perceptions, in which an ego is turned toward an object. This is consciousness in the mode of actuality (*Aktualität*).[83] But, as Husserl says, "the stream of experience can never consist wholly of actualities."[84] When we attentively perceive an object we are also aware of other objects around it and this awareness is also a process of consciousness, albeit in the mode of inactuality.[85] Moreover, both types of mental processes are intentional, are consciousness *of* their respective objects,[86] even though in the latter type the glance of the ego is not specifically directed through it towards its intentional object. But this "implicit" awareness of background objects can be turned into an explicit awareness through a turning of the mental glance, therby modifying an inactual mental process into an actual one. Looking ahead, we can anticipate the significance of this modification for the being-on-hand of the world, especially for its aspect of availability. However, at this point in his discussion Husserl is not yet asserting that these inactual mental processes make a background to be available to us, nor do his observations imply this. To say, for instance, that the pencil lying next to the piece of paper I am now attending to is also, in a sense, "seen" by me, and that this seeing is a mental process does not necessarily imply that its being there to be seen, whether attentively nor not, is due to these non-attentional or any other mental processes. Naturally this remark applies also to the attentional mental processes. The intentionality here is not *constitutive* in the sense explained above, since to experience these mental processes is not tantamount to having their objects on hand. What is on hand on its own is merely *seen* through them.[87]

Counting the two types of perceptual consciousness just discussed to be among the "moments on the side of consciousness" mentioned in the summary of the meaning of Husserl's thesis above,[88] we note that Husserl's observations about them do not yet show them to correspond to the particularity of their objects. By the end of section 41 of *Ideas*, this situation is remedied. This development is announced in section 36 where Husserl says: "It lies in the very essence of an experience not only *that* it is a consciousness of [something], but also *of what* it is a consciousness, and in what determinate or indeterminate sense it is this."[89] This is said in order to dispel any thought that intentionality is a real relation between an experience, as a factual reality in the world, and a similarly factual, real object, for instance a psychophysical connection.[90] What Husserl seems to mean is that in a "real" relationship the coming-into-relation of a given experience and a given object would be governed by some natural law (in the broad sense of "natural," including psychological events as natural events). Each, the experience and the object, would have its proper nature determined independently of its connection with the other. The experience, in particular, would be a consciousness-of, but not, as to its own nature, of anything in particular. It would only be an experience of a particular object because the law governing occurances connected it with some particular object and would thus derive the particularity of its intentional relatedness *from the object*. It is precisely this which Husserl wants to deny in the passage quoted above. To support this, Husserl engages in a further analysis of perceptual experiences which fill their empty "consciousness-of" with content such that these experiences begin to correspond to the particularity of their objects. Among these contents are the "adumbrations" mentioned in the first statement of his argument.

Husserl begins his discussion of the components of a perceptual experience by distinguishing between the "perceived thing" and the "physical thing." Neither of these, he finds, belongs to the really intrinsic components (*reelen Bestande*) of a perception.[91] By "perceived things" Husserl means the things which are there in our environment as we perceive them in our everyday lives, things which, together with their perceived properties and characteristics and the space in which we perceive them, we normally take to be part of the world itself. But if we adopt a scientific attitude toward these things, recalling theories of physics, we understand the entire content of these things, their "secondary" as well as their "primary" qualities, as being "mere appearances" and "merely subjective" in contrast to the "true" physical thing whose description is ultimately given solely in mathematical terms. Likewise, "perceptual space" is to be distinguished form "physical space." Thus, in terms of "true being," the perception of a thing gives only the mere "this," "an empty X which becomes the bearer of mathematical determinations," something which does not exist in perceptual space and for which the perceived thing is merely a sign.[92]

Husserl's discussion here parallels certain sections in *Crisis* in which he is also gradually leading the reader toward the transcendental realm.[93] Thus, when Husserl tells us to consider exclusively the "perceived thing" from this point on in his analysis in *Ideas* by saying "we shut off the whole of physics and the whole domain of theoretical thought,"[94] he is guiding us to perform what he calls the "epoche of objective science" in *Crisis,* a move which takes us to the "life-world."[95] When Husserl, in contexts like this, calls the perceived thing "merely subjective" or the life-world "subjective-relative,"[96] he usually puts these words in quotation marks to indicate that they express the way things are considered in objective scientific thought. He is not saying that they are relative to consciousness in the sense which his world-constitutive thesis claims they are, nor that they are appearances in the strictly phenomenological sense which he is about to develop at this point in *Ideas*. Thus, performing this epoche does not presuppose an acceptance of the world-constitutive conception of consciousness.

"A thing," Husserl writes, "is necessarily given in mere modes of appearing [*Erscheinungsweisen*]...."[97] Within the psychological sections of *Ideas*, these "modes of appearing" refer chiefly to "modes of experiencing" (*Erlebnisweisen*) although, as Husserl tells us, they can also have a correlative "ontic" sense.[98] Although he does not make this explicit, it seems that this double reference of the expression "modes of appearing" points to the distinction made in later, transcendental portions of the text between the really intrinsic (*reell*) (hyletic and noetic) and the intentional (noematic) components of an experience.[99] This distinction can help us to understand Husserl's explication of the statement quoted above. A thing "can 'appear' only in a certain 'orientation', one which necessarily predelineates systematic possibilities of ever new orientations, each of which again corresponds to a certain 'mode of appearing', which we perhaps express as being given from this or that 'aspect', and so forth."[100] A perceptual experience, then, is an adumbrating (*abschat-*

*tend*) experience, one which does not give something completely, but which "sketches out" its completion in advance.

In *Ideas* as a whole, and in the sections we are dealing with in particular, the term "adumbration" (*Abschattung*) refers mainly to certain really intrinsic components of a perceptual experience which are classified among the "data of sensation"(*Empfindungsdaten*),[101] namely those which Husserl calls "hyletic data."[102] However, hyletic data are not "adumbrations" in themselves but are only called such when they perform a presentive (*darstellende*) function, i.e., when, "animated" by certain other really intrinsic components of experiences called "apprehensions" (*Auffassungen*) (the specifically noetic components), they function to present an object.[103] Although a datum of sensation is an experience,[104] or is a moment of an experience, it is not in itself intentional according to Husserl,[105] it is not an experience *of* anything. It is only through an apprehension, i.e., through the "noetic" phase of an experience, the phase which bears in itself the specific characteristic of intentionality and which "bestows sense" on such sensory contents, that an experience can be the experience *of* something.[106] Thus, a certain sensory content could not be called, let us say, a "shape-adumbration" unless it functioned to present an object *having* a shape in one of its possible orientations, unless, then, it were animated by an intentional phase of the entire concrete experience. Only then could the sense datum be "adumbrative," i.e., function to predelineate other experiences of the same object which would present its shape in different orientations.

Before proceeding with this rather abstract discussion, let us try to gain a concrete understanding of what hyletic data and apprehensions are. As an example, I will first relate something that happened to me and then describe it in Husserl's terms. I was seated in a very large dining hall with a number of fellow diners, prior to the serving of our common meal. The various courses of the meal were passed from the kitchen through an opening in the wall some distance to my right to one or two of us who served the rest. I was engrossed in talking with a friend when I began to experience a smell to which I paid hardly any attention and which I in no way connected with what we were all there for —to eat. Moments later my friend announced: "Here comes the spaghetti." At that moment the smell I was experiencing "turned into" the smell of spaghetti, a smell which then seemed to be beginning to fill the room from its source at my right. Since, by chance, I was engaged in a study of Husserl's theory of hyletic data at the time, I immediately reflected on this course of events before it ceased to be alive in my retentive memory. In this reflection, I was sure that when I first experienced the smell, or better, had the smell-experience, it was in no way the smell-experience *of* anything. I do not mean that it was not the smell-experience of anything *in particular*, yet *was* the smell-experience of something but of something I did not identify or recognize. It was not a smell-experience *of* at all. Nor was the "smell" located in the room. It seemed rather to be something purely temporal and located "nowhere," as it were, something whose only quality was to be a "smell" and a rather particular "smell." It seemed to simply have been something I was undergoing, an *Erlebnis* in Husserl's terms, and a non-intentional one. Once I heard the word "spaghetti," the smell-experience, it seemed, became the smelling *of* spaghetti, and simultaneously, the smell seemed to be located *in* the room and even seemed to be coming *from* my right. In becoming the smelling *of* spaghetti, it did not seem that a kind of "smell in general" became particularized as happens when a vague figure, say a "postman" coming my way becomes identified as "my postman." It had already been rather particular. What happened was not the same, then, as the transformation of the perception of a type into the perception of a particular instance of that type. Rather Husserl's expression "sense bestowal" seemed to be a more fitting characterization of what happened. Influenced by the word "spaghetti," and seemingly without any "effort" on my part, totally "passively," my experience was transformed through an "apprehension" which embued it with sense or meaning into the smelling *of* spaghetti, presenting me with the "smell of spaghetti coming from my far right." As such, the smelling became adumbrative, predelineating other smellings which would present the smell in other "orientations," such as the stronger, yet strangely often less enticing "smell of spaghetti right under my nose."

According to Husserl, data of sensation are not to be identified with features of the object which they may function to present. In our example, the smell-datum which functioned to present the spaghetti's smell is not to be identified with the smell itself, nor even with the way the spaghetti smelled in a particular smelling of it (its smell from a distance versus close up, for example). The latter two pertain to the object which is experienced, while the former pertains to the experiencing of the object.[107] Thus, such data of sensation, along with the apprehensions animating them (which also have a specificity of their own[108]) constitute the really intrinsic components of a perceptual experience[109] *whose specificity, then, is correlated with the specificity of the object*. Thus if I am experiencing a red, triangular object in a certain orientation, there are really intrinsic components of my experiencing of that object correlative to those specifications. It is, in part, due to such really intrinsic components of an experience that it is intentional in the sense Husserl meant when he said that it "lies in the very essence of an experience not only *that* it is a consciousness of, but also *of what* it is a consciousness, and in what determinate or indeterminate sense it is this.[110]

However, one cannot fully understand the meaning of this statement as it applies to perceptual experiences nor the first statement of Husserl's argument until the noematic side of the double reference of the expression "modes of appearing," is considered. There is a serious question, however, of whether one can speak of a noema in a *pre*-transcendental context. In *Ideas*, Husserl does not introduce the term "noema" until section 88, well beyond the beginning of the transcendental parts of the book, i.e., after effecting the transcendental epoche. Furhtermore, we find Husserl saying: "For the apprehension of the noema all affirmations bearing on actuality must be suspended."[111] No doubt this statement refers to the transcendental epoche. Clearly, the transcendental concept of noema cannot be introduced into an argument which attempts to show that consciousness constitutes the world. I believe, however, that a concept of noema can be extracted from certain aspects of Husserl's analyses which is consistent with the psychological framework that we are maintaining here. The following discussion aims, in part, to do just that. Since this discussion will rely in places on the transcendental parts of Husserl's texts, I will use the phrase "transcendental noema" when referring to the noema as it is discussed in those parts. Otherwise, "noema" will be used.

It will be instructive to start this discussion with Gurwitsch's definition of the perceptual noema. He defines this as "the thing perceived exactly and only as it appears to the perceiving subject through a given act of perception."[112] Actually, this defines only that part of the transcendental noema which Husserl calls the noematic "nucleus." This nucleus plus the noematic "characters" constitute the full transcendental noema.[113] However this definition contains an ambiguity whose clarification is very important for understanding the noematic concept of adumbration and the sense in which perception is said to be "inadequate" in the first statement of Husserl's argument. The definition may be understood in two ways. It may be interpreted as referring to the object of a perception in light of the "predicates" which the object is perceived to have in that particular perception. Alternatively, it may be taken to refer to the *appearance* of the object and of its "predicates." These two interpretations focus on two different dimensions of the noema which will be referred to as the "object dimension" and the "appearance dimension" respectively.[114] I will discuss the object dimension first.

If the above definition is taken to refer to the object of a perception, whether or not that object exists in actuality, in light of the "predicates" (i.e., features) which the object is experienced to have in a particular perception, then it defines what Husserl calls the "sense" (*Sinn*) of a perception. Husserl also refers to this as the "perceived as such" (i.e., as perceived),[115] and as the "object in the how of its determinateness" (*Gegenstand im Wie seiner*

*Bestimmtheiten*).[116] The above phrase "whether or not it exists in actuality" indicates that the concept of noematic sense is developed under the phenomenological epoche.[117] As such, the terms "object" and "predicate" do not refer to entities as straight-forwardly encountered actualities which are in the world, but to reflectively encountered ideal components of a perceptual experience,[118] or as Husserl metaphorically puts it, to something which one has " 'in mind' " when conscious of something.[119] Husserl means that if I reflect on my perceiving of an object and if I suspend my belief in the actuality (or non-actuality, as the case may be) of that object there is still a *phenomenon* left which is *what* I am perceiving and which belongs essentially to my perception. The features of this "what" can be described in terms like those I would employ if I did not suspend belief, except that the terms would have a meaning radically different from the one they have in their normal use.[120] This is because, in using these terms to describe what is reflectively intuited, one does not intend them, in accordance with the way in what they express is reflectively intuited, as referring to actualities, but rather to phenomena of actualities. The word "phenomena" is employed here to denote the irreal ontological status which that which is reflected upon is intended to have as a consequence of the phenomenologist's change of attitude. "Senses," as Husserl says, "are not things."[121]

This phenomenon or noematic sense is that "content" of the transcendental noema by virtue of which the noema, and through the noema, consciousness, is related to an object.[122] The noematic sense is correlated specifically with the "sense-giving" moment (the apprehension) on the noetic side of consciousness,[123] and refers to the same object to which that noesis refers.[124] The object referred to, considered in abstraction from its predicates, is also said to be part of the transcendental noema and of its sense.[125] It is the " 'determinable subject of its possible predicates' – the pure X in abstraction from all predicates...," the identical moment in different transcendental noemata which refer to a "same."[126] By "predicates," Husserl means determinations of the perceived *object*, and not, as we shall see, of the *appearance* of the object. In the case of a mere thing, these predicates would comprise whatever could be said of an object in formal or material ontological terms on the basis of a given perception, for example, it is a "thing," it has this or that "shape" and "color," it is "hard," "rough," etc.[127] Thus, the noematic sense is that part of the transcendental noema which is "described in objective terms only."[128]

It must be emphasized that the predicates in question are those features which an object is *experienced* to have in a *given* perception. This means that the description of the noematic sense is a "definitely limited description."[129] However the description is not limited just to those features which are *directly* given in a particular perception, i.e., which appear. For instance, in seeing a thing from one point of view the sides of the object facing one are directly given, yet the thing is experienced to be something which *has* other sides and other features not directly given. The specifics of the other side and other features may be quite indeterminate, but nonetheless, in their indeterminacy they figure in the sense of the given perception. Other perceptions of the same object from different points of view could have different noematic senses wherein those predicates only indicated in the first preception are directly given. They may also contain new predicates which did not figure in the first perception at all. In this fashion, one perception points to certain others through whose actualization the indeterminacies in the given noematic sense would become filled out, the object becoming further and more closely determined. Such pointing references make up what Husserl calls the "horizon" of a given perception.[130] The horizon consists of the co-intendings to all the other predicates of the object which the object is experienced to have in a given perception but which are not directly given. Noematically speaking, then, the sense of a perception contains implicit moments which are foreshadowed by the explicit ones.[131] Thus a single perception of an object (or even a finite series of perceptions) can be said to be "inadequate" in that an explication of its contents through acts of thought would yield an incomplete *knowledge* of the object. I will call this inadequacy "epistemic inadequacy" to distinguish it from another inadequacy I will discuss, namely the inadequacy which perception has due to its being perception through appearances or adumbrations. In order to have a concise way of referring to this second concept of inadequacy, I will make use of the previously coined adjective "appearential" and call it "appearential inadequacy."

The second way of understanding our definition of the noema concerns the appearance dimension of the noema. Within this dimension lies the adumbrational concept of the noema in terms of appearances. Husserl says almost nothing about this dimension of the noema in *Ideas*, and thus his account of the adumbrational nature of perception, as presented above in the discussion of hyletic data, and of perception's appearential inadequacy is almost solely in noetic terms. However, in section 132 of *Ideas*, Husserl distinguishes the noematic sense from the "full" noematic nucleus, the former being said to be a "kind of abstract form that dwells in" the noema. As the full nucleus, Husserl mentions a second concept of "object in the how of its determinateness" which takes into account the "how of its modes of givenness" (*der Wie seiner Gegebenheitsweisen*).[132] In the body of *Ideas*, Husserl mentions "saturation-differences in clearness" as the only example of this.[133] Among these seem to be such differences as between the way a sense is "filled out" primordially when an object is given in a "now," as opposed to the same sense which is retained in consciousness, and also differences in the mode of such filling out, such as the same sense judged versus intuitively given in a perception.[134] Such differences do not determine the *object* itself, nor is a different sense involved, but they do qualify the transcendental noema.[135]

These considerations do not yet bring us to the appearance dimension of the noema. In a note to section 132 of *Ideas*, written a few years after its publication, Husserl noted a deficiency in his treatment of the full noematic nucleus.[136] In that note he points to something in the transcendental noema which specifies the "as perceived" in "the perceived as perceived" in a way other than "in the light of its predicates" and which is the noematic correlate not just of the apprehension moment of the full noesis, but of the apprehended hyletic data. This is the mode of appearance or the perspectival adumbration of the perceived object or of its predicates. Certain changes in the hyletic data correspond to changes in the transcendental noema, noematic changes which are not the same as, but which have to do with, the different orientations the object is perceived as having with respect to us. In other writings published after *Ideas* Husserl analyzed this dimension of the transcendental noema extensively. The following brief and simplified account of these analyses draws from those later writings.[137]

The best way of presenting this dimension of the noema is through an example. Let us imagine that we are seated at one end of a long rectangular table looking at its top surface, whose color is brown, and that we perform the phenomenological epoche, i.e., we reflect on what we see, but in our reflective act we refrain from participating in the "actuality" of what we see.[138] We say: "In this perceiving there is a 'table' which is 'rectangularly shaped', is 'in front of me' and is 'brown'." This is a description of the noematic *sense*, the single quotation marks serving to signal the change of meaning the words have as a consequence of the epoche, and indicating in each case that we are now talking about a "phenomenon of...." 'In front of me' denotes what Husserl calls the "orientation" of the object. Other orientations, some of which could be realized if we changed our position, are 'above' and 'below,' 'right' and 'left', 'near' and 'far'.[139] These also belong to the transcendental noema and to the noematic sense in its "fullness,"[140] although they are not predicates of the object *per se*, but are objective determinations of the situation. In addition to these, the table is experienced to be one having many other predicates not directly seen, for instance, four legs, an underside which has some color or other, perhaps not the same as the top, etc. Such predicates make up the implicit moments of the noematic sense.

Let us concentrate now on what is visible to us of the table, seated, as we are, before it. We suppose this to be only the top surface. Husserl calls this a "side" (*Seite*) of the object.[141] If we walked around the table, viewing it from different distances, we would experience a continuum of sides. Let us suppose that we rise from our seated position, but do not move from the table, so that it is still only the top of the table that is visible, no new determinations of the table coming into view. During our movement the same side is given, and the shape of the side (i.e., of the table top) is experienced to remain unchanged. Yet, something changes. If our mental glance is properly directed we may note, for instance, that as we rise the angles formed by the left and right edges of the table top and its far edge seem to get "smaller," and that, from our standing position, the left and right edges seem more "parallel" than before. These changes are not experienced to be changes in the table *itself*, i.e., in the "side," but in the mode of givenness of the side. Husserl calls a mode of givenness of a side an "aspect" (*Aspekt*),[142] or a "perspective."[143] "Aspects" are adumbrations on the *noematic* side of consciousness,[144] and are correlative to the (apprehended) hyletic data on the noetic side, i.e., to the noetically understood adumbrations.[145] We are not usually aware of such perspectival changes, but of the unchanged side or of our objective change in orientation with respect to the object. However, such changes in orientation are not the same as the perspectival changes described above, although, according to Husserl, changes in orientation are necessarily given *through* such perspectival adumbrations,[146] are things generally.[147] From this point on I will often refer to a perspectival as adumbration as an "appearance" or as a "perspectival appearance."[148]

The difference between what has just been called an "appearance" and the noematic sense must be emphasized, since it is of crucial importance for what will be said soon concerning the inadequacy of perception. One way of making that distinction has just been employed, namely, by showing that certain changes may occur in an appearance which, although connected with, are not the same as changes in the noematic sense. Thus, to use our previous example, even if different determinations of the table top were to come into view as we rose from the table, thus bringing about a change in the noematic sense, that change would not be the same as the one which we noticed in the appearance. Furthermore, although it is true that there is an objective change given through the change in the appearance, namely our change in orientation, that change is also not the same as the change in the appearance.

The difference between an appearance and a noematic sense is indicated by Husserl in another way in an unpublished manuscript.[149] There, Husserl distinguishes a "side" from an "aspect" by noting that an aspect, unlike a side, has no inner or outer horizon. This means that the aspect has no details which could come into view if one "stepped closer" to it, nor can it be seen in another perspective. He also distinguishes the "phantom," which, as the unified totality of sides, pertains to the noematic sense, from the "*Apparenz,*" which, as that continuum of aspects which would result when a thing is seen from all sides in such a way that each side is given only once, belongs to the appearance dimension of the noema. He calls the *Apparenz* a "mere image (*Bild*)," a "between-object" (*Zwischengegenstandlichkeit*). An *Apparenz* is also an appearance in our sense, although one of a higher order than an aspect.

Recalling our discussion of adumbration in noetic terms, we can ask what the difference is between the two kinds of adumbration. We can verbally distinguish them, calling the noetic an "appear*ing*" of, and the noematic an "appear*ance*" of an object, but that still leaves the question of what difference is indicated by the different grammatical forms. What difference is there between certain apprehended hyletic data and an aspect? Husserl seems to maintain that there is a difference.[150] Hyletic data, apprehended or not, do not belong to the noema; rather, the apprehension of hyletic data, to use Husserl's word, "achieves" corresponding components in the noema, some of which stem specifically from the hyletic data, namely, that which comprises the perspectival dimension, and others from the apprehension.[151] The latter are those components included under the concept of noematic sense.[152] I believe that this question of the identity of, or the difference between, apprehended hyletic data and noematic perspectives can be dealt with in somewhat the same way as the question of the identity of, or difference between, a perceived object or perceived property of an object and their reflected upon bracketed noematic counterparts. In both cases there is an identity *and* a difference. Let us take up the latter problem first.

In section 97 of *Ideas* Husserl writes: "The color of the tree-trunk, as we are aware of it under the conditions of pure perception, is precisely 'the same' as that which before the phenomenological reduction we...took to be that of the real tree. Now *this* color, as bracketed, belongs to the noema."[153] Here, the real color and the noematic color are identified. However, Husserl also says: "The *tree plain and simple*, the thing in nature, is anything but the *perceived tree as such*, which as perceptual sense belongs to the perception...."[154] From the context of this quote it is clear that the statement applies to all properties of the tree. Thus, the color in nature and the noematic color are different. The *difference,* I believe, is in ontological status (real vs. irreal); the *identity* is in that which has the differing ontological status. The ontological difference arises from the different ways in which "the same" is viewed, and the difference in ways of viewing, in turn, is due to the different attitudes with which "the same" is viewed, the real color in the straight-forward (or reflective) natural attitude, the noematic color in the reflective phenomenological attitude. The identity that is maintained through these ontological differences is, I believe, an *experienced* identity, i.e., as a matter of fact, the object perceived is experienced to be the same as the noematic sense when we switch from the natural to the phenomenological attitude.

The identity and difference between apprehended hyletic data, appearings of something, and noematic perspectives, appearances of something, is also, I submit, a matter of experienced identity through ontological difference. The identifying and distinguishing in question are performed by a reflective act which, I believe, confronts an essentially ambiguous situation. This situation may be grasped either as a temporal object, an appearing of something, or as an ideal object, an appearance of something. Depending on whether the situation is grasped as the former or the latter, the reflection is called noetic or noematic respectively. As the latter type of reflection seems more natural, I will deal with it first.

Let us use our previous example of "rising from the table," and assume that we are at first seated, staring at the table top; then we rise, continuing to look at the top, and finally sit again. If we focus our reflective glance properly while this is happening, and keep our own objective movements and the identical unchanged table outside the sphere of our interest, we may note that the appearance of the table top changes its shape in the way that was described before, and then, in a reversal of this process, it again takes on the same shape it had in the beginning. In this reflection we are aware of a numerically self-identical, yet changing object, the appearance, over/against the temporally distinct and non-identical phases of our *reflective* perceiving of it. If we were to close our eyes and then open them again, or turn our head away and then back, rising and sitting again, we would experience the same, numerically identical appearance again going through an alteration of its shape in these distinct, non-numerically identical reflective acts. In addition, we grasp this appearance as an irreal object and the changes it undergoes as irreal changes. As irreal, and as numerically identical both in the numerically distinct temporal phases of the reflective act and in different reflective acts, the appearance is experienced to be an "ideal" object.[155]

There is another mode of reflection in which one can grasp the *same* series of changing shapes not as different shapes of a numerically identical, *ideal* object, i.e., the appearance, but as the changing content of the reflected upon perception, a *temporal* object. Instead of reflectively seeing a self-identical appearance changing *its* shape, one sees a temporally extended perception undergoing a series of content changes. As components of the perception, the "shapes" are seen to have their identity tied to their temporal locus. Thus, should another series of contents be reflectively seen at another time, even though it might be totally similar to the first series, it would not be grasped as another alteration of the shape of an object (the appearance), which object, in turn, would be identified as numerically identical with that which changed in the first series. Rather, the second series would be grasped as the changing content of a numerically *distinct* perception. Even in the case where there is no change in the content, such as if one sits still and stares fixedly, the content of each phase would be seen to be numerically distinct from that of every other phase. Thus one would not reflectively see one self-identical unchanging ideal object, but phases of a perception whose totally *similar* content-phases succeed one another. In cases where the series of changing contents are totally similar to those of another series, or, as in the last example, where one series has totally similar content from phase to phase, one may speak of an identity of sorts, but not of numerical identity. One could speak, rather, of identity in the sense of a one to one correlation of undistinguishable contents. This temporal boundedness of contents marks them as really intrinsic (*reell*) components of a perception. To quote Husserl, "We call that in an experience which is tied to phenomenological time a really intrinsic moment of the experience."[156] Thus in the reflection described here, one is reflecting on apprehended hyletic data.

It is this type of reflection in which Husserl is often engaged when *he* talks of "appearances of an object." This is usually when he is contrasting the mode of being of a perception with that of the thing perceived, or with that of the noematic sense, and where there is usually no mention of an appearance dimension in the noema. Thus, for instance, in *Ding und Raum*, Husserl *equates* appearance (*Erscheinung*) and perception (*Perzeption*).[157] There he designates the content of the appearance, or equivalently, of the perception, as really intrinsic content,[158] and talks of its having a temporal extension.[159] Similarly, in *Ideas*, when he talks of color adumbrations, shape adumbrations, or in general, of the appearing (*Erscheinen*) of the objective qualities of objects, he means certain really intrinsic components of experiences which are constantly changing and where there is no strict numerical self-identity.[160] It may seem strange to talk of temporally flowing shapes, colors, etc., but I believe these can be grasped in reflection. What may seem even stranger is to cite these as components of a perceivi*ng* of an object. It is more "natural" to consider them, or, more accurately, to consider what is grasped *as* them to be ideal entities and not parts of perceiving of objects. This, I think, is because it is more natural for us to carry out the first type of reflection discussed above. However, I believe that the temporal flow of such shapes, colors, etc., of an appearing of an object, is precisely what Husserl means by perception, i.e., perceivi*ng* an object.

I have tried to show that there is a certain ambiguous situation which reflection encounters. That situation is most neutrally described as change—certain figural, chromatic, etc., alterations. These can either be viewed as having the ontological status of temporal objects, which basically means that they are objects which cannot be reflectively *perceived* again as numerically identical, or they can be viewed as ideal objects, alterations of something which remains numerically self-identical, which can be reflectively perceived again, and whose various forms can also be perceived again. The latter way of viewing this ambiguous situation is the one Husserl usually takes when he is analyzing the various levels in the constitution of a thing, such as in *Ideen* II.[161] In switching from one mode of reflection to the other, one grasps the same change, now as having the ontological status of a temporal object, then as an ideal object. The identity of what is grasped as different in the change is made manifest through what is perhaps a second order reflection. Thus, as in the case with the components of the noematic sense and perceived natural objects and their properties, there is an experienced identity through ontological difference. For our purposes here, however, further consideration of these two points of identity/difference is of less importance than is a study of the hiatus that is left. While we may speak of identity *and* difference with respect to appearings and appearances of objects and with respect to the objects (and objective features) as noematic constituents and realities in nature, there can be no such "bridging" talk between these two identity/difference dimensions themselves. For the connection between adumbration and perceived object (or perceived determination) we must look in another direction. It is this connection that we must now pursue, by way of distinguising two senses of perceptual inadequacy which correspond to these two dimensions.

"Epistemic" inadequacy concerns the object dimension of the noema, and it is so called because it has to do with our knowledge of an object. In any perception only some of an objects's features actually appear to us, although the object is experienced to be one having other features which are not, strictly speaking, given.[162] It is this contrast between what is, and what is not, actually given which forms the basis of the epistemic inadequacy of perception. Perceptual inadequacy in this sense is not overcome by passing from perception to perception for two reasons. First, in such a passage what is given and what is not merely change places, the structure of empty and filled moments in the noematic sense remaining intact. The roots of this structure can be traced first to the appearance through which what is given of the object appears, and then to the noetic apprehensions and hyletic data. The appearance is limited, and lets appear only so much of the object. Its limitedness is rooted in the hyletic data whose apprehension, however, reaches beyond these limits so that we always experience more than we actually perceive.[163] Second, no finite number of perceptions could even sequentially bring a thing to givenness in the completeness of its actuality.[164] Ultimately, then, epistemic inadequacy concerns the contrast between what comes to givenness in a noematic sense or in a finite number of noematic senses pertaining to one thing, and what Husserl calls the "Idea" of the complete givenness of that thing.[165] The concept of thing which determines this inadequacy is thing as consisting of infinitely many determinations.

What I call "appearential inadequacy" does not concern the incompleteness of what *is* given as compared to what *could be given* (or the Idea of what could be given), as does epistemic inadequacy; it concerns an inadequacy of the appearance of something with respect to what *is* given through that appearance. As far as I know, Husserl does not formulate a concept of "appearential inadequacy" *per se*, although a number of his analyses imply such a concept and require it. Before defining appearential inadequacy I will discuss one of these analyses.

This analysis occurs in section 44 of *Ideas*, a pretranscendental section. In the first two paragraphs of the section, Husserl explains what I have called the "epistemic inadequacy" of perception, connecting it with perspectivity. His account dwells on the manner in which *different* perspectival appearances bring to givenness *different* determinations of a thing. Then, in the third paragraph he discusses what I take to concern appearential inadequacy, i.e., how the *same* determination is necessarily given in *different* appearances, none of which can claim priority over the others as giving it as it really is in itself.[166]

To explain this assertion, Husserl contrasts reflective perception of experiences (immanent perception) with straight-forward perception of things (transcendent perception). He notes that the reflective perception of an experience is also inadequate, in the sense that the whole of an experience cannot be perceived in its completeness.[167] This is so because we only strictly perceive the "now" phase of an experience and do not perceive those of its phases which are retained in memory and those which are no longer retained. But this inadequacy, Husserl maintains, is not the same as the inadequacy of transcendent perception, for unlike the perception of spatial objects, the perception of experiences is not perception through appearances.[168] Viewing an experience reflectively, "I have before me an absolute; it has no sides which might present themselves now in this way and now in that....that which is there in the seeing look is there absolutely with all its qualities, its intensity, and so forth."[169] He contrasts this with the perception of a violin tone. If I approach or move away from the violin, or listen to it from outside the concert hall, the same tone would be given through different appearances. But, "no way of appearing claims to rank as giving its data absolutely, although a certain type, appearing as normal within the compass of my practical interests, has a certain advantage; in the concert hall, at the 'right' spot, I hear the tone 'itself' as it 'really' sounds."[170] But this, Husserl explains, after generalizing to all givennesses of things, only points to "a kind of secondary objectification of the thing."[171] "If we were to hold to the 'normal' form of appearance as the one and only form of appearance and cut away all the other multiplicities of appearance...no vestige of the sense of the givenness of the thing would be left over."[172]

With the example of the violin tone in mind, let us observe that the point here is not that a single appearance fails to give certain determinations of an object which other appearances would give, although that may be true. Nor is it that appearances do not give objects or their determinations themselves at all. Rather, the point is that no appearance, not even the "normal" appearance, can rightly be singled out as giving whatever determination it *does* give as it "really" is "itself" in contrast to all other appearances which also give that determination, although not as it "really is itself." What does this mean, and why does Husserl raise this issue? I will discuss its meaning first.

Concerning ourselves, for the sake of simplicity, with only the volume of the violin tone, let us suppose that the violin emits one long note that does not vary in volume. As we approach the violin from a distance, at first we can barely hear the tone; it is too soft. Once we step close to the violin and place our ear next to the strings, it is much too loud to listen to comfortably. We move back, find the distance where the volume is just right, and settle down to listen. Actually, our description is not quite correct, for as we approached the violin we did not experience the tone *itself* getting louder. It would not be correct, even, to say that it "seemed" to get louder, for *it* did not seem to do so. Our words "soft" and "loud," then, do not express differences in the objective determination of the tone; they actually refer to different *appearances* of the volume of the tone. Objectively speaking, we heard a tone invariant in volume, at first located some distance away, and then close by. Throughout, we experienced the tone to have a specific and unchanged volume. That specific volume, as I interpret what Husserl says, is not to be identified with the degree of "loudness" heard from the "right" distance, nor from any other distance.

Why does Husserl raise this issue of the "normal" appearance in *Ideas*? in section 42, Husserl asserts that the perception of spatial objects is necessarily perception through adumbrations.[173] Then in section 43, he discusses a "fundamental error." This error would be to think that perception fails to come into contact with things themselves, i.e., to think that "in principle, there belongs to everything existing the possibility of intuiting it as what it is, specifically, of perceiving it in an adequate perception which gives us the bodily self without any mediation through 'appearances' " but that we humans are denied this type of perception.[174] This view is wrong, he says. We do perceive things themselves, but things are perceivable, in principle, and not just in fact for humans, only through appearances[175] A perception which would intuit something without any mediation through appearances would give us something "absolute."[176] Husserl's discussion of perception through the "normal" form of appearance, then, is first of all aimed at dispelling the idea that perception of spatial objects under certain conditions can achieve absolute givenness. One aim of the discussion, then, is to reject a possible counter example to his claim that the perception of spatial objects is necessarily through appearances. In its wider significance, the discussion aims to point out that there can be no such counter example in principle, since it is fundamentally mistaken to equate itself-givenness with absolute givenness, i.e., givenness without the mediation of appearances, in the case of spatial objects. For spatial objects, itself-givenness must be givenness of something identical through different appearances or else the objects would lose their very character of being spatial.

Applying this interpretation to our example of the tone's volume, the point is that the degree of "loudness" heard from the "right" distance is just as much an *appearance* as any other degree of "loudness," and thus, perception from the "right" distance is just as much perception through an appearance as any other perception. In the succession of perceptions there is no sudden point of discontinuity where the "loudness itself" impresses itself upon the mind directly, without the mediation of an appearance. If one of the series of "loudnesses" coincided with the specific volume of the tone, there would be no grounds for a distinction between appearance and actuality. The "right" degree of "loudness" would then either be the actuality itself, resulting in a discontinuity in the series of appearances and thus the perception of an absolute, or a privileged member of the series of appearances, there being *no* distinguishable actuality perceived through it, and thus perception would fail to come into contact with the volume itself. In the latter case, the account of how the other appearances were appearances of the volume would become unintelligible, as they would have to be appearances of the privileged appearance. Husserl rejects both these alternatives and the coinciding which gives rise to them. The "normal" appearance" is not the actuality itself, nor is the "actuality itself" a member of the series of appearances. Rather, the volume itself is the identical factor given through *each* member of the series of appearances.

The point can be further illustrated through an analogous example from the visual sphere. Suppose a friend approaches me on the sidewalk form some distance away, until we are finally face to face. I do not experience the friend to grow larger as she approaches, but to remain identical in size. Yet something "grows larger"—the appearance. Now there may be some distance from which

I can see my friend "best," for instance, the distance from which I could see the greatest number of determinations of my friend. That would relate to epistemic inadequacy. However if I select one determination, her size, it would not be correct to say that her size, as it "really" is, is given only through one of the series of "sizes" of the appearance. Rather, her size as it "really" is is given through all of the appearances, and is the identical factor in all of them. This point is perhaps not as easy to see in the case of the tone's volume, because the "secondary objectification" Husserl writes of refers to what is experienced in a narrower range of distances in that example and thus the objectification is especially effective. "Secondary objectification," I believe, is the pointing of all other members of the series of appearances pertaining to one thing or thing-determination to one member of the series, a reference such that the other appearances are seen as "deviant" variants of the one. Such objectification is especially noticeable in the case of certain spatial forms where only one orientation gives the "normal" appearance, rectangular table tops, for example. But this kind of objectification is different from what Husserl refers to as the "total objectification" of the thing, for the one appearance to which the others refer in secondary objectification is not the *identical* factor given *through* each. Rather, the relationship is one of norm and deviance from norm. Secondary objectification is called "secondary," perhaps, because it presupposes the result of the other objectification, i.e., it presupposes that the various appearances form *a* set in the first place, by being appearances of the same.

What I call the "appearential inadequacy" of perception is the "inability," as it were, of any of the possible perceptions of a thing, of a feature of a thing, or more generally, of anything spatially extended, to give that entity directly, without the mediation of an appearance. This means that something spatial is necessarily given through appearances, none of which can "coincide" with it.

It was mentioned above that Husserl does not formulate a concept of appearential inadequacy *per se*, i.e., as a separate concept of perceptual inadequacy. This is because his account of the "failure" of perception to give anything spatial directly, without the mediation of appearances, is in terms of the epistemic inadequacy of perception. I do not believe that the matter should be dealt with in this way for reasons which I will give below, after presenting a summary of Husserl's account. For the reasons I will give, I believe that what I have called "appearential inadequacy" is distinct from epistemic inadequacy.

That Husserl accounts for what I have called "appearential inadequacy" in terms of epistemic inadequacy is especially clear from his discussion of the "normal" appearance in *Ding und Raum*.[177] The aim of that discussion is also to show that no perception, and especially not one through a "normal" appearance, gives a thing or a feature of a thing "as it is in itself," i.e., "absolutely." What Husserl mainly seems to mean there by "as it is in itself," however, is "in its completeness." He argues that whether one considers an appearance in relation to an object as a whole or in relation to one of its parts, one could always have more determinations of the object or the part given through another appearance.[178] This, he says, is as true in the case of the normal appearance as it is of any other appearance. Thus, in our terms, a perception which gives something through a normal appearance, like any other perception, is epistemically inadequate.

Husserl supports his argument further by showing what the "as it is in itself" *really* amounts to when one thinks that one form of appearance gives the object in that way. It is not that the object or feature of an object is given completely, but that a certain form of appearance satisfies an interest of the perceiver best in comparison to other forms. A certain form of appearance becomes regarded as "normal" *because* it does this. But this value, Husserl argues, is not grounded in the essence of the appearances themselves. The appearance which becomes regarded as giving the object or feature "best," as the "normal" appearance, is determined solely by the requirements of the interest.[179] Theoretically, then, any form of appearance might become so regarded with respect to some interest or other. So, for example, the sound of a piano is heard "best" by the concert-goer from a distance, and hence, through an appearance, which would not satisfy the interest of the piano tuner. To be sure, something about a certain appearance allows it to best suit a particular interest, but that something, by itself, does not confer on that appearance any special value in contrast to any of the other possible appearances of the same. It is from the interest alone that the value is derived. The result of attributing this value is the "secondary objectification" of which Husserl wirtes.

When Husserl analyzes what makes the givenness of an object or feature of an object through a certain appearance "best" or "normal" with respect to a certain interest he always seems to think of this in terms of the completeness of givenness of those determinations most relevant to that interest. He points out, for instance, that the lay persons's interest in a flower is different from that of a botanist. For each, the best appearance is different, as is what constitutes fullness of givenness.[180] Indeed, we may have noticed that whenever we show some object we own to an "expert" in such objects, the expert often looks at it in "peculiar" ways, from "odd" angles and distances. This is because the expert is looking at different features and different features of features than does the layperson.

However this may be, I do not think that Husserl's analyses sufficiently deal with the phenomenon which inspired them, i.e., the circumstance of thinking, when perceiving something under certain conditions, that one then has this something "itself" and as it is itself. I believe that a second concept of inadequacy is required to deal with this phenomenon, an inadequacy having its locus in the appearances and which is not resolvable into a matter of epistemic inadequacy.

To present my objections to Husserl's account I will employ a new example. Suppose we are looking at a rectangular door from a few yards away, which when closed is oriented in our fronto-parallel plane. Suppose we do not change our position while looking at it. Whether the door is closed, half open, or fully open, we perceive it to be "rectangular." In all these positions, then, 'rectangular' is a component of the noematic sense. Despite the different positions of the door, the angles where the sides meet the top and bottom are perceived to be "right angles," the top and bottom are perceived to be "parallel," as are the sides. These terms are put in double quotation marks because they are not meant in a strict geometrical sense. They are just labels which serve to bring to mind certain familiar shapes and relationships. Now, when we see the door oriented in our fronto-parallel plane we may be inclined to think that the "look" of the door's shape then is as the shape really looks, i.e., that *that* is how rectangularity *looks*. In contrast to this, we may think that the look of the rectangular shape in any other orientation is not the true look of rectangularity. We may then go on to consider the latter looks as appearances of the shape and consider the former look as not being an appearance. If we then wonder how it is that, no matter what orientation the door has, we still see the door to be rectangular, we might say that the various "appearance-looks" somehow refer us to the true look and that we see it through them (secondary objectification). Let us consider this matter in terms of the appearance and object dimensions of the noema, assuming, for the moment, that the "true" look is also an appearance.

When we say that in all but one orientation the look of the shape is not the true look, our word "look" does not refer to the orientation itself, which may be considered part of the noematic sense. We are referring to the "shape" of the *appearance*. Also, although it is true that, when oriented in the fronto-parallel plane, more determinations of the door may come into view, thus enriching the noematic sense, that enrichment in determinations does not constitute the *correctness* of the "right" look. There is, of course, another "enrichment" which takes place as the door swings from an open to the closed position. This is the increase in "fullness" of the breadth of the door which reaches a maximum when the door is closed. Of the door? That is not correct. The door is not experienced to increase in breadth, but to remain the same in that respect. The change is not one in the noematic sense, but in the appearance. Although correlated with, it is not the same as the changing orientation of the door.

It is also possible to imagine that the increase in fullness takes place without an enrichment in the noematic sense, i.e., without any new determinations of the door itself coming into view. It is, then, independent of such enrichments. This maximal fullness of the appearance goes together with the correctness of the shape of the appearance. But neither of these, in themselves, is a matter of the noematic sense. If someone were to think that the maximally full and correctly shaped "appearance" was, in fact, not an appearance at all, but the shape given directly, that person would not mean that the shape of the door or of the front surface of the door is given with a maximal number of determinations distinctly given, whether this is relative to a certain interest or not. Rather, the person would mean that the *look* and the actuality coincide, and that the former is just the latter.

I believe that a similar analysis could be developed for all of what Husserl refers to as non-independent moments of spatial objects. In each case it could be shown, as here, that what provides the basis for the norm character of the normal appearance, and thus, what provides the orientational center for secondary objectification has its locus in the appearance, and not in the noematic sense. The correctness of the look of something is not an epistemic value. Fullness of the appearance is not a fulfillment of empty intentions, at least not in an epistemic sense. The door, for example, is seen and known all along to be rectangular, so that the maximally full appearance does not bring with it an increase in knowledge or a confirmation of something "merely" intended.

To continue the analysis, we see that it is quite conceivable that one of the looks of the shape of the door other than the one of the fronto-parallel orientation, say of a half-open door, could be the norm for someone. Of course, one would be surprised if, when one asked a person to draw the shape of a rectangular door, that person drew the door in what seemed to us to be 45 degree perspective. That might be surprising, but it is not impossible. Such a person would surely see objects very differently than we do. With this possibility in mind, and following the outlines of Husserl's analysis of the normal appearance, we can go on to point out that there is nothing intrinsic to any of the appearances (looks) which gives any one of them priority over the others as giving the shape of the door as it "really" looks. Theoretically, any look could become the norm. No doubt there is something about the maximally full appearance which allows it to become the norm, but that something alone does not constitute a norm. The value comes from outside. Whether the bringing about of secondary objectification in a particular way in this case can also be attributed to an interest or not, and if no, what sense of "interest" is involved, is a question we cannot take the time to pursue here. If it is an interest in some sense, I doubt that it is a cognitive one. However much the details of the account of secondary objectification might have to differ from Husserl's due to the change in the locus of the basis of the norm and to the different meaning which "as it is itself" has in our account, the aim is the same, namely, to show that the normal look is just as much an appearance as any other look and that it has no intrinsic priority over any other look in being the "real" look of something. All this, in turn, serves the wider aim of showing that itself-givenness is not to be equated with givenness without the mediation of appearances in the case of spatial objects and their determinations. The perception of things is necessarily inadequate in the appearential sense, and appearential inadequacy is distinct from epistemic inadequacy.[181]

Before completing our discussion of the first statement of Husserl's argument, let us review the steps that have brought us to where we are. We began with a discussion of the nature of the intentional relation which consciousness has to objects, noting that this relatedness has a specificity which is not imposed upon consciousness "from the outside," but is intrinsic to it. Since intentionality, especially its specificity, is a central factor in the world-constitutive theory of consciousness, we sought those components of perceptual experience which accounted for that specificity. Following Husserl's psychological reflection, we first found these components on the noetic side of consciousness, in the hyletic data and the apprehensions animating them, which together constitute the "modes of appearing" of objects. It was here that we first entered into a discussion of the adumbrational nature of perception. This was our special concern because the inadequacy of perception mentioned in the first statement of Husserl's argument was connected with it. Then, we sought to discover "modes of appearing," or rather, "modes of appearance" on the noematic side of consciousness. This led us to Husserl's transcendental concept of noema. In line with our desire not to abandon the presuppositions of a pretranscendental account of consciousness, we questioned whether one could speak of noemata in a psychological context. Our concern there was that affirming Husserl's statement about perceptual inadequacy would lead us into circularity if the account of that inadequacy presupposed a transcendental conception of consciousness. But then we distinguished two dimensions of the noema, the object dimension (the noematic sense) and the appearance dimension (noetic adumbrations). This allowed us to differentiate two senses in which one could speak of perception being inadequate, the epistemic and the appearential. It is the latter inadequacy which primarily figures in the first statement of Husserl's argument, although as we shall see later, epistemic inadequacy also plays a role.

In what follows, a concept of noema will be developed on the basis of our discussion of the appearance dimension of the noema. This concept will not include the noematic sense as a noematic constituent. This is important because the concept of noematic sense presupposes the transcendental epoche, and thus the transcendental conception of consciousness. While this will allow us to affirm the first statement of Husserl's argument without circularity, it will leave us unable to completely account for the intentional relation. This will bring us to the psychological formulation of the problem of cognition. It was, we will recall, the problem of cognition for which Husserl's theory of consciousness as world-constitutive is to provide the solution. Let us now proceed with the rest of our discussion.

The perception of spatial objects, according to Husserl, is necessarily through appearances. This finding takes our previous discussion of appearance and actuality one crucial step further.[182] The "normal" appearance which Husserl mentions in *Ideas* is the same as what we previously discussed as the object or feature of an object as it is given under "optimal conditions," and which we will now, following Husserl, call the "optimum."[183] In our previous discussion it was said that when something is given under optimal conditions it is given directly, without the mediation of an appearance.[184] Optima were of central importance for our definition of the concept of actuality, in that they provided the extension of that concept. Under non-optimal conditions subjective appearances were said to arise, *through* which actualities are given. These subjective appearances were said to be correlated with appearential modes of consciousness, whereas optima were said not to be. It was because of this that we were allowed to say that the being-on-hand of actuality is not due to consciousness. We can now ask whether we can extend our psychological reflection to incorporate Husserl's finding that all spatial objects are necessarily given through appearances, without endangering its status of being a *psychological* reflection, i.e., one which, among other things, abides by the natural attitude and does not presuppose that consciousness is world-constitutive.

It should be clear that, to a certain extent, we can identify "appearential consciousness" and "non-illusory subjective appearances" with what we here have called "appear*ing* of an object" and "appear*ance* of an object" respectively. Although the previous presentation of the results of Husserl's reflections on noematic appearances relied somewhat on transcendental parts of his texts, there seems to be no reason why appearances cannot be reflectively focused on and analyzed outside of that context, without presuming the world-constitutive thesis or departing from the natural attitude. But in the light of our previous discussion of appearance and actuality, the question of a complete identification of the above pairs of concepts arises when one wants to classify the optimum as a subjective appearance. How are we then to formulate the concepts of actuality and being-on-hand in a way which allows us to say that the world (actuality) is there for us independently of consciousness?

Our deliberations above have already prepared the answer for this. Let us accept the optimum as a subjective appearance and thus grant that perception is appearentially inadequate. Given the specific meaning of this inadequacy, it should be clear that a concept of actuality is already contained in it, and that the *meaning* of this concept is still the same as it was before: an object, a feature of an object, event, etc., itself, as it is in itself, apart from its appearance. If we do not include such actualities, nor their bracketed counterparts that are within the transcendental noema (the noematic senses), as components of experiences, but consider only appearances to be such components, then actuality is still what is on hand independently of consciousness. Thus, for example, the size of my friend which remains the same as she approaches me and which I see, or the invariant volume of the tone which I hear as I approach the violin, can be said to be actualities. These can be said to be on hand independently of consciousness precisely because the moments in experiences which correspond to them, and through which they are given, the appearances, fail to correspond to them in their particularity. This deficiency in the particularity of the correspondence concerns what in Chapter 2 was called the "ontic moment" of the world, i.e., its status as transcendent actuality.[185] The deficiency is one consequence of the appearential inadequacy of perception. Let us see how this is so.

First, we must consider what it means to say we perceive an object "through" an appearance. A distinction between the "object" and "content" of an experience and between the different ways we attend to each can help us here. Let us use the familiar example of the "converging" railroad tracks. If one were to stand between a pair of railroad tracks, one could make the following statements without inconsistency or contradiction:

1. The tracks look like they converge.
2. The tracks look like they are parallel and stretch out into the distance.
3. The tracks diverge.[186]

These statements would not be inconsistent or contradictory if the first reported on the appearance-content of one's experience, the second on *what* one saw, and the third on what *in fact* was the case. If the third statement were true, the other two could still be true as they both could report on an appearance, but in different senses of "appearance." The second statement is made on the basis of a straight-forward perception and states how the tracks look to be, seem to be, or appear to be. If the tracks were in fact not parallel, one could none-theless have seen what looked like parallel tracks. But in this case one's percep-tion was not veridical. What was seen, then, was an illusory subjective appear-ance.[187] But the first statement would not normally be one stating how the *actual* tracks look, seem or appear to be. Convergence is not predicated of the real tracks, but of the "tracks" in the appearance which make up the *content* of the perception. The first statement would not normally motivate the ques-tion "Are the tracks really convergent?" as would the second. Should the third statement be true, the "perception" which "sees" the convergence could not be said to be nonveridical. What is reported on in the first statement is a non-il-lusory subjective appearance, or what we now call the "content" of a percep-tion. The experience which attended to this content, then, was not directed to the real tracks or to what looked like real tracks. *Its* object was the content of the straight-forward perception. As such, it was a reflective or "immanent" perception. The appearance-content of the straight-forward perception can only become an object in such a reflective perception.

That we cannot experience the appearance-content of a straight-forward perception as an object except when we reflect upon it, however, does not mean that while perceiving straight-forwardly we do not experience it *at all*. Rather while perceiving straight-forwardly we do experience this content in the sense that we "live" it, or "undergo" it. As Husserl puts it, "Every Ego lives [*erlebt*] its own experiences, and in these is included much that is real (*reell*) and inten-tional. The phrase 'It lives them' does not mean that it holds them and whatever is in them after the manner of immanent experience (*Er-fahrung*)...."[188] Thus, taking our previous example of the violin tone, we straight-forwardly hear a tone invarient in volume, now from afar and then from close up. It is this that is object and objective for our experience, and which, in our present psychological context, lies outside our experience. It is encountered (*erfährt*). That to which our words "soft" and "loud" apply, however, is the appearance-content of our perception and it is lived (*erlebt*) by us.

Let us now relate these considerations to the question of what it means to say that we perceive an object "through" an appearance. The word "through" is a metaphor which attempts to convey the way in which the content of a percep-tion, as lived, functions to make an experience intentional, i.e., one of a specif-ic object. In that an experience becomes constituted in our mental life as having a certain appearance-content, we perceive a specific object. In this sense, "through" signifies "by means of." Thus a theory of intentionality can be formulated within the confines of a psychological conception of conscious-ness. Husserl's comment that "(i)t lies in the very essence of an experience not only *that* it is consciousness of [something], but also *of what* it is a consciousness, and in what determinate or indeterminate sense it is this,"[189] can be interpreted, in the case of perception, to refer to the appearance-content. Within the psychological sphere, then, the appearance-content of a perception plays the same role as the transcendental noema does within the transcendental sphere. It is irreal, it can be said to be the "correlate" of apprehended hyletic data (in that it is ontologically different from it), and it is that by means of which we are referred to an object. Because it functions in this analogous way, I will call the appearance-content of a perception the "psychological (perceptual) noema," forming this concept from the appearance dimension of the transcendental noema and leaving behind, as pertaining to the transcendental noema alone, the noematic sense. Later, after a discussion of the doxic moment of perception, another component will be added to the psychological noema.

In addition to signifying "by means of," the word "through" in the statement "We perceive objects through appearances" points to a certain translucency in the medium by means of which objects are perceived. "Translucent," too, is a metaphor, used to express the idea that when we perceive something there is a certain awareness of the medium. The appearances are experienced when we perceive an object straight-forwardly in the sense that they are "lived," but when lived, they are not encountered. That they are lived means that they are *something* for us, but they do not constitute what is object (*Gegenstand*) and objective for our experience.[190]

The givenness of an object or a feature of an object, we have said, is necessarily through a multiplicity of different appearances (or as we now call them, psychological noemata), none of which can be said to coincide with what is given. It is because of this that one cannot make the sort of "bridge" between the appearance and that of which it is the appearance which was previously made between appearings and appearances, and between realities and noematic senses. An appearance cannot be identified with that which appears through it. This consideration puts us in a position to say how consciousness, conceived psychologically, is not yet world-constitutive consciousness. Within the confines of our psychological reflection we seem to be able to say that the specificity of the intentional relation is secured by factors within consciousness, particularly the psychological noema. However, this psychological conception of intentionality still lacks something, and what it lacks is related to the previously mentioned deficiency of the particularity of the correspondence between things in the world and consciousness with regard to the former's ontic moment. It is especially the moment of actuality which concerns us here. We perceive an object in that we live certain appearance-contents, i.e., in that a certain experience is constituted in our mental lives having certain hyletic data, an apprehension, and a correlative psychological noema. But since none of the components of the psychological noema "coincide" with the actuality which is given through them, the mere experiencing of a perception is no guarantee that anything actual *is* given through it.[191] Could we not have the same hyletic data, apprehension, and psychological noema and be hallucinating or otherwise suffering an illusion? There seems to be nothing in our description of consciousness thus far which corresponds to the ontic moment of the world as actuality. Since consciousness in the psychological sense fails to correspond to the particularity of the world in this respect, we must say that actualities are still on hand independently of consciousness, and thus, consciousness is not yet world-constitutive. The psychological conception of consciousness fails to meet the reality criterion.

We can also formulate this as the psychological conception of the problem of cognition. The problem of cognition was first mentioned in this work as Husserl's motivation for the development of a world-constitutive theory of consciousness. Stated concisely, the question is: How is cognition of transcendent objects possible? In trying to understand the meaning of this question, one version of the problem has been discussed, the "naive" version. What I call the psychological version goes as follows. Intentionality can be considered as a kind of "aiming" at an object, and, most significantly for cognition, at something *actual*. How does perceptual consciousness achieve its aim? *That* it does seems evident on the basis of everyday experience. But behind our question we can hear a skeptical voice from the history of philosophy which says: "Whether perception reaches its aim...." Husserl wishes to avoid this abyss, but not before stepping closer to it, as we shall see as we turn now to the second statement of Husserl's argument.

### 3. The Possibility of Illusion and the Coherence-Thesis

The first statement of Husserl's argument asserts that the perception of a thing is necessarily inadequate since it is perception through adumbrations or appearances. The second statement is: Because of this inadequacy, any perceived thing could be inactual, which means that the perception of a thing is a believing or doxic consciousness.

The first part of the second statement, "Because of this inadequacy, any perceived thing could be inactual," is asserted by Husserl in section 46 of *Ideas* (the rest of the statement will be discussed later): "It is, as we know, an essential feature of the thing-world that no perception, however perfect it may be, gives us anything absolute within its domain; and with this the following is essentially connected, namely, that every experience (*Erfahrung*), however far it extends, leaves open the possibility that what is given, despite the persistent consciousness of its bodily self-presence, does *not* exist. It is an essentially valid law that existence in the form of a thing is never demanded as necessary by virtue of its givenness, but in a certain way is always contingent."[192] This means, Husserl continues, that "it can always happen that the further course of experience will compel us to abandon what, on the basis of experience, has already been legitimately posited. It was, so we afterwards say, mere illusion, hallucination, merely a coherent dream, and the like. Moreover, in this sphere of givenness the open possibility remains of changes in apprehension, the turning of an appearance over into one which cannot unite with it harmoniously, and therewith an influence of later experiential positions on earlier ones whereby the intentional objects of these earlier positings suffer, so to speak, a transformation...."[193]

What Husserl means by this seems fairly evident at first. His examples provide us with a ready interpretation. Because the perception of things is necessarily through appearances, no matter what perception we may be having of a thing at a certain time, no matter what appearance that perception may be through, there are always other perceptions of the thing, through other appearances, that we could be having.[194] In the normal course of a perceptual process, in which we perceive a thing or a whole field of things from different orientations and under different circumstances, certain of these possible perceptions become successively realized, each of whose appearance-content "unites harmoniously" with that of earlier ones. Although this is what normally happens, there is the "open possibility" that it might not.[195] If it does not, then we may say depending on the nature of the circumstances, that we had had a hallucination, suffered an illusion, etc. In other words, we perceived what we have called an illusory subjective appearance. Thus Husserl seems to be saying that, because of the nature of perception, it is possible that at any given moment what we are perceiving is not a worldy actuality but a mere apparition of one.

Perhaps Husserl's most well-known example of the failure of subsequent perceptions to unite harmoniously with previous ones is the case of perceiving a person who turns out to be a manniquin.[196] Let me supply an example that goes in the opposite direction. I once stopped to look at a display in a store window. While I was admiring the beautiful clothes on the very life-like manniquin, it changed its position. The intentional object (manniquin) underwent a transformation (into a person) through a change in apprehension motivated by "the turning of an appearance over into one which" could not "unite with it harmoniously" (movement). Here, the transformation concerned *what* the object I was perceived was, i.e., there was *something* actual which was perceived all along, but it was not a manniquin, it was a person. The second statement of Husserl's argument, of course, concerns the case where nothing actual is in fact perceived.

Our example can be used to bring out an aspect of perception which is not mentioned in the above quotes but which is presupposed by what is said in them and which Husserl deals with elsewhere. This is the anticipatory nature of perceptual experience. One can imagine how surprised I was when the "manniquin" moved. My surprise, and the surprise-phenomenon in general, indicates that certain expectations were not fulfilled, and in addition, that what I perceived ran counter to those expectations. Let us call this occurance the "disappointment" of expectation. The expectations involved here are not "explicit" expectations, i.e., they are not separate *acts* or awaiting something; they are implicit moments of the perception itself, which form part of the apprehension of hyletic data.[197] Their effect is to prefigure what appearances should come next if I were to explore the object perceptually,[198] and thus preannounce what should be given through those appearances. They also anticipate no change in appearance should I not explore the object. It is in union with these expectations that the hyletic data become "adumbrations" in the noetic sense, i.e., prefigurings. It is also by virtue of the, at least partial, fulfillment of anticipations that there can be a "uniting" of perceptual contents into a sustained perceptual *process,* so that one can speak of perception being a "synthesis."[199]

Is the above interpretation of Husserl's remarks correct? Led by the suggestion of his examples, the interpretation implies that the disappointment of expectations only has the effect of cancelling the actuality of what was perceived during a limited and continuous extent of time. Even if that which is cancelled as to its actuality were a whole perceived environment, including what was perceived to be one's own body and behaviour, as in the example of a coherent dream, the cancellation only extends back through a circumscribed duration of time. This being so, any familiar objects or environments which seem to appear in the negated experiences are not cancelled in *their* actuality. Rather, we might say, what was experienced was, in fact, not those actualities, but only something we took to be them. When I realize I have only been dreaming of having a meeting with a friend in my home, I do not think that my home and my friend *themselves* never existed. However there are passages in Husserl's texts which suggest that we should interpret his statement that "every experience, however far it extends, leaves the open possibility that what is given...does *not* exist" to apply to just such objects. For example, on the page just following the one from which the above quote was taken, Husserl states that what could be cancelled in its actuality is "everything which is there for me in the world of things"[200] and "in the world of realities generally."[201] Surely my friend and my home count as things in the world of realities. Under this more radical interpretation we would understand Husserl not to be saying that, due to the nature of perceptual experience, what we may be perceiving at a certain time or any limited stretch of time might not be worldly actuality itself, but to be saying that it is possible that future experience could be such that *all* that is and ever was on hand to me as worldly actuality could turn out not to be and not to have been actual. This interpretation seems unavoidable when we find Husserl asserting that "it is always imaginable that experience would run counter to all expectation and that instead of what was anticipated, something else ensues, and ultimately, something which devalues what exists to the status of not existing. Everything which appears in the mode of being [*Sein*] through appearances is undecided between being and not being, namely as always open [*bereiter*] possibility...of not being. And that, I could show, holds also for the mundane universe [*das Weltall*], as the 'object' of universal experience."[202]

The difference between this and our previous interpretation can be brought out by considering the following distinction which Husserl makes in *Erste Philosophie* between "empirical illusion [*Schein*]" and "transcendental illusion." "During the course of our normal experiencing of the world, wherein we are certain of its existence, we occasionally meet with an empirical illusion, an illusion for which we can ask the explanation, i.e., the truth which *underlies* it and which is only concealed. We are certain before even inquiring that this question is meaningful, is *decidable*. But the matter is completely different in the case of transcendental illusion. The possibility is always open that the world, which at this very moment is itself given, in fact does not exist, that what is itself given is an illusion, a transcendental illusion. But in the case of the illusion which we call transcendental, it would be completely senseless to seek a correction in terms of a corresponding true state of affairs, to ask for some true being which is to be posited *instead of, in place of* this non-existing world."[203] What Husserl means here, I believe, is the following: The concept of illusion that we normally employ gains its very sense from the fact that there are experiences that count for us as genuine, as experiences through which the true state of affairs can be ascertained. So, for example, if I am wondering whether a familiar object is really before me or whether I am hallucinating, the sense of my puzzlement is conditioned by my knowing that I have had and can have experiences in which the familiar object is itself given. My question is: Is this one of those experiences? I know that this is, in principle, a decidable question. It is *possible* for me to confirm whether the object is before me or somewhere else. In contrast to illusion in this "empirical" sense, Husserl mentions a possible illusion of a fundamentally different kind. In transcendental illusion, to use the same example, the question is not whether a particular experience is one in which the familiar object is itself given; rather, the question is whether those experiences in which the familiar object *is* itself given, i.e., those experiences that give sense to and *rightly* provide the measure for all empirical illusion, are themselves illusory. But "illusion" here has a completely different meaning. It is not a matter of the familiar object being somewhere else, which some truly self-giving experience could ascertain. It is not the self-giving character of the experience which is the issue, but the existential status of the "self" which is given. The question is: Does the familiar object itself exist. But even this question must be understood in a certain way to grasp the proper sense of transcendental illusion. The question must not be understood as asking whether *all* of my experiences of the object have been experiences in which a wordly actuality has been itself given, for this is once again a matter of empirical illusion. Understood this way we would be asking, for instance, if there really was anything actual there every time I experienced the object, or was there in truth, just an empty portion of space. But this question once again asks for a correction in terms of worldly actuality; it asks for what the world was like *instead of* the way I perceived it to be. Transcendental illusion does not concern the issue of *whether* a wordly actuality is given through an experience, it concerns whether experiences which *do* give worldly actualities are illusions, whether worldy actualities are indeed actualities.

Husserl strongly emphasizes that posing the possibility of transcendental illusion does not constitute a skeptical argument that the world does not exist. The open possibilities inherent in perception do not allow one to say that the world we experience "perhaps" does not exist or that it is "likely" or "probable" that it does not exist. "The existance of the world," he says, "is *completely doubtless.*"[204] There is absolutely nothing in our experience that says that the possibility that the world does not exist will be realized. "The proposition that this world may be a pure nothing, a mere transcendental illusion is compatible with our empirical and doubtless perceptual certainty of the factual existence [*Dasein*] of the world."[205] Suppose there were a subject, Husserl imagines, who lived through courses of consciousness within which "there is nothing lacking which might in any way be required for the appearance of a unitary world and a rational theoretical knowledge of the same. We ask now, presupposing all this, is it still *conceivable*, is it not on the contrary absurd, that the corresponding transcendent world should not be?"[206]

The section of *Ideas* from which the just-quoted passage was taken (section 49) contains a discussion which seems to support the more radical interpretation of the second statement of Husserl's argument. Since this interpretation concerns the possibility of "transcendental" illusion, it will be called the "transcendental interpretation;" the other interpretation, since it concerns "empirical" illusion, will be called the "empirical interpretation." Section 49 of *Ideas* comes after the point in the text where Husserl announces that his psychological investigation of consciousness has "reached its climax" and that he has laid down the "premises" of his argument. The sections which follow, including section 49, concern certain "conclusions" which he is drawing on the basis of those premises.[207] However, the section where Husserl asserts that any perceived thing could be inactual, and where he cites examples of empirical illusion to explain what he means (section 46), falls within those where he is establishing his premises. Thus it is not perfectly clear which interpretation we are to adopt for the purpose of evaluating the *premises* of his argument. A reading of a section of *Cartesian Meditations* which is parallel to the "premise" sections of *Ideas* only reinforces the thought that there is a problem of interpretation here, for there Husserl once again cites examples of empirical illusion.[208] Although I believe that Husserl's argument for world-constitutive consciousness requires the transcendental interpretation of the second statement of the argument, I wish to leave the issue of the correct interpretation open at this point. Later, we will explore the implications of each of these interpretations. This discussion will prove interesting in its own right in terms of elucidating the distinction between a psychological and a world-constitutive conception of consciousness. In addition, it will show why we must adopt the transcendental interpretation. Before proceeding to this, however, I will first elaborate further the second statement of Husserl's argument, doing so, as much as possible, in a way which is neutral to the two interpretations.

The second statement in essence expresses what I have called the "coherence-thesis."[209] This thesis is the pivotal point of Husserl's argument. The thesis can be formulated by the following propositions.

1. Our perceptual experience of an object which we regard to be actual has an anticipational structure such that later perceptions can either fulfill or disappoint these anticipations.
2. If the anticipations are fulfilled *in certain ways,* we will continue to experience the object to be something actual.
3. If the anticipations are disappointed *in certain ways*, we will consider the object to be inactual.
4. With respect to any perception, it is always possible (in the sense of open possibility) that anticipations could be disappointed in these "certain ways."
5. The existence of this possibility, so long as it is not realized, makes the actuality of any perceived object a "presumptive" actuality, and the mode of consciousness of it presumptive certainty, which is a form of belief.

The following explanations of these propositions will suffice for our purposes now.

The anticipational structure of perception is an ever-present theme in Husserl's writings. According to him, every perceptual experience of an object (and every experience generally) has an "intentional horizon of reference to potentialities of consciousness."[210] These potentialities of consciousness are possible experiences of the object other than the one presently enjoyed. Among them are other perceptions of the object which we are about to have in the immediately coming phases of the perceptual process which we are, in fact, engaged in and which "explores" the object in a particular way, and other perceptions we *could* have if we actively directed the course of perception otherwise than we in fact do.[211] References to the former type of potentialities are anticipations proper. These are references to potentialities that are "aroused" when a particular course of perceptual exploration is pursued, while the rest of the horizon lies in "dead" potentiality.[212] Husserl sometimes calls the latter type of references expectations also, no doubt because of their capacity to be aroused. He then distinguishes between actual and potential expectation.[213] The horizon of reference is somewhat indeterminate, although that indeterminacy is predeliniated in conformity with the present perception and with the kind of object experienced.[214] Thus, in addition to the fairly determinate references based, for instance, on past experience with a particular object or with objects of the same kind, there is a certain openness to something new to emerge in the perceptual exploration of an object.[215] In Husserl's transcendental theory, references to the other perceptions of the object are correlated with the implicit moments in the noematic sense.[216]

Normally a perceptual process runs its course harmoniously. This means that the anticipations aroused in one phase of the process are fulfilled in subsequent phases.[217] "However," Husserl notes, "every expectation can be disappointed, and disappointment essentially presupposes partial fulfillment."[218] Two types of disappointment must be distinguished, those that involve a partial "break" in the unity of the perceptual process and thus lead to a modalization of perceptual belief, and those that do not.[219] The latter type is involved in the perception of change in an object. Here disappointment sets in with a regulated style and thus becomes itself predelineated. The former is involved in illusion in the broad sense, where the disappointment indicates that the object is and was not as expected, but is and was otherwise. We are concerned with disappointment of this type.

It should be obvious that not *all* kinds of disappointments of expectation would affect our experiencing something to be actual. Some disappointments would only affect our experience of something as having certain features which it need not have in order to be actual or even to be the kind of object that it is. Let us refer to such features as constituting "how" an object is, as opposed to "what" it is or "that" it is. To use one of Husserl's examples, we may, for a while, perceive a ball to be uniformly red and uniformly spherical, but on perceiving a side of it not previously seen, it turns out to be partly green and dented.[220] Other sorts of disappointments could affect what kind of object we experience something to be, yet also not alter our experience of perceiving something actual. Our example of the mannquin that turns out to be a person is a case of this. Clearly, then, when Husserl maintains that the disappointment of anticipations can result in our experiencing something to be completely inactual, these disappointments must be along other lines than those involved in how or what an object is. It is for this reason that the phrase "in certain ways" was included in points 2 and 3 above.

As has already been indicated, when perceptions disappoint anticipations which are involved in an earlier phase of the perception of an object in such a way as to modify our experience of either how, what, or that the object is, this affect is retroactive. This means that we not only experience something after the disappointment to be different than it was taken to be prior to the disappointment, but as well, the disappointment has the affect of cancelling the how, what or that of before, so that we take the object to really have been *all along* as we take it to be after the disappointment.[221] This affect, which Husserl calls "retroactive cancellation,"[222] is a key element in the coherence-thesis.

Presumptive actuality," mentioned in the fifth proposition, is the name Husserl gives to objects whose non-actuality is always an open possibility. It is in contexts where Husserl discusses this concept that the transcendental interpretation seems most appropriate.[223] In using the name "presumptive actuality," Husserl expresses the idea that the actuality of some object or of the world itself is one "until further notice."[224] The "notice" which could always come would be brought by further experience, experience which could convey " 'stronger rational motives' " to outweigh and overcome the "force" with which experience up to that point, through its harmony and coherence, supports the experience of the actuality of a particular object or of the world.[225] Thus, according to Husserl, every object experienced by us to be actual is perceptually given, at bottom, in a passive doxic consciousness whose certainty of belief is the ground for the centainty of all active or egoic modes of consciousness of the object.[226] The type of certainty involved here is "presumptive" certainty which Husserl distinguishes from "apodictic" certainty. Whereas in the former the nonbeing of the object perceived is an open possibility, the latter kind of certainty "entails the exclusion of nonbeing.... There are no opposing open possibilities here, no realms of free play...."[227]

Apodictic certainty is the mode of transcendental self-experience, i.e., the reflective experience of one's own mental life under the transcendental reduction.[228] However, as Husserl indicates, the range of the apodicticity of this experience is not unlimited. It certainly extends to the "I am,"[229] but its range as to "what" and "how" I am requires investigation.[230] Is this mode of position-taking, which excludes the possibility of cancellation, properly called "belief?" There is evidence in Husserl's texts that he thinks it is not. Speaking, in *Ding und Raum*, of the absolute givenness of experience to reflection under the transcendental reduction, he remarks that not only are disbelief and doubt excluded as modalizations of such consciousness, but "in a certain sense even belief is excluded, namely, belief in the usual sense of a mere aiming at being."[231] Here, Husserl calls this belief in the usual sense "*doxa.*" In immanent perception, he says, the "having" and the "positing" cannot be analytically separated. Its positing is "*related*" to belief; it is that kind of positing which excludes disbelief...."[232] It would seem from Husserl's extensive discussion of belief in *Ideas* that doxic consciousness necessarily admits of being modalized into question, doubt, etc., and finally, admits of negation wherein the ontic correlate of simple belief, actuality, can become cancelled.[233] The term "belief," then, would seem inappropriate for the apodictic factor in immanent perception. In contemporary terms, the difference between apodictic and doxic positing would be that between "knowing" and "believing," where "X knows that p" implies "that p" (p is true). If it is thought that the only kind of knowing possible under this definition is of necessary truths, then Husserl's use of "apodictic," given the association of this term with necessity, is appropriate.

In light of these considerations, let us call "belief" only consciousness which necessarily admits of being transformed into disbelief, i.e., where the correlative object admits of cancellation of its being. Given this definition, experiences which are basically doxic in modality are those having and anticipational structure which is such that it is always possible for the anticipation to be disappointed in a way which would cancel the actuality of the object experienced. It is Husserl's claim in the coherence-thesis, then, that our perception of worldly objects is basically a doxic consciousness. This doxic consciousness is the same as that which was referred to before as the belief which Husserl finds to be at the core of the natural attitude.[234] As such, the truth of the second statement of Husserl's argument (...any perceived thing could be inactual, which means that the perception of a thing is a believing or doxic consciousness) depends to a large extent on the truth of the forth proposition of the coherence-thesis (With respect of any perception, it is always possible... that anticipations could be disappointed in these "certain ways.").[235] We will see that the fate of Husserl's argument as a whole depends on the truth of that proposition of the coherence-thesis.

With the completion of this brief elaboration of the coherence-thesis, the issue of whether the empirical or the transcendental interpretation of the second statement of Husserl's argument (and of the coherence-thesis) is correct, must now be considered. In the light of some of the quotations and texts cited above, however, it may be asked if there really is a viable issue here. The evidence seems to favor the transcendental interpretation. Husserl's examples, it may be said, are only intended to suggest what he means through analogy. Furthermore, there seems to be no discussion of this as an issue of interpretation in the literature on Husserl's writings. However, as much as it may seem obvious that the transcendental interpretation is correct, we shall see that many of Husserl's statements concerning illusion and perceptual coherence can be profitably given the empirical interpretation. When this is done, a rather coherent psychological (phenomenological) theory of perception emerges from Husserl's writings. Considering the "parallelism" which Husserl thought to hold between psychological and transcendental phenomenology, it may be that he intended many of his remarks about illusion and perceptual coherence (including those in section 46 of *Ideas*) to be applicable to both empirical and transcendental illusion.

Therefore, let us consider what the issue is for us. There can be no doubt that Husserl has a concept of transcendental illusion, and that he does claim in places that the world could be a transcendental illusion. Our question is whether it is the possibility of transcendental illusion or of empirical illusion that figures in those pretranscendental parts of his texts in which he is laying down his argument that consciousness constitutes the world. Which possibility is meant in the passage from *Ideas* quoted earlier as Husserl's assertion of the second statement of his argument?[236] Which one must be meant in order for the argument to hold? Other issues also arise in this connection. When Husserl's statement in that passage that "every experience, however far it extends, leaves open the possibility that what is given, despite the persistent consciousness of its bodily self-presence, does *not* exist" is considered closely, is it perfectly clear what it means under *either* interpretation? If, under the empirical interpretation, it means that it is possible that *every* perception might be a hallucination, part of a coherent dream, etc., what is the meaning of "possibility" here? What is the nature of this "possibility" if it is to be a possibility for what are, in fact, genuine (i.e., veridical) perceptions, as must be the case if it is to be universal and if empirical illusion is to have the very sense it has (which requires that there be such perceptions)? Is the existence of this possibility merely the consequence of a particular theory of perception, or can it be verified independently of any such theory? Can a meaning be given to the possibility such that it can be so verified. Similar questions can be raised in the case of transcendental illusion. Furthermore, if it is a matter of transcendental illusion, what *experiences* could I have such that the world would become an illusion for me? And if this is not to be an empirical illusion, then what sort of illusion is it, and who or what is the "I" who is the subject of this illusion and its discovery? Let us try to give meaning to our two interpretations and explore some of their implications, beginning with the empirical interpretation.

*a. The "Empirical" Interpretation of the Coherence-Thesis.* Let us start with a provisional characterization of the two ways of interpreting Husserl's assertion that any perceived thing could be inactual. Under the empirical interpretation, this assertion would mean that what is perceived is only an apparition of something, an unreal "imitation" of an object which, if it exists, is somewhere else in the world. I will call such objects "phantasms." A phantasm, then, is an object which does not fulfill certain criteria which other objects do fulfill, namely the originals which the phantasms imitate and which they may be taken to be. The possibility that what we are perceiving at any given moment of our lives is a phantasm I will call the "permanent possibility of empirical illusion." Sometimes this will also be referred to as the "phantasm-possibility." On the other hand, it may be that the object is not a phantasm, but is an original. It may be precisely the specific object of the world or precisely one of the sorts of objects of the world it was taken to be. Still, the object could be inactual, but not, as in the former case, because it could fail to fulfill certain criteria which some other objects or objects *do* fulfill. Rather, it could be inactual because nothing fulfills these criteria. This is the possibility of transcendental illusion. The following example will serve to clarify this distinction.

Suppose I am perceiving a table that I have never perceived before. It could be that what I see is only a phantasm and does not fulfill whatever criteria something must fulfill in order to *actually* be a table, as could be discovered through further experience. However, there are objects, real tables, which do fulfill these criteria. On the other hand, the table I am perceiving could be inactual because there are not and never have been any tables. Should this possibility be realized, all tables which I have ever actually experienced would turn out to merely have been "presumptive tables." The very criteria which they have previously met are now themselves thought to have been, in a sense, fictions. What is meant here is not that the "tableness" *of those objects* has been a fiction, and that the objects existed all along but were simply not tables. Nor is it meant that the *concept*, "table," was a fiction, in the sense that there never really were any objects in that concept's extension *and* the objects I thought were tables really existed but were instead some other sort of objects (e.g., elephants). Rather, what I mean is that those objects *were* tables just as much as anything is the sort of thing that it is, but tables (or any other *sort* of thing) do not exist (in a sense to be explicated later), nor have they ever existed. It is not a matter, as with empirical illusion, of an expereince being a spurious table-experience, an eventuality whose sense requires that there be genuine table-experiences. Rather, it is a question of the spuriousness of genuine table-experience. Here there can be no comparison with a *genuine* genuine table-experience, for the iteration is sensless.

The following discussion of empirical illusion will resume our previous development of the psychological conception of consciousness. We recall that in that development a problem arose concerning our account of the intrinsic intentionality of consciousness which was called the "psychological problem of cognition."[237] It was said that through experiencing certain appearance-contents of consciousness we perceive a specific object. However, it seemed quite possible that an illusory or hallucinatory experience could have appearance-contents which do not differ in any essential way from those of a genuine perception. How, then, are we to account for the intrinsic intentionality of consciousness in the most significant sense of "intentionality," namely, consciousness, not just of an object in general, but of something *actual,* of a worldly reality? It is true that we are sometimes "deceived" by our perceptions, but as our very awareness of this fact shows, these deceptions can and do become uncovered. Most of the time we live our lives totally unconcerned about the possibility of such deception. How, then, are genuine and illusory perceptual experiences to be distinguished *intrinsically*? How does the theory of intentionality account for both the possibility of and the disclosure of deception and for our usual unconcern as to whether our perceptions are providing us with knowledge of the world? The following example of a phantasm-experience will serve as a focus of our discussion.

Let us suppose that I am standing at a window in a room of my house excitedly awaiting the arrival of a friend. Suddenly I sense my friend's presence in the room behind me. Although I do not see or hear him, I "know" that he is there, looking at me and waiting for me to turn to greet him. His presence changes the space of the room, polarizing it into his sphere and mine; a line, along which I will look once I turn, divides the room into two parts. I turn, see him, and walk over to greet him. Suddenly I hear the doorbell ring loudly. The ringing tears me from my engagement in the greeting process, and as I become reoriented, I find that I am still standing at the window. Apparently I had been hallucinating. I go to the door to find my friend there, having just arrived. The object I saw in the room and the room itself as I perceived it was a phantasm, the product of my "imagination," I might say, which was stimulated by the excitement I felt while awaiting my friend's arrival. But what I see now is no phantasm, it *is* my friend. Yet in terms of their appearance-content, my perceptions of my friend do not differ in any essential way from those through which what I took to be my friend was given.

The psychological problem of cognition emerges here as a problem for the development of an intentional theory of consciousness, and is conceived in the specific terms of that theory. Likewise, when the problem was discussed during the presentation of the second statement of Husserl's argument, it was expressed in terms of Husserl's theory of perception. However, the idea of the permanent possibility of empirical illusion is not unique to Husserl's thought; it has been employed in many diverse philosophical contexts. It occurs, for instance, in Descartes *Meditations*, as does also, I believe, the idea of transcendental illusion.[238] In contemporary philosophy, reference to the possibility of empirical illusion has often been made to support the argument that the immediate objects of perception are not real things, but "appearances," "sense data," or some other kind of "mind dependent" objects. This argument is known as the "argument from illusion."[239] The fact that the idea of the permanent possibility of empirical illusion has played a role within diverse philosophical contexts indicates that there may be a way of formulating the possibility and of verifying its existence as a permanent possibility without reference to any specific theory of perception. If this could be done, then formulations and discussions of the possibility in the specific terms of some theory could be viewed as efforts to further clarify the issue and to provide an account. Different theories could then be evaluated in terms of their adequacy in this regard. In what follows, I will present a formulation of the possibility in question which does not presuppose any specific theory of perception. Then, I will consider some of Husserl's analyses in the light of this formulation. A comparison of the theory which can be gleaned from Husserl's writings with other theories, although it would be highly interesting, would take us too far beyond our present concerns.

The approach to be taken here is based on understanding possibility as imaginability. Let us return to our example, giving it a new twist, to illustrate this. Suppose the events that were described as occuring before the ringing of the doorbell actually occured and were not hallucinated, while the rest of the story was pure fiction. As it really happened, there was no phantasm-experience. My friend was in the room, we greeted one another, and spent many hours together in enjoyable conversation. At the present time I return in memory to the period beginning with my awareness of my friend's presence in the room and ending just before the (now considered) fictional ringing of the doorbell and say that what I perceived during that period "could have been" a phantasm. I mean by this that I can imagine myself having had a plausible sequence of perceptions and other kinds of experiences which began just after that period and which terminated in my imagined self coming to the belief, warranted on the basis of the perceptions, that what was perceived during the period had been a phantasm. The original version of our story describes just such a plausible sequence of experiences. With "possibility" understood in this way, the claim that what I was perceiving "could have been" a phantasm is equivalent to the claim that the having of such a sequence of experiences is imaginable.

Before generalizing this formulation, let us consider two objections which might be raised against this way of understanding the matter. First, it might be said that something stronger is needed, namely, not merely that my having such a sequence of experiences is *imaginable,* but that, at the time in question, I *really* could have had those experiences. The idea here would be that the experiential situation at the time was so constituted that experience really could have developed either in the way it did, confirming the actuality of what was perceived, or in the imagined way, cancelling the actuality of what was perceived, and that *both ways* could have consisted in veridical perceptions. In this way, the possibility of empirical illusion is seen to pertain to real experience and its context, and the existence of the possibility as a permanent possibility is seen to tell us something significant about these, not about what could happen if reality were otherwise. However, the specifics of this proposal cannot be adopted, because if they were, we would no longer be talking about *both* a possibility that is permanent and an illusion that is empirical. By "permanent possibility" is meant a possibility which holds with respect of *every* perception. Since empirical illusion is at issue, according to the previous discussion, some perceptions must be veridical. Thus, the possibility holds with respect to all veridical perceptions. This means that in some sense it is "possible" that what is perceived is a phantasm even in cases where, in fact, it is not a phantasm. Now if "possibility" is understood in the way just proposed, the only way the possibility could exist at a given time is if the actuality of the perceived object were somehow undetermined in itself at that time, for if it were already determined, then only one of the two ways in which experience could develop could consist of veridical perceptions. However, if the actuality of the object perceived were undetermined, then it would not, in principle, be a *decidable* issue as to whether the perception is genuine or illusory. Consequently, empirical illusion would no longer be at stake.[240]

The objection, however, raises an important issue. We seek to understand the possibility that what one is perceiving at any given time could be a phantasm in terms of the imaginability of *having* a sequence of experiences which disconfirms the actuality of what is perceived. In saying that "having" such a sequence is imaginable, what is meant is not only that one can imagine what the experiences would be *like* and how they would proceed *if* they were to occur, but also that one can imagine them actually ensuing from a given experiential situation, i.e., from the experiential nexus of which the perception in question is a part. The difference here is like that between imagining what one's life would be like now *if* one had taken a certain course of action at some point in the past, and imagining, in addition, oneself actually having taken that course of action within that past context. The latter case involves difficulties that do not beset the former, since the former proceeds on the hypothesis that the course of action has been taken, while the latter involves imagining how that course of action could have been taken given the situation at the time. It may well be that in some instances one cannot imagine oneself actually having taken a course of action in the past because the situation simply did not permit it. In this connection one thinks, for instance, of the common complaint: "If only I had known then what I know now, I would have acted differently." While one may well be able to imagine oneself having acted differently, and also how one's life would have gone differently, *presupposing* that one knew then what one "knows now," it may be that one cannot imagine oneself having known then what one knows now. One reason for this could be that one could *not* have known then what one knows now, for instance, if the only way one could have learned what one knows now was by having done what one actually did. To apply this to our present concern, it is one thing to imaginatively "come up with" a sequence of experiences which, *if* it occured, would disconfirm the actuality of what is presently being perceived, and another to imagine that sequence ensuing from the present experiential situation, especially if it is also to be possible that the object of one's present perception *is* actual. Since it is the latter imagining which is the issue for us, these considerations lead us to add something to our formulation. The imagined disconfirming sequence must be imagined to start with a real experiential situation which becomes, then, part of the imagined sequence, and the ensuing of the purely imaginative part of the sequence from the real situation must be plausible.

By understanding the imaginability of a disconfirming sequence in this way, the intention of the proposal made in the objection above is satisfied, while the undesirable consequences of its specifics have been avoided. The intention was to formulate the possibility of empirical illusion in such a way that its existance as a permanent possibility would tell us something about the experiences that we actually have. This has been achieved by requiring that the same *actual* experiential situation which, let us say, gives rise to a confirming sequence of perceptions, remains the same situation from which our imagined disconfirming sequence must take its departure. Clearly, if the disconfirming sequence can be imagined under this condition, there must be *something* about the common starting point which permits the actual occurance of a confirming sequence (should the object not be a phantasm) and enables one to imagine a disconfirming sequence. A discussion of what this is, however, does not concern the formulation or the verification of the phantasm-possibility; it concerns the theory of how that possibility is a possibility. Husserl's contribution to this theory will be discussed later. The implication that the actuality of an object perceived is undetermined is avoided simply by understanding "possibility" as imaginability. Clearly, to assert that something can be imagined to occur is not to assert that it could really occur, since the latter assertion involves claims about the nature of the real conditions under which things do or do not happen which the former does not involve.

The second objection concerns claims that something can or cannot be imagined. It may be said that such a claim cannot be evaluated objectively, since its verification, namely, the result of the imagining process, the imagined state of affairs, is accessible only to the subject who imagines. If X says to Y that S cannot be imagined, and Y replies, "Yes it can, I've just done it", what more can be said? X cannot inspect the state of affairs Y has imagined. Of course X is not to be understood as saying that Y in particular, because of a lack of "imagination," cannot imagine S. Rather, to claim that something can or cannot be imagined, as we will understand it, is to claim that there is or there is not a way of setting out a merely posited matter concretely, and in detail, through an imaginative process, such that it will remain the matter it was posited to be in the way it was posited to be. For instance, someone I know once claimed that one cannot imagine a human being experiencing a certain non-Euclidean space. This claim was put forth to support the assertion that this non-Euclidean space was impossible as the experiential milieu of a human being. To counter this claim, I reminded my friend of the efforts of Poincaré and Helmholtz to imagine this matter, efforts which I thought were successful.[241] He said that they had not imagined the matter in question; rather, they imagined how this non-Euclidean space would look through "Euclidean eyes." He meant that the space imagined was only a translation of the non-Euclidean space into Euclidean terms. The fact that this debate was possible shows that the objection we are considering can be overcome. Poincaré and Helmholtz had made the results of their imaginings public in the form of stories. One could evaluate their claims as my friend did, by reading their stories, itself an imaginative process. After our discussion, I reread the stories and decided that my friend was correct.

Nevertheless, the objection raised to considering possibility as imaginability was well-founded. I do not know exactly what Poincaré and Helmholtz imagined, i.e., what they held before their imagining "eyes," nor did my friend. I also do not know exactly what my friend imagined as he read the stories, nor he what I imagined. All we have are the stories. However, the stories do make it possible for the alleged verification of the claim to be evaluated objectively. To be in a position to make this evaluation, it is not necessary that one have access to the very images of Poincaré and Helmholtz; it is sufficient that one read their stories.

Let us make use of these results to reformulate the way we shall understand the possibility of empirical illusion. The claim that an actually perceived object could be a phantasm shall be understood as the claim that a story can be told which describes a plausible sequence of perceptions and other kinds of experiences which begins with the actual perception and terminates with the subject of the story coming to the belief, warranted on the basis of the perceptions, that the object perceived was a phantasm. The possibility that *anything* perceived could be a phantasm, then, amounts to saying that such a story can always be told, no matter what it is that one is perceiving and no matter what the conditions of perception are.

This way of formulating the phantasm-possibility may not be free of all philosophical presuppositions, but at least it seems not to presuppose any specific theory of perception. It further has the merit of indicating a method of verifying the existence of the possibility. One simply asks: given that I am perceiving this, under these conditions, can such a story be told? But its chief virtue is in its emphasis on the importance of the *details* of the story. All too often one finds it asserted that this or that is possible because it is imaginable and only the briefest of hints of what the state of affairs would be like is given. Rarely is it asked: is this *really* imaginable?

I have not set it as my task to verify the existence of the phantasm-possibility as a permanent possibility, but only to formulate it. I should say that I do believe a story can be told in every case. I also think that one could develop a general formula of a story, or at least a few general formulae, which would cover all possible instances by substituting the specifics of each case. The attempt to develop such a formula or such formulae would no doubt be quite illuminating and theoretically suggestive, not only with respect to a theory of the experience of illusions and realities, but more generally. One would have to deal, for instance, with such problems as what constitutes a "plausible" story and what constitutes warranted belief. For our purposes here, we will simply assume that such problems can be solved and that the possibility of empirical illusion does exist as a permanent possibility.

Let us now turn to Husserl's analysis of perceptual consciousness to see how the existence of the permanent possibility of empirical illusion can be accounted for. First we recall that the second statement of Husserl's argument connects the possibility that any perceived thing could be inactual to the "appearential" inadequacy of perception, i.e., to the circumstance that anything spatial is necessarily given through appearances, none of which can "coincide" with it.[242] In his various discussions of this connection, Husserl often brings the epistemic inadequacy of perception into the issue, and, in my opinion, in such a way as to obscure the specific contribution of appearential inadequacy *per se*, i.e., that which is contributed to the possibility in question by the sheer fact of givenness through appearances, apart from the relation of this fact to epistemic inadequacy.[243] This contribution concerns the requirement that the experiences related in a story, most importantly the perceptions, begin with the actual perceptions with respect to which the possibility of empirical illusion is raised. The question here is: How is it that those perceptions could be genuine (as they are in most cases), and thus be followed by a sequence of veridical perceptions wherein the actuality of the perceived object remains unquestioned (as it does in most cases), *and* can also become the starting point of a story, in which their object turns out to have been a phantasm (as we suppose they can)? The importance of this question becomes clear when one considers an opposing theory of perceptual illusion. This theory maintains that if one believes one is perceiving a certain object which exists (like my friend), and it turns out that the experience was a phantasm-experience, then the experience was not a "perception of that object" (a "perception of my friend"). Either one was not, in fact, *perceiving*, or one's experience was not *of* that object, but of something else which one mistook to be that object. In this theory, perception is defined as "successful" perception. If this theory were correct, experiences which are related in the beginning of a story could not really be the same as the experiences which one actually has, in the case where they are, in fact, veridical perceptions. The storyteller would be mistaken in identifying them. To use our example again, in reality my experience was a "perception of my friend," while in the story the corresponding experience either could not really have been a perception (perhaps it was some form of imagination), or, if it was a perception, it could not have been one *of* my friend, but of something I mistook to be my friend. In terms of this theory, then, the kind of stories by means of which we have proposed to understand the possibility of empirical illusion are inherently countersensical and cannot really be told.

We learn from this that a theory of perception which is to corroborate the existence of the possibility of empirical illusion as we have understood it, and explain how the possibility exists, must meet the following condition: within the theory it must be "possible" to affirm that one can have a perceptual experience of an object, and *also* deny that the object is actually present. Thus, in terms of our example, it must be possible for me to assert that I had a perceptual experience of my friend, while asserting that my friend was not there during the time of that perceptual experience. In this way, the factual presence or absence of an object, X, is irrelevant to the identity of the perceptual experience as a particular perceptual experience of X, and to the identifying of the "two" perceptions, the one related in a story, and the other actual.

The possibility in question here is a form of logical possibility, but not mere freedom from formal contradiction. The requirement is that it must not be *countersensical* to say that an experience is 1) perceptual, 2) of an object, and 3) of an object that is not, in fact, itself present to the perceiver in the perception. This requirement is met by Husserl's concept of transcendent perception, in particular perception of spatial objects, as appearentially inadequate. As we saw earlier, the distinction between appearance and what appears allows the formulation of a concept of perception as intrinsically intentional. Thus, a "perceptual experience" could be defined with *reference* to an object ("A perceives" means "A perceives X") without *requiring* that the object (X) be actually present to the perceiver through the perception. Thus, a perceptual experience of a specific object could be constituted in someone's mental life whether or not that object is *actually* present. All that is necessary is that the experience contain an appearance of that object, something which is ontologically distinct from the object itself. A consideration of a concept of perception similar to the opposing theory discussed above, but which does not have to meet the requirement will serve to reinforce the point being made here.

We recall that Husserl distinguished transcendent from immanent perception, i.e., reflective perception of one's own experiences. Concerning immanent perception, Husserl writes: "perception and perceived essentially constitute an unmediated unity, that of a single concrete cogitatio. Here, the perceiving so conceals its object in itself that it [the perception] can be separated from it [the object] only abstractively, only as something essentially incapable of subsisting alone."[244] This means that a reflective perception *of* an experience (e.g., another perception) cannot exist without the actual presence of that experience to the perceiver through the reflective perception, or as Husserl says, that which is grasped in a reflective perception "is, in principle, characterized as something which...is and endures within the gaze of perception...."[245] Husserl expresses the same idea when he states that "(e)very immanent perception necessarily guarantees the existence of its object,"[246] and that through immanent perception "I apprehend an absolute Self...; it would be countersensical [*Widersinn*] to maintain the possibility of an experience *given in such a way* not truly existing.''²⁴⁷ It is quite clear from the context of Husserl's remarks that by the ''existence'' of the object of reflective perception he means not only that the experience perceptually reflected upon is ''really lived'' and exists ''now,''²⁴⁸ but that it is actually itself there in the reflective perception.

Why is it countersensical, in the case of immanent perception, to say that there is a perception of an object, but the object is not, in fact, itself present to the perceiver in the perception? It is because such experiences are intentional *only* by virtue of the actual presence of their objects. In *Ideas*, Husserl says that the fundamental difference between immanent and transcendent perception is in the ways that their respective objects are given,²⁴⁹ i.e., in the latter case through appearances, and in the former not.²⁵⁰ We saw earlier that, in *Ideas,* Husserl emphasizes that this difference in mode of being given does not concern the *incompleteness* of givenness (epistemic inadequacy), for in both cases, the object is not given completely.²⁵¹ In another text, Husserl discusses the incomplete givenness of experiences to reflection and notes that the temporal phases of an experience could also be called ''appearances.''²⁵² But, he adds, the concept of appearance here is radically different from that which pertains to spatial objects. In the case of experiences as objects of reflective perception, he writes that ''appearance and what appears cannot be distinguished,'' whereas in the case of spatial objects they can.²⁵³ When Husserl says that ''appearance and what appears cannot be distinguished,'' he seems to mean that the temporal phase of an experience (the ''appearance'') ''through'' which the experience is given in reflective perception, for instance, the ''now'' phase, ''coincides'' with the experience itself as it is in the ''now.''²⁵⁴ Lacking an appearance-content which is distinct from the object which appears, such a perceiving is a transparent attentive consciousness which can be intentional, i.e., *of* a certain object, only by virtue of the actual presence of that object to it. It would be countersensical to say, then, that there was a perceptual experience of a certain object, but the object was not itself actually present to the perceiver in the perception.

As we have seen, it is not countersensical to say the same in the case of the perception of spatial objects. Husserl's analysis thus enables us to understand how perceptions which form the starting point of a story, in which the object of those perceptions turns out not to have been present, may be identified with perceptions one is actually experiencing, whose object might very well be present. The identification may be made because the difference between the actual and the imagined perceptions, the presence versus the absence of the object of the perceptions, is irrelevant to the identification. All that is relevant is what constitutes the essence of ''a perceptual experience of a certain object.''

As we know it thus far, this is its having a certain appearance-content, i.e., the unity which results when certain hyletic data are apprehended in a certain way. The specificity of this appearance-content qualifies the experience as intrinsically directed toward a certain object. Thus it is legitimate to imagine a perception, which is in fact genuine, as a component of a situation where the same perception is in fact illusory.

These considerations seem to satisfy one aspect of the challenge presented by the theory mentioned before that "perception" is "successful" perception, and that when one suffers an empirical illusion, either one is not perceiving, or one is not perceiving the object one thought one was perceiving. However, the challenge can be pressed further. With respect to our example, it has been said that the object of the imagined perceptions "turns out to *have been* a phantasm" at the end of the story. Does not this mean that from the very beginning of the story, the object of the perceptions was not my friend, and therefore *not* the same object as that of the actual perceptions? Does it not seem, then, that the difference between a genuine perception and its "corresponding" illusory perception is that, in the former, the object one believes one is perceiving is really there, and in the latter, that object is not there and in its place is *another* object, which could be called an "inactual object" or a "phantasm." Is it not *this* object which is the true object of the perception? Empirical illusion, in this view, is just a case of an erroneous belief as to the *identity* of the object of one's perception.

The view just presented cannot be disputed in so far as it maintains that, in "genuine" (or "veridical") perception, the object one "thinks" one is perceiving is actually present, and in the corresponding illusory perception it is not. This is precisely the way we have distinguished these two types of perception. However I believe it would be consistent with Husserl's theory to say that, in the case of illusory perception, there is not some *other* object present (called a "phantasm" or "inactual object") *in the place of* the object one believes one is perceiving, which is the true object of the perception (and which is misidentified). Rather, no such *replacement* object is there, and in this sense one could say that in such cases one is not perceiving anything. In saying that no such replacement object is there, I do not wish to contradict the testimony of those who have experienced hallucinations and who find that there *is* something present to them during such experiences. However this "something" which is present is not the "true" object of the perception which is there *in place of* the object which one believes is there. Rather, what is there is present in the case of *both* a genuine perception and its corresponding illusory perception. I will call this "something" a "phenomenon of the self-presence of X," where "X" is the object of the perceptual experience in Husserl's sense, i.e., the object one believes one is perceiving or what Husserl calls the "intentional object."[255] A genuine perception (which, let us suppose one is actually experiencing) and its corresponding illusory perception (which becomes an element of a story) have the same intentional object and the phenomenon of the self-presence of that object.

The following passage from one of the provisional drafts of Husserl's *Encyclopedia Britannica* article analyzes empirical illusion in a way which is particularly helpful with respect to this point. "Whether the thing perceived in a perception is itself present or not, the intentional process of meaning [*intentionale Vermeinen*] of the perception, in accordance with the kind of grasping which perception is, is directed nevertheless to something which exists as being itself present. Every illusory perception makes that clear. Only because perception, as intentional, essentially has its *intentum*, can it be modified into an illusion about something."[256] What is here called the "*intentum*" is the intentional object of a perception; it is that object toward which the perceiving is directed and which "exists" in the sense of being intended as an object in the world. An illusory perception can have the same intentional object as a genuine one, and, as the passage emphasizes, it must have if the perception is to turn out to be illusory. Furthermore, an experience can be directed to its object "as being itself present," whether or not the object is, in fact, present. Indeed, it is this intrinsic *way* of being directed towards its object which qualifies the experience as a perception,[257] and not, at least in the case of transcendent perception, the actual presence of the object. This noetic "way of being directed" has as its noematic correlate, I would maintain, the phenomenon of the self-presence of the intentional object. That which is illusory about an empirical illusion is precisely this phenomenon, and it is this phenomenon, and not the intentional object, which the second statement of Husserl's argument refers to as possibly being inactual under the empirical interpretation of that statement. Empirical illusion, then, is not a case of erroneous belief as to the identity of the object of perception, it is an "erroneous belief" as to the *self-presence* of the object of a perception.

Both the theory presented here and the opposing theory we are considering hold that belief plays a role in genuine and illusory perception, but they differ as to its nature and function. As belief concerning the identity of the object perceived, the opposing theory would seem to have to posit the "real" object of the perception formed independently of this belief, which then functions erroneously in misidentifying the object. It would seem, however, that the "real" object (the "phantasm") would have to be perceived prior to the functioning of this belief in order to be the object of the misidentification. Then, a second experience, formed by the mistaken belief, would have to be said to arise, in order to explain how the object one believes one is perceiving seems to be actually present. Among the difficulties which this theory would encounter is one concerning the perception of the "real" object. In order to be a *perception*, of course, it must be a correct perception. However it also seems that its object must go unnoticed. But how can one speak of a *correct* perception if the subject of that perception does not notice its object? The only "noticing" that is achieved is through the other experience containing the belief. But this experience cannot be a perception, since perception means successful perception. But this experience only notices what it constitutes through its misidentification. It remains mysterious, then, how the "real" object is given to *be* misidentified. The nature and role of belief in Husserl's theory of perception is quite different from this, and to that subject we now turn. In doing so, we shall meet the other side of the challenge presented by the opposing theory, namely, how an illusory experience can be a *perceptual* experience.

So far this discussion has concentrated on explaining the intrinsic *intentionality* of a perception, i.e., how, even if its object is not actually present, a perception can be an experience *of* that object. But how an experience can be intrinsically perceptual under such a condition has not been explained. There is also one more matter to be cleared up in connection with our formulation of the permanent possibility of empirical illusion. The formulation was expressed in terms of being able to tell a story in which the "object" of one's perception turns out to have been a phantasm. Related to this, we recall that the second statement of Husserl's argument says that "...any perceived thing could be inactual..." The word "thing" was included because Husserl had announced in the beginning of his psychological analysis in *Ideas* that the analysis was to concern things, and not events, processes, etc.. "Things," of course, are among the "objects" of perceptions which figure in the stories. However, in our latest discussion it has been said that it is not the *intentional* object of one's perception which turns out to have been inactual in empirical illusion, and it is not that object which "could be inactual" under the empirical interpretation of the second statement of Husserl's argument. Rather, it is the "phenomenon of the self-presence of the intentional object." Thus, from a theoretical point of view, this phenomenon is the ultimate referent of the word "object" in the formulation of the permanent possibility of empirical illusion and of the expression "perceived thing" in the second statement of the argument. But is this phenomenon an "object" which is "perceived?" If not, how do these expressions arise in the discourse about empirical illusion? These questions are intimately connected to the issue of the intrinsic perceptual character of an experience and of the role Husserl assigns to belief in perceptual experience. As all these subjects also concern the third statement of Husserl's argument, that statement should be introduced first.

The third statement of Husserl's argument is: Whatever *could be* inactual and is on hand, is on hand through consciousness. From this statement and the second statement (...any perceived thing could be inactual...), the fourth statement (any perceived thing is on hand through consciousness), which is one of the conclusions of the argument, can be inferred.[258] This inference, however, requires that the referent of the expression "perceived thing" in the second and fourth statements be identical to the referent of the word "whatever" in the third statement. Under our present interpretation, this common referent is the "phenomenon of the self-presence of the intentional object of the perception." For the sake of brevity, I will refer to this phenomenon as the "self-presence phenomenon," or the "phenomenon of self-presence." This self-presence phenomenon is something common to both a genuine perception and its corresponding illusory perception. The phenomenon is "actual" when the intentional object of the perception is, in fact, present, and the phenomenon is "inactual" when the intentional object is not factually present. Since this phenomenon is "on hand" in a sense soon to be explained, the third statement of the argument asserts, in effect, that in the case of every perception this phenomenon is an "achievement" of consciousness.[259] This is brought out explicitly in the fourth statement of the argument.

The second and fourth statements seem to refer to something which is an object of straight-forward perception, as does the word "object" in my formulation of the permanent possibility of empirical illusion. Likewise, it may seem that the third statement is about something which is on hand to straight-forward perception. However the self-presence phenomenon, as we are about to see, cannot be the intentional object of a straight-forward perception. Nonetheless, as we shall also see, there are grounds for the way in which our discourse about empirical illusion has been expressed.

There is a sense in which the phenomenon of self-presence can be both an object of and on hand to perception, namely, in the case of reflective perception. This might happen in a reflection "in memory," as when, after uncovering an illusion, we recall our previous perception, and, reflecting on it, we grasp the phenomenon which was "in" the perception and speak about it as having been a "mere phenomenon." We can also conceive such a reflection coming about in a situation like the following. Our storysteller relates a story to demonstrate the possibility of empirical illusion. In the story, the "object" he is perceiving at the very time of the telling of the story turns out to be a phantasm. He is perceiving his friend, who, let us say, is a phenomenologist. His friend finds the story quite plausible, but asks,

"Surely you don't mean that *I* turned out to be a phantasm?"

"No...."

"You mean a certain phenomenon did, a phenomenon which is still present to you, don't you?"

"Why yes."

"So when you say that what you are perceiving could be a mere phantasm, you mean that only the phenomenon is present, and I am not."

"Yes."

"And right now that phenomenon is present, and so am I."

"That's true."

"Then I am not identical to the phenomenon."

The storyteller agrees to this. In the course of the conversation he has come to grasp the self-presence phenomenon intuitively, through reflection on his present perception. Further reflection shows that the phenomenon was already there, "in" the straight-forward perception, to be grasped. Like the appearance-content of a straight-forward perceptual experience, the self-presence phenomenon "in" such an experience becomes an object of perception only when the attentive glance is diverted from the intentional object of that experience, and it is on hand with respect to that reflective attending. Also, like the appearance-content, the phenomenon is not, according to the third statement of Husserl's argument, on hand independently of consciousness. Phenomenological analysis clarifies what the storyteller is doing. It shows that in the telling of a story there is an implicit reference to the phenomenon of self-presence, and that it is that phenomenon, not the intentional object, which turns out to be inactual.

Is it true that the self-presence phenomenon is an object, i.e., an intentional object, only of reflective perception? What about when a visual hallucination persists after being uncovered as such? Does one not then "see" the phenomenon of self-presence itself? This cannot be the case. What is seen on such occasions is not the self-presence phenomenon. It must be remembered that he phenomenon in question is the phenomenon of the self-presence of the *intentional object* of a perception. If I discover that I am hallucinating my friend, and the hallucination persists, there is no longer a phenomenon of the self-presence of my *friend*, for I no longer believe my friend is present. What is it, then, which is seen? What is perceived on such occasions is the proper referent of the term "phantasm," and it is in situations like this where the retrospective talk of the perceived object "having been a phantasm all along" arises. After an illusory experience is discovered to be illusory, and something is still perceived, the intentional object of the straight-forward perception is no longer the same as what it was before. It is no longer my friend, but a "phantasm."

Husserl calls such perception "*Schein-Wahrnehmung*," and says about it that "in a certain narrow sense nothing appears in such a perception, rather something is there *as a mere appearance* [*Schein*]... It is a mere 'image' [*'Bild'*]...",[260] i.e., a "fiction" [*Fiktum*].[261] Retrospectively, this object may be thought to have been there all along *in the place of* the intentional object of the previous perceptions. Such an inference is based on a common way of understanding empirical illusion. In that understanding the phantasm-object is thought to be like a real object in a certain respect, namely, as something which has a being-in-itself apart from its being perceived and from the way it may be perceived. As such, it can be misperceived and taken for something which it is not. It is this understanding of the phantasm-object as "having been there all along" which forms the basis of the opposing theory which has been under discussion. This understanding is not purely arbitrary, however, rather it is based on the way such objects present themselves. But this manner of presentation and the very presence of the phantasm-object itself are the constitutive achievement of a certain mode of productive consciousness and thus have their "being" only when that consciousness is at play. The phantasm-object "is" only when it is perceived, i.e., when it is the intentional object of a perception.[262] It is for this reason that it was denied above that the phantasm is what is really there, in place of the intentional object of a perception, when we are "deceived" by an illusory experience.[263]

The common understanding of empirical illusion also determined my formulation of the permanent possibility of empirical illusion and of some of the statements of Husserl's argument. This was fitting in the case of the former, since I wished that formulation to be as free as possible from any theory of perception. It may be thought that the common understanding of empirical illusion involves a theory of perception. However "theory" in *this* sense was not what I have intended to avoid. Indeed, no formulation could avoid being theoretical if "theory" is understood in such a broad manner. The formulation of the various statements of Husserl's argument in terms of this understanding follows the way Husserl at first also introduces these issues, and is also fitting since the argument is aimed at someone who has not yet attained phenomenological clarity. Our results in that direction have shown that during the time one is "taken in" by an illusory experience, there is no *object* there which later, when the illusion is uncovered, "turns out to have been a phantasm," nor is what turns out to be inactual the *object* of the illusory perception.

Someone who has experienced a visual hallucination may ask at this point: "Well, if the phantasm which I saw after I discovered I was hallucinating was not there before this discovery, if the intentional object of my perception was not present, and if the self-presence phenomenon was not perceived, then what

*did* I see while I was hallucinating?'' If the questioner is asking what was ''real-
··· there'' during the hallucination, this question has already been answered.
Nothing was there; the questioner did not see anything. But at this point the
questioner probably wants to know what the visual ''sight'' was which seemed
to have filled a portion of the surrounding space. This ''sight'' was the
phenomenon of the self-presence of the intentional object of the perception,
which although it was not perceived in the sense of being itself an intentional
object, was on hand and therefore not nothing. In being ''on hand,'' it was
present, and it was available to be perceived through reflection. In that it was
present, it was something ''there.'' The hallucination was a visual perception
of a certain object. That which made it such was just what makes any
experience a visual perception of an object, namely, the self-presence phenomenon and the correlative way of being conscious which achieves the being-on-
hand of that phenomenon. Whether an experience is genuine or illusory, it is a
perceptual experience on intrinsic grounds. In illusory experience, the intention
''misses the mark,'' the intentional object is not really there. In genuine perception the object is there. However it is only through the intrinsic ''way'' of
being conscious and its correlative self-presence phenomenon that the actual
self-presence of the intentional object can be *given* to a subject. It is quite possible for an object to be really present and not to be given as such. For example,
someone could believe they are hallucinating the object even though it is really
there.

It remains for us now to consider what it is that makes a perceptual experience intrinsically perceptual. What is the nature of that ''way of being conscious'' which is correlated with the self-presence phenomenon and thus
through which an object is given as itself-present? Before turning to Husserl's
inquiry into this, let us first analyze the meaning of the expression ''itself-
present.'' The expression points to two features of perception, namely, that the
object *itself* is given, and it is given as *present*.[264] Concerning the first feature,
Husserl writes that ''perception is that act which puts something before us as it
itself [*als es selbst*], [it is] an act which *originally* constitutes the object.''[265] In
being direct and original consciousness of an object, perception contrasts with
other forms of consciousness which, either in their non-immediacy or their
non-originality, bear an intentional reference to perception. These include
being conscious of an object representatively, for instance, as in recollection,
signitively, as in naming or judging, and pictorially, when we are conscious of
something through a picture of it. In contrast to the latter two of these, Husserl
writes, ''Perception is the consciousness of viewing and having the object itself
in person [*leibhaft selbst*]...it is not given as a mere sign or depiction [*Abbild*],
we are not mediately conscious of it as something merely signified or as ap-

pearing in a depiction; rather, we are conscious of it as it itself, in the way it is meant, and it is there personally [*in eigener Person*], so to speak."[266]

In addition to giving an object "itself," outer sensory perception gives it as "present," and for this type of perception, this means here, *in the present*.[267] Perception, Husserl says, is the self-giving of the present [*Gegenwart*],[268] it offers its object as bodily present [*leibhafte Gegenwart*].[269] That this feature of being temporally present is distinct from self-givenness can be seen in the case of primary memory (retention). According to Husserl, primary memory, the consciousness of the just-past phases of a temporal object, is a perceptual consciusness in the sense of giving the object itself.[270] He writes: "There is originary consciousness not only of the Now, but also of the Just-past."[271] "For only in primary remembrance do we see what is past; only in it is the past constituted, i.e., not in a representative but in a presentative way."[272] Of course, what is given in retention is not given as itself-*present*, but as itself-*past*.[273] This is in contrast to secondary memory or recollection, where the object is also given as *past*, but where, rather than being given originally, the object is given "representatively."[274] In terms of these two characteristics, "as itself," and "as present," the counterpart to perception, as we shall see, is imagination and particularly, phantasy.

As described earlier, a perceptual experience contains sensory (or hyletic) data which are apprehended in a specific manner. The unity of sensory data and apprehension I have called the "appearance-content" of a perception, and this content has been discussed above in both noetic and noematic terms.[275] Is it either of these factors making up this unity which makes an experience a perceptual experience? Husserl poses the question in this way in *Logical Investigations*. There, he calls this unity a "representation," and its two components the "representative content" and the "matter" of an intentional experience.[276] He also distinguishes a third component of the unity called "representation," namely, the "quality" of an experience. In *Logical Investigations* his way of pursuing the question is by asking whether the difference between perception and imagination can be accounted for by referring to any of these three variables, for, he says, imagination differs from perception in that, in imagination, an object is not given as itself-present; rather, it appears in a likeness or image (*Bild*).[277]

Imagination, along with recollection and anticipation, is a form of "presentification" (*Vergegenwärtigung*), i.e., it is a non-original and, as we shall see, "reproductive" mode of consciousness. Husserl uses the term "imagination" to denote a number of different types of experiences, chiefly phantasy (*Phantasie*) and picture-consciousness (*Bildbewusstsein* or *Bildlichkeits-bewusstsein*). Picture-consciousness differs from phantasy in that the presentifying is based on the perceptual conciousness of a physical object, for example, of a painting on a wall when we are conscious of a person through a portrait. Here, consciousness of the painted picture, made possible by the perception of the painting as a physical thing, provides the "likeness" through which the person is given.[278] In phantasy, however, for instance in "daydreams," there is no dependency on such an underlying perception.[279] Nonetheless, in *Logical Investigations* and in other early writings on imagination, Husserl conceived of phantasy (and other forms of presentification) as a kind of picture-consciousness in that he thought of it as involving the consciousness of an image in the sense of a likeness.[280] Thus, in *Logical Investigations*, Husserl ignores the differences between these kinds of imaginative experiences in his pursuit of the distinction between imagination and perception.[281]

Husserl distinguishes the matter from the quality of an act in the following manner. The matter of an act is "that element in an act which first gives it reference to an object, and reference so wholly definite that it not merely fixes the object meant in a general way, but also the precise way in which it is meant. The matter...is that peculiar side of an act's phenomenological content that not only determines *that* it grasps the object but also *as what* it grasps it, the properties, relations, categorial forms that it itself attributes to it."[282] Thus, it is because of its matter that an act is intentional.[283] Relating matter to apprehension, Husserl says that the "matter after a manner fixes the *sense* in which the representative content [e.g., sensory content] is interpreted [*aufgefasst* – "apprehended" in our terminology]."[284] The quality of an act, Husserl says, "determines whether what is already presented *in definite fashion* [i.e., through the matter] is intentionally present as wished, asked, posited in a judgement, etc."[285] The examples given here, and the word "quality" itself, suggest that the quality of an act is simply the "type" of act, i.e., in the sense in which perception, imagination, judgement, etc., may be said to differ in "type."[286] However, this is not what Husserl is referring to. By "quality" he means primarily the different ways in which intentional experiences do or do not ¨osit their objects.[287]

In *Logical Investigations*, Husserl concludes that the essential difference between perception and imagination does not lie in either the matter or the quality of an act.[288] Clearly, the same object can be "meant" (or "intended"), and meant as having the same determinations, in both a perceiving and an imagining, and thus, the two kinds of acts can be alike with respect of matter.[289] In terms of quality, it is doxic positionality or belief that Husserl discusses in this context. By "belief," he means belief in the actual existence (or actuality) of an act's intentional object.[290] In this sense, both perception and imagination may doxically posit their object. In this regard, Husserl points to the obvious fact that one can imagine an object which one believes to be actual.[291] Thus he distinguishes the "qualitative" from the "imaginative modification," i.e., two different dimensions along which acts may differ while having the same matter. The former, which is called the "neutrality-modification" in *Ideas*,[292] concerns the modification of an act which posits its object as existing into one which lacks that position-taking and which "merely presents" the same object.[293] The latter modification, however, concerns the change from having an object itself present (and thus perceiving it), to having it "present" through an image (thus imagining it). The modification which affects the quality of an act, then, the neutrality-modification, does not transform one "kind" of act (e.g., perception) into another kind (e.g., imagination). This is shown by the fact that when imagination itself undergoes the neutrality-modification, it remains imagination.[294] Such considerations show that the difference between perception and imagination lies neither in the quality nor the matter of an act. Thus Husserl says, "Quality and matter we took to be absolutely essential to acts,... but we originally pointed out that other aspects could be distinguished in them. Just these come into consideration... in connection with the distinction... between perception and imagination [*Eben diese kommen... für die Unterschiede... zwischen Perception und Imagination in Betracht*]."[295]

Husserl does not resolve the issue of the difference between perception and imagination in *Logical Investigations*. To be sure, in many places one finds the distinction expressed in terms of the self-presence or non-self-presence of the intentional object, but this is only the starting point of analysis. As to the "other aspects" of acts mentioned above, two emerge in *Logical Investigations* as relevent to the issue, the *mode* of apprehension and the representative contents. The latter was mentioned above as one of the three essential components of an act. In the case of perception and imagination, Husserl divides these representative contents into sensations and sensory phantasmata [*sinnlichen Phantasmen*] respectively.[296] These, he says, "owing to the purely imaginative or perceptual interpretations that they sustain, point unambiguously to definitely corresponding contents in the object, [and] represent these in imagined or perceived perceptual slantings [*2 bschattungen*]."[297] We see then, that both the apprehended contents and the modes of apprehension are differently named. Does this difference in naming point to a two-fold essential difference between perception and imagination? In one place Husserl says "(i)f there are essential descriptive differences between sensations and images [*Phantasmen*], if the usually mentioned differences in liveliness, consistancy, elusiveness etc., are sufficient, or if a varying mode of consciousness must be brought in, cannot be discussed here. Anyway we are sure that possible distinctions of content do not make up the difference between *perception* and *imagination*, which analysis shows, with indubitable clarity, to be a difference of acts *qua* acts."[298] Husserl's point here seems to be that even if one could find descriptive differences between sensations and phantasmata, taken in abstraction from the other components of an act (and the implication here seems to be that one may not be able to), *these* differences would not alone constitute the essential difference between perception and imagination, because such a difference is a difference in *intentionality,* and the apprehend contents are not the intentional moment in an act.[299] Thus, Husserl says that the difference lies in the apprehension-form (*Auffassungsform*).[300]

Husserl introduces the concept of apprehension-form in order to distinguish something about an apprehension which is different from matter. The latter, since it determines the *sense* in which the representative contents (now called "apprehended contents") are apprehended, is called the apprehension-sense (*Auffassungssinn*).[301] This distinction is made because "when the content functions representatively, more precisely, as representing in this or that way and as representing this or that object, we are differently 'minded' each time, thus we speak of a change in apprehension."[302] Here we see that the change in apprehension can either concern what we are conscious of, and be a change in the apprehension-sense, or the *way* we are conscious of it (e.g., perceptually or imaginatively), and be a change in the apprehension-form. Concerning the apprehended contents, Husserl says that these concern "whether the object is presented... by way of this or that representative content [e.g., sensations or phantasmata]. In [this] case, if we consider the matter [i.e., the issue] more closely, the laws connecting intuitive representatives with matter and form, entail that we are also concerned with differences that affect form even where the matter remains constant."[303] The implication in the last sentence of this passage seems to be that the apprehension-form and the apprehended contents might *covary,* and, in connection with what seems to be some hesitation on Husserl's part concerning whether sensations and phantasmata can be distinguished *in themselves*, and apart from the other components of an act, the further implication seems to be that, within the *unity* of form, matter, and content, the descriptive nature of the apprehended contents might be determined by the apprehension-form. This would mean that where the apprehension is perceptual, one would find sensations, and where it is imaginative, the "same" contents would emerge as phantasmata.[304]

It seems from the above study of Husserl's thoughts in *Logical Investigations* on the difference between perception and imagination, that what makes a perceptual experience intrinsically perceptual does not lie in the quality or the matter of an experience, but in its apprehension-form and its apprehended content, and perhaps most fundamentally in the former. However, Husserl occasionally experiments with the idea that quality may be involved. This occurs once in *Logical Investigations*. After pointing out that an imaginative act can be modified from a positing into a non-positing one and still remain imaginative, he writes: "It is most doubtful whether anything similar occurs in its purity in normal perception: whether perception can preserve the rest of its phenomenological features, but be qualitatively modified, so as to lose its normal positing character. It may be doubted whether the characteristic perceptual apprehension of the object as 'itself' (bodily) present would not at once pass over into a pictorial apprehension [*Bildauffassung*], where the object, much as in the case of normal perceptual picture-consciousness [*perzeptiven Bildlichkeit*] (paintings and the like) appears portrayed rather than itself given."[305] In this passage Husserl surmises that there may be *some* connection between the self-presence character of an object of normal perception and that experience's positing (i.e., its quality). He does not, of course, say that the former would be the correlate of the latter. As we have seen, the positional moment in an experience, as Husserl usually conceives it, is a belief in the actuality of the intentional object, and thus it is that moment which is correlated with the object's character of being *actual*. We have also seen that "self-presence" and "actual" are distinct characters.

In *Ideas*, Husserl delves into the subject of positionality more extensively. There, he finds the neutrality-modification of normal perception to be the neutral consciousness of a picture-object (*Bildobjektbewusstsein*),[306] for example, our perceptual consciousness of the figure in a portrait which normally, because of an additional moment of presentification, we experience as depicting an actual person. Consiousness of the picture-object alone is achieved by a falling away of the presentifying moment.[307] When this occurs, the intentional object is no longer the object depicted, but is what *was* the depicting object, now deprived of its character of depicting (i.e., the "picture-object"). In such cases, according to Husserl, we are conscious of the picture-object as something given "itself,"[308] and we are conscious of it in a neutral manner, i.e., neither as existing nor as non-existing.[309] Thus, the qualitative (i.e., neutrality) modification of perception would *not* lead to the experience of an object as portrayed, as Husserl surmised it would in the above quote from *Logical Investigations*; rather, the object would remain itself given. It is no doubt due to his further studies of the phenomenon of neutralization, reflected in *Ideas*, which led Husserl to insert into the second edition of *Logical Investigations* the following passage after the one quoted above: "Yet one might here point to many sensible appearances, e.g., stereoscopic phenomena, which one can treat, like aesthetic objects, as 'mere phenomena', without adopting an existential stance, and yet treat as they themselves [*sie selbst*], and not as portraits of something else."[310] It seems, then, that the self-presence character of an object of perception is unrelated to the positing moment in the experience (i.e., the quality). We are thus referred back again to the apprehension-form and the apprehended content for a resolution of the issue.

Of course, when we speak of "perception," as Husserl reminds us, "the normal sense of the word does not only indicate generally that this or that thing appears to the Ego *in embodied presence* [*leibhafter Gegenwart*], but that the Ego is aware of the appearing thing, grasps it as actually existing, posits it."[311] Thus, *normally*, the intentional object of a perception is outfitted with two characters, self-presence and actuality. This would also be the case in illusory perception (when we are "deceived," of course). But we have seen that it is its seeming to be itself-present (the self-presence phenomenon), and not an intentional object's actuality, which constitutes the illusory nature of empirical illusion. I have focused on the characteristic of perception to give its object as itself-present as the essential characteristic. This determination seems to be confirmed by our study of Husserl's writings on the subject. The "way of being conscious" which is correlated with the self-presence phenomenon would seem to be what Husserl calls "apprehension-form." In this regard, he mentions "perceptive" apprehension as opposed, for example, to "imaginative" apprehension. But the question is, what is the nature of that apprehension which is called "perceptive" and how does it differ from an "imaginative" apprehension? How can we give an account of this difference other than by appeal to the way an intentional object appears? The answer to this would seem to provide us with an account of what makes a perceptual experience intrinsically perceptual.

Thus far in our quest we have looked toward the proper *components* of experiences in order to discover that which makes a perceptual experience intrinsically perceptual. This focus is in conformity with the conception of an intentional experience which we developed prior to entering into this inquiry, and it is in conformity with Husserl's approach in *Logical Investigations*. However, one will search in vain in Husserl's subsequent writings for an answer to the question in such terms. This is because Husserl came to radically change his view on the *way* in which perception and imagination differ, and to that subject we now turn.

Phantasy, according to Husserl, is the "neutrality-modification of 'positing' presentification, of memory [*Erinnerung*] in the widest conceivable sense."[312] The explication of this formula will help us understand Husserl's final conception of the difference between phantasy and perception. Let us consider phantasy as presentification first, apart from the neutrality-modification involved.

A perceiving of an object is an "impressional" consciousness, i.e., it is an experience which is actually being constituted as an immanent temporal unity in inner time-consciousness.[313] Inner time-consciousness is that non-thematic, non-reflective awareness which we have of our own experiences through which they first become present as what fills a duration of our mental life.[314] Inner time-consciousness has three inseparable aspects, primal impression, retention and protention.[315] Through the latter two, we are aware of the elapsed and the coming phases of an experience respectively.[316] Through the primal impression, we are aware of a phase of an experience as itself present (*gegenwärtig*), as bodily Now, in the most original sense.[317] A perceiving is said by Husserl to be "impressional," no doubt, because to experience (*Erleben*) a perception is to be aware of it through a primal impression (and through retention and protention also), i.e., to be aware of it as actually presently existing in one's mental life.[318] But of course every experience, as a lived experience, is impressional in this sense, and this includes phantasizing and all other modes of presentifying.[319]

Unlike perception, however, presentification is a "reproductive" mode of consiousness, i.e., it is a consiousness in which there is, as it were, a doubling of experiences such that there lies within the impressional presentify*ing* a second, non-impressional, presentifi*ed* experience.[320] Thus, if I am presently engaged in phantasizing some object, my phantasizing is an impressional consiousness; I am aware of it as being originally engendered as the living present of my conscious life. In short, I am actually experiencing the phantasizing. However, *in* the phantasy the object becomes "visible" to me through a seeing which I am aware of as not actually being originally engendered in the present. I am aware that I am not *actually* experiencing that seeing. The same is true of a visualizing which is involved in recollecting or anticipating.

The different forms of positing presentification are distinguished by the different ways in which we are conscious of the time of that which is presentified in them. Each presents this time in a different temporal locus with respect to the Now of the actual present, i.e., of the presentifying. In a recollection of an object which was perceived, the Now of the perceiving and of the perceived is presentified as a different Now than that of the recollecting, and specifically, as an actually past Now.[321] In anticipation, the presentified Now is presented as a future Now which is actually coming.[322] What is meant by "time" or the "Now" here?

With regard to perception, one can speak of time in many senses. The perceiving is a filled duration of *immanent time*, in fact, "(e)very concrete lived experience is a unity of becoming and is constituted as an object in internal consciousness in the form of temporality."[323] This immanent, "subjective" temporality of experiences can be regarded as distinct from "objective," world-time.[324]

Considered in this way, one could say that in recollection, the purely immanent, subjective temporality of the perceiving is reproduced and presentified as a past duration of conscious life. But "immanent time, in which lived experiences are constituted, is...at the same time the form of givenness of all objects given in them...."[325] Thus, if I have perceived two stationary objects one after the other, and I recall them both, I recall them as having succeeded one another, but not, of course, in objective world-time, rather, in what Husserl calls their "givenness-time" (*Gegebenheitszeit*), which is a time that "belongs to the immanent sphere."[326] However, the immanent sphere itself may be viewed as partaking in objective time. Thus, when Husserl states that, in perception, "(t)he Now of the perceiving is identically the same as the Now of what is perceived,"[327] from one point of view this may mean that the givenness-time of the object is identical to the immanent time of the perceiving. On the other hand, it may mean that the perceiving, taken as a psychic process of a person in the world, can be seen to partake of the objective world-time (e.g., as occuring yesterday, or a minute ago), and that the immanent time of the perceiving (and thus the immanent givenness-time of the object perceived) is objectively simultaneous with the objectively present state of the object.[328] One can say, then, that in recollection I presentify a past objective time, a slice of my "life-time" in so far as it partakes of objective time. When it is said that, in presentification, the "time" of what is reproduced is differently placed with respect to the "time" of the presentifying, what is primarily meant is that the immanent time of the reproduced perceiving and the givenness-time of the perceived object (which is the same time) are differently placed with respect to the immanent time of the presentifying (the actually present Now).[329] However, depending on one's point of view, immanent time here may be regarded as either purely subjective or as partaking in objective world-time. In the following discussion it will not always be important which point of view is adopted, but when it is, attention will be explicitly drawn to whether the "time" refered to should be understood purely subjectively or objectively.

In recollection and anticipation there is a disparity between the presentified Now and the Now of the presentifying. There is a third type of presentification in which this disparity does not exist, where the objective Now of the object presentified is identical with the (objectively understood) Now of the presentifying. Husserl calls this intuitive "co-presentation" (*Mitgegenwärtigung* or *Gegenwartserinnerung*).[330] Examples of this are the visualizing of the unseen backside of an object one is perceiving and of one's surroundings that are out of view. Such a visualizing presentification may be based on a recollection, although when it is, we are not conscious of the object as what was previously seen in its mere being-past (as in recollection), but we are conscious of it as enduring now, in the actual objective present.[331]

Let us now consider the other aspect of phantasy, its being the neutrality-modification of positing presentification. What is the positing whose neutralization defines the essence of phantasy? It would be the positing *proper* to the three forms of presentification just discussed. This positing is not the positing of the *actuality* of a presentified object. Although such a positing could also be present, it need not be.[332] A recollection could be the recalling of a phantasm which was once experienced. The positing proper to recollection is not the positing of the actuality of that object, nor even the actuality of *its* time; rather it is the positing of the actuality of the reproduced *immanent time*, i.e., the reproduced temporality of the reproduced experience and the reproduced givenness-time of the object. This positing consists in positing the reproduced immanent time as having a certain relation to the time of the reproducing, namely as actually *having been* a present time in one's life-time. As Husserl expresses it, "Recollection...posits what is reproduced, and in this positing it gives it a position with respect to the actual Now and to the sphere of the originary time-field to which the recollecting itself belongs."[333] Likewise, in anticipation, the Now of the reproduced immanent time is posited as a Now which *will be* a present Now.[334] In both cases, then, the immanent time is posited, and that means posited as having a relation to the actually present Now of the reproducing consciousness.[335] What is posited in the case of co-presentation?

Co-presentation seems to be different from recollection and anticipation in this regard. In co-presentation the presentified immanent time is not posited as actual. This means that the presentified perceiving is not posited as having been, as being, or as going to be, nor, then, is the givenness-time of the object.[336] Rather, the actuality of the presentified perceiving is a "conditional" possibility.[337] One might express this by saying: "If I were there now, I would be seeing...."[338] However there is a positing proper to co-presentation. The object as presentified is posited as enduring in the objective present, as being now here, there or somewhere in our immediate or remote environment.[339] Thus in co-presentation the presentified objective temporality of the object is posited as the present time.

It is of the very nature of co-presentation to be consciousness of something in the world, and for this reason its specific positing is easily confused with the positing of the actuality of the object. The fact that positing of actuality in the case of mundane objects involves attributing objective temporality to them only encourages the identifying of these positings. Thus it is important to call attention to the difference between them. Let us consider this issue within the context of positing presentification in general.

In recollection and anticipation there is a positing of the actuality of the presentified immanent time of the presentified experiences. This is most obvious in the case of recollection. Reflecting in memory, I grasp the reproduced flowing appearance-content as being the very flow once lived by me. In the case of anticipation there is something analogous to this. The reflectively grasped flow of appearance-content presents itself as one which will be lived by me, and hence I can say, "I am expecting to see this particular object looking this particular way, etc." It is important to note that in these two cases the positing of the presentified flow of immanent time is identical to the positing of the actuality of the experiences presentified, since actual existence in the case of temporal objects means elapsing at a locus in time. Reflecting on a recollection or an anticipation, it would be impossible to distinguish a positing of the actuality of the presentified experience from a positing of the "having been" or the "going to be" of the presentified flow of time. But what is impossible here is possible in the case of co-presentation.

In co-presentation, we are conscious of the *object* as enduring in the present objective time. Let us take an example of this. We may frequently pass by a house which we have never been in, and each time, on the basis of a description provided by someone else, presentify its interior. If the description was extensive, we may have a rather detailed and vivid "picture" of it in our mind. That we think this "picture" represents what endures therein is shown by the way the same "matter" (in Husserl's technical sense) is taken up in anticipations should we get invited to the house and begin to enter it, and by the subsequent experiences of partial fulfillment and partial disappointment of our positing expectations. Thus in picturing this interior, we think that the very image which we have represents what endures there now, and in and through the image we bring to intuitive clarity the knowledge we have derived from someone else.[340] What we represent to ourselves is what we would see if we were now inside the house.

It can be said, then, that like recollection and anticipation, co-presentation contains a certain cognitive claim. In each case, the cognitive claim is embodied in the positing of the *reproduced* temporality. Since in recollection and anticipation the positing of the actuality of the experiences presentified is the same as the positing of the presentified temporality, the cognitive claim can be said to be contained in the positing of actuality. In positing the actuality of presentified experiences, I posit the presentified flow in its concreteness as what has been or will be. However, in the case of co-presentation, the claim that the image I have represents what endures there now is not embodied in the positing of the actuality of the intentional object of the presentation, even though that positing involves a positing of the object's temporality. In other words, the positing in a presentification of the object as actual and as enduring in objective time is distinguishable from positing the *represented* temporality and does not embody any claim to knowledgde of how the object is *now*. This is because, in the case of spatial objects, the object "itself," as what is identical in, and endures through time, is distinguishable from the way that it might be at any *particular* time. The positing of the object's actuality in co-presentation is the positing of this identical "substrate" as an actuality, and that implies its being in time.[341] But the positing which is peculiar to the co-presentation as such, is the positing of the determinate represented content as enduring now.

One can infer from this analysis that it should be possible for there to be a presentification which posits the actuality of a spatial object, but which does not do so in regard to the presentified temporality. Just this is the case in certain kinds of phantasy. We recall that it was said above that although some phantasies involve purely fictitious objects, others do not. Daydreams, for example, often involve ourselves, people we know, and other elements from our everyday world, as do the dreams we are sometimes aware of when we are "sleeping." Of course in these cases the events phantasized are not posited to be actual. But if phantasy is the neutrality-modification of positing presentification, and if the positing neutralized is precisely the positing of the presentified particulars, we should expect phantasy-consciousness to be neutral in regard to these particulars. However, if the above analysis is correct, we also know that phantasy can be consiousness of something actual and it can so posit it. Thus, we may say that, on the one hand, phantasy-consiousness is not *complete* neutrality, but, on the other hand, no knowledge is gained or illustrated in phantasy; its determinations are totally fictions.

Husserl finds the specific nature of the positing in positional presentification to be belief.[342] This seems correct, if belief is understood in the way previously discussed, namely, as a mode of consciousness which can pass over into its opposite, into disbelief, i.e., where error is possible.[343] As Husserl says concerning recollection, "If I trust the memory, then I am sure that the memory is a presentification of an earlier perception."[344] But one could be mistaken, and in a variety of ways.[345] My "recollection" could be, in truth, a mere phantasy.[346] In anticipation, the experiences presentified and believed to be coming could fail to materalize.[347] Likewise, the co-presented object may not at all be as presentified.

Husserl seems to have conceived of *all* intuitive presentification as the reproducing of a complete act supplied with its Now, with the past and future horizons of that Now, and with a *positing* of that Now.[348] If the presentification is a recollection, the presentified Now is posited as being a past Now with respect to the Now of the presentifying, *and*, the positing is seriously engaged in.[349] However, if everything else remains the same, but the positing is *not* seriously engaged in, then there is the *phantasy* of a recollection.[350] Likewise, in anticipation and co-presentation. In the phantasy-of each of these, the positing of time is there, but it is not seriously engaged in. Rather, as Husserl expresses it, it is a completely neutralized "as if" or "quasi" doxic positing, and thus, we are not conscious of what is phantasized as *actually* present, past or future.[351] In phantasy, time is presented, "but it is a time without actual, strict localization of position—it is, precisely, a quasi-time."[352] It is for just this reason (and perhaps it was Husserl's reason) that I have chosen phantasy, and not the other forms of presentification, as the counterpart of normal sensory perception in this search for that which makes this type of perception intrinsically perceptual. Perception gives an object "itself" and gives it as something in and with *actual* temporal presence. With all else remaining the same, the corresponding phantasy of the object lacks precisely these features.

We have come to understand how phantasy is related to positing presentifications. Now we must see what can be learned from this regarding our question of the difference between phantasy and perception, and, more importantly, regarding the question of what makes a perceptual experience intrinsically perceptual. Let us compare a visualizing phantasy and a visual perception of the same object, and try to discern what would be involved in an actual transformation of the phantasy into a perception.[353] The phantasy in question, let us say, is precisely the phantasy of the percetion. We can think of it as a very vivid daydream.

We recall first that the phantasy is a neutral *presentification*, and not a neutral perception. Husserl is quite emphatic about maintaining that a neutralized perception of an object is not a phantasy of that object.[354] In neutralized perception, the positing of the *actuality* of the object is affected, but the character of bodily presence is unaffected. In phantasy, the intentional object could be believed to be something actual; however the object is not experienced to be actually itself present—it is only *as if* it were present. Let our example, then, be a phantasy of someone we know.

Purely as presentification, and apart from its neutrality, the phantasy we are considering is very much like a co-presentation, and thus the phantasy differs from its corresponding perception in the same way in which a co-presentation would, namely, we are (non-reflectively) aware of the perceiving which presents the person as an experience which is not actually being lived, as non-impressional. One of the things involved in the transformation of a phantasy into a perception, then, would be the conversion of this non-impressional, presentified perception into one which is actually lived.

What would be the effect of this? Consider what it would be in the case of a co-presentation. Suppose I am now perceiving a person I know who is standing some distance from me in the middle of a room with her back to me. Suppose further that I co-present her front-side, visualizing how she looks now. It is conceivable that I could become engaged in that co-presentation in such a way that I experience myself to be on the other side of the room looking at her from that point of view and merely co-presenting the side of her I previously was actually seeing. Unusual as such an occurance might seem, it is entirely conceivable that it could happen. Indeed, I would venture to say that the so-called "out of body" experience which some people have had, where they seem to be actually perceiving themselves from a place in space other than the one where their body is perceived to be, is just a case of this.[355] The effect of this transformation is evident: what had been merely presentified becomes presented as itself given.[356]

Since the transformation of a co-presentation into a perception involves becoming "aware" of the (previously) presentified perceiving as an actually lived experience, we can say that this awareness is the intrinsic factor "in" a perceptual experience which is correlated with the "itself" character with which an object is given in perception. "In," however, is not quite an appropriate term, since this "awareness" seems not to be itself "in" an experience in the sense in which Husserl described the components of an experience in *Logical Investigations*. In so far as phantasy is presentification, at least, the difference between phantasy and perception is not ultimately traceable to a difference in this of that component of an experience, whether it be its quality, matter or representative contents. Rather, all these components are in a sense the same, because visual phantasizing involves the reproduction of an *entire* perception of an object, and thus, the reproduction of all of the components of the perception *intact*.[357] The difference concerns whether the act presenting the object is impressional or non-impressional, a difference which holds for the entire act, including each of its components. That which is responsible for this difference is not a component of an act; it is an entirely difference dimension of consciousness, namely, internal time-consciousness.

The examination of what would be involved in the transformation of a co-presentation into a perception allowed us to isolate the intrinsic factor which is the correlate of the object-character of self-givenness because the character of being what is (objectively) temporally present remains constant in that transformation. We know that the correlate of this latter character is the positing of the objective temporality which is given in an experience. In the phantasy of a perception, the temporality which is given is not posited as the actual present time, it is a quasi present time. This would mean, then, that the transformation of a phantasy into a perception involves two changes. The non-impressional presentified perceiving becomes impressional, and thus the object is given "itself." Also, there is a deneutralizing of the positing of the "present time" which is given, i.e., an engagement in positing that time as being the actual objective present. *Impressionality and time-positing, then, acting jointly, are the correlate of the self-presence phenomenon. Together, they are that which makes perception intrinsically perceptual.*

This result concludes our search for the intrinsic factors in perceptual experience which make it intrinsically perceptual. This search was undertaken in order to explain one aspect of how, in the course of attempting to verify the permanent possibility of empirical illusion, one could "tell a story" wherein perceptions one is actually having, which may in fact be veridical perceptions, turn out to be illusory perceptions. The problem was how an illusory perception (before being uncovered as such) can be both *of* the same object as its corresponding genuine perception, and be perceptual, considering that its object is not, in fact, present. This problem was posed by a theory which opposed the one presented here, and which maintained that "perception" means "successful perception." To meet this challenge, it was shown earlier how perceptual experience can be *of* a certain object even though that object is not, in fact, present. The second aspect of the problem has now been dealt with through the elucidation of factors in the perceptual experience of spatial objects which make such experiences intrinsically perceptual. The theory presented here, then, which is based on Husserl's analyses, confirms the story-teller's procedure and theoretically grounds it. The import of this, of course, is to ground the formulation I have given of the permanent possibility of empirical illusion, a formulation wherein "possibility" is understood as "imaginability."

The opposing theory which was discussed attempted to maintain that illusory perception is simply a matter of mistaken belief as to the identity of the object perceived. In this context it was mentioned that Husserl's theory assigns a different role to belief. Let us proceed to discuss this aspect of Husserl's theory. Before this can be done, however, a supplement needs to be added to our results.

First, let us confirm that the two factors which were identified as the correlate of the self-presence phenomenon are truly distinct, i.e., not merely separable conceptually, as has already been shown, but also in experience. We already know from the examples of positing presentifications that there can be non-impressional time-positing experiences. Is the opposite possible? Can there be an experience which is impressional and perceptual, in the sense of giving the object itself, yet neutral in regard to the actuality of the "present time" given in it? Such an experience can occur, I believe, while watching a non-documentary motion picture, providing that the acting is flawless and one is so immersed in the fictitious characters and their actions that one's awareness of being in a theater and of the screen is reduced to a minimal, marginal consciousness. Then, the characters and their actions are perceived, in the sense of being themselves given, but the time is given as a fictive time. This would not be a presentificational picture-consciousness, for in picture-consciousness we are conscious of something as *absent* through the mediation of the perception of something as actually present. In the case envisioned here, what would be absent? If the fictitious characters and their actions are absent, how *would* they be themselves given? The only way for "The Tramp" of *Modern Times* to be himself given to someone is for that person to be at the movie, viewing it in the proper attitude. Of course there can be picture-consciousness when viewing a movie. This could come about by becoming aware of the *actors* as acting. The actions viewed would become seen as the real activities of the actors in the performance of their roles. The absent actors and actions would be presentified through the meditation of the images "on" the screen, and would not be given perceptually. The temporality of the actors and actions would be posited as an actually past duration of objective time.

This separability of impressionality and time-positing should make it possible for a phantasy to be transformed into a sort of perception solely by an alteration of its presentifying factor. The merely reproduced perception would become impressional and the object would become itself given. If the phantasized object was experienced to be a fiction to begin with, the result would be a "perceptive" consciousness of a fiction, or what Husserl calls "perceptive phantasy" (*perzeptive Phantasie*).[358] However, if the phantasized object was not a fiction, as in a daydream about an acquaintance, and if we suppose the neutrality of the time-positing to be maintained, the alteration of the presentifying factor would seem to have to be accompanied by a neutralization of the belief in the actuality of the object, for it seems impossible for an actuality to be itself given, yet in and with a fictive time. The result in this case would be a neutralized perception. But the results of both of these transformations seem to be the same, so that we can say that perceptive phantasy and neutralized perception are exactly the same phenomenon. This is apparently Husserl's view too, since he uses the same examples to illustrate both.[359] The neutralization of normal perception, then, a process which does not alter the impressionality of the experience, involves *two* changes: neutralizing the positing of the actuality of the intentional object, and neutralizing the positing of the temporality which is given. When Husserl discusses neutral perception he usually only mentions the first of these factors. This is justified, in a way, since with impressionality held constant, if either of the positings is altered, is seems that the other is of necessity altered too. Under the stated condition, then, these positings are separable only conceptually, and not in experience.

These observation now allow some comments to be made about Husserl's concept of the belief moment in perceptual experience. Above, Husserl's expression *"perzeptive Phantasie"* was quoted. Obviously the word *"perzeptiv"* here is used to designate the self-giving aspect of an experience. In *Ding und Raum,* Husserl calls that which remains of *"Wahrnehmung"* (perception) – which he emphasizes is a *Für-wahr-Nehmen,"* a taking for true or real – after one abstracts from *"Glaube"* (belief), *"Perzeption"* (also perception).³⁶⁰ In using this Latin derivative, he wishes to emphasize the essential character of perception, which, he says, is "to be 'conscious' of the bodily presence of an object."³⁶¹ He adds, "To perceive a house – that means to have the consciousness of, the phenomenon of, a house standing there bodily [*leibhaft dastehenden*]. Concerning the so-called existence [*Existenz*] of the house, its true being, and what this existence means, nothing is expressed about that in this."³⁶² What "house" is Husserl talking about here? As with most of his examples when he is discussing the role of belief in perception, we are presented with an anonymous object – *"a* house," *"an* apple tree in a garden," etc., but not *"my* house," *"the* tree in my garden which I look out upon every day," etc. Let us suppose it is Husserl's house he is talking about. He goes on to say that if we take the word *"Wahrnehmung"* in the usual sense, we find the *"glaubhaft"* (believed in) and the *"leibhaft"* (bodily, in person) fused together. He adds, "The perception [*Wahrnehmung*], the phenomenon of a house bodily standing there is at the same time belief [*Glaube*] that it stands there [*dass es dastehe*]."³⁶³ To show that belief is not essential to perception in the sense of *"Perzeption,"* he cites the case of a hallucination which has been uncovered, and where there is disbelief, yet the phenomenon of an object bodily standing there remains. Let us suppose Husserl has just discovered he has been hallucinating his house. What does he now disbelieve? Is it a matter of the "true being" of *his* house? Does he now believe that his house does not exist? Of course not. He believes that his house is not really "standing there," and thus we should take *"dastehen"* literally, as meaning "standing there," and not figuratively, as meaning "exists."³⁶⁴ But does the "phenomenon of the bodily standing-there" of *his house* still persist? According to our analysis, no. He now perceives a phantasm, perhaps an apparition of his house. But in perceiving a phantasm, he no longer has the same intentional object as before, and thus the phenomenon of the self-presence of his house does not persist. Thus it seems that without the *"glaubhaft,"* he does *not* have the same phenomenon, the same *"Perzeption"* as before.³⁶⁵

Before his discovery, Husserl "believed" that the intentional object of his perception (his house) was actually there, and afterwards, he no longer believes this, although he still perceives something. What has changed here? The impressionality of the experience remained constant, and the time-positing was neutralized (a phantasm has a quasi temporality). Above it was said that this change should bring with it a neutralization of the belief in the actuality of the intentional object, but of course it was persumed there that the intentional object remains the same. We now see that when it does not, there is a different result. The result is a neutral perception, but not one *of* the same object. Furthermore, the previous belief in the standing there of his house becomes retroactively cancelled, layered over as it is revived in memory by disbelief, and the correlate of the belief, the phenomenon of the self-presence of his house, is cancelled in its actuality.

It seems, then, that the "belief" involved in normal perceptual experience (*Wahrnehmung*) which Husserl discusses in *Ding und Raum,* is simply the moment, or rather the moments, of such an experience which I have identified as the correlate of the self-presence phenomenon, namely, the joint functioning of impressionality and time-positing, it being understood, of course, that the intentional object is posited as actual. However, if this is the case, one cannot abstract the *"glaubhaft"* from the *"Wahrnehmung"* and retain the *"leibhaft,"* i.e., have the bodily presence of the same intentional object (the same *"Perzeption"*). A neutralization of belief in this sense would not result in a "perceptive phantasy" of the same object. That could only be brought about by the neutralization of the positing of the actuality of the intentional object, i.e., by the "qualitative-modification" of *Logical Investigations*. However, from an examination of the way Husserl analyzes perceptual experience in *Ding und Raum*, and the way he discusses belief, it seems that by "belief" he means the same factor which he designated "quality" in *Logical Investigations*, and which he identifies with the thetic character of an act in *Ideas*.[366] Our earlier discussions have shown that Husserl conceived this to be the positing of the actuality of the *intentional object*. Thus it appears that in *Ding und Raum* Husserl is not distinguishing a second moment of positionality in perceptual experience as I have done drawing from Husserl's own analysis of perception.

It also seems that in thinking that the *"Perzeption"* can be the same after a hallucination has been uncovered as such, Husserl holds the same view which I called the "common understanding" of empirical illusion and which was rejected earlier when I presented a theory of empirical illusion I claimed to be consistent with Husserl's theory of perception. Thus, there in an inconsistency in Husserl's theory, *if* his remarks in *Ding und Raum* are taken to apply to a case of empirical illusion. Have I been led by the example of hallucination into an "empirical" interpretation of Husserl's remarks, as I indicated was possible earlier, where a "transcendental" interpretation would have been more appropriate?[367] Was the anonymity of the "house" a clue which I failed to pick up? If we assume the "house" was not Husserl's house, but a house which he never saw before, it might very well be that when he discovered he was hallucinating Husserl would have believed that the "house" he saw did not exist. In this case, it would be the *intentional object* of his previous perception which would be retroactively cancelled as "inactual." This is still not transcendental illusion as I have characterized it, but it is certainly a phenomenon which, in the "empirical" sphere, is somewhat analogous to it. Perhaps Husserl intended his example to be understood only in that way. Under the new hypothesis about the identity of the "house," would Husserl now have the same *"Perzeption"* as before? Perhaps not, but if not, the significance of this is quite minor in comparison to what it was before.

This discussion brings us back to our main concern, Husserl's argument and its two interpretations. The issues just discussed will be raised again in another context. Let us now look at Husserl's argument as a whole, under the empirical interpretation, in light of the results obtained thus far.

The five statements of Husserl's argument can be formulated in terms of the empirical interpretation in the following manner.[368]

1. The perceptual experience of a spatial object is necessarily inadequate in the sense of being perception through appearances.
2. Because of this inadequacy, it is always possible that, although such an object seems to be itself present in perception, the phenomenon of the self-presence of the intentional object could be inactual, i.e., the object may not, in fact, be itself present; this means that perception is, in part, belief, namely, belief that the object is itself present.
3. Whatever could be inactual and is on hand, is on hand through consciousness.
4. Therefore, the phenomenon of the self-presence of an object of perception is an achievement of consciousness, and,
5. The phenomenon of the self-presence of the world is an achievement of consciousness.

The first three of these statements have already been discussed. In reference to the fourth statement, it has been shown how the self-presence phenomenon is an achievement of consciousness through the identification of its intrinsic correlates, the impressionality of an experience and its time-positing. Thus we may expand our conception of the psychological noema by adding the self-presence phenomenon to it. The fifth statement generalizes from the self-presence of spatial objects to the self-presence of the world, following Husserl's precedure in *Ideas*.[369] The legitimacy of this generalization will not be discussed here. We will simply assume that the generalization can be made, and that the intrinsic moments of consciousness which have been identified also suffice to explain the phenomenon of the self-presence of the world. A consideration of one more issue in connection with the argument will lead us to a discussion of the transcendental interpretation of the argument. This issue concerns the coherence-thesis which, as mentioned earlier, elaborates the second statement of the argument.

The coherence-thesis was said to be the pivotal point of Husserl's argument. It was formulated earlier in a manner which attempted to be neutral to the two interpretations of the argument. It can now be formulated in terms of the empirical interpretation.[370]

1. Our perceptual experience of an object which we regard to be *itself present* has an anticipational structure such that later perceptions can either fulfill or disappoint those anticipations.
2. If these anticipations are fulfilled in certain ways, we will continue to perceive the object as itself present.
3. If these anticipations are disappointed in certain ways, we will no longer perceive the object to be itself present, and we will believe that it was not itself present prior to the disappointment.
4. With respect to any perception, it is always possible (in the sense of open possibility) that anticipations could be disappointed in these "certain ways."
5. The existence of this possibility, so long as it is not realized, makes the self-presence of any perceived object a "presumptive" self-presence (i.e., the actuality of the self-presence phenomenon, a presumptive actuality), and the mode of consciousness of the object, as being itself present, presumptive certainly, which is a form of belief.

It was stated earlier that the truth of the second statement of Husserl's argument depends to a large extent on the truth of the fourth proposition of the coherence-thesis, and that the fate of the argument as a whole depends on the truth of that proposition.[371] We now see the point of that remark in the case of the empirical interpretation of the argument. The argument that the phenomenon of the self-presence of the world is an achievement of consciousness turns on the assertion that it is always possible that the self-presence phenomenon is inactual. This assertion depends on the existence of the permanent possibility of empirical illusion, which is what the fourth proposition of the coherence-thesis affirms. I have tried to show how the existence of the permanent possibility of empirical illusion can be demonstrated through the telling of "stories" which, in effect, show that the anticipations built into perceptual experience *can* always be disappointed in the requisite "certain ways." What these "certain ways" are has not been said, but they could be discovered, I believe, through the above-mentioned attempt to develop formulae of stories, i.e., story-forms from which concrete stories would result by the substitution of the specific details of each case. The idea here is that the permanent possibility of empirical illusion exists because of certain general features of perceptual experience having to do with its anticipational structure, and that the attempt to develop formulae of stories would yield clues to those features.

The study of the "negative" side of consciousness, its inherent "potentiality" for error, must not obscure the fact that the conclusion of Husserl's argument expresses something positive about consciousness, its "achievement" in making the world itself-present to us. For the most part, the anticipations are fulfilled, and the "belief" in the self-presence of objects is sustained. Viewed in this way, the search for the "certain ways" in which anticipations could be disappointed yields at the same time the "certain ways" that they are *fulfilled*, and thus provide clues to the general features of perceptual experience through which consciousness succeeds in "hitting the mark," that is, assures itself that it does not "merely intend" its objects, but *has* them in its grasp. Thus a discovery of the "certain ways" would yield clues to how consciousness functions in continual syntheses of verification which motivate and sustain the belief in the self-presence of its objects, and thus, in turn, would show how the theory of intentionality can overcome the psychological problem of cognition.[372]

With this remark, our investigations have reached a crucial turning point. It has been indicated, at least in outline, how a psychological-phenomenological theory of consciousness can resolve the psychological problem of cognition. A fairly articulated psychological conception of consciousness has been developed by interpreting many of Husserl's analyses in a particular way. The question must now be asked: Is this conception of consciousness the world-constitutive conception? Does Husserl's argument as "empirically" interpreted, granting its soundness, establish that consciousness "constitutes" the world, that the being-on-hand of the world is an achievement of consciousness?

*b. The Insufficiency of the "Empirical" Interpretation.* As we think back over the psychological theory of consciousness which we have developed, do we not sense that in some way the world remains beyond the reach of what has been identified as "consciousness"? There seems to be some essential correlate missing on the side of consciousness which could account for the world's being-on-hand. To be sure, the non-attentional modes of consciousness which we have discussed function as pregiving, as do the components of the horizon structure of perception, and it has been shown how consciousness brings objects intuitive self-presence. Yet as we recall the course of our development of the psychological theory, remembering especially the naive concept of being-on-hand of the world which provided our starting point, did there ever come a point where we, as theorists, felt that this concept had yielded to another? Did *we* not continue to assume all along that the world, as actuality, and as it is in itself, remains on hand independently of consciousness, and did not this assumption condition our very understanding of what emerged as "consciousness?" Let us articulate this problem.

The theory that has been developed seems to show that the phenomenon of the self-presence of the world is an achievement of consciousness. The question is whether this achievement is identical to that of world-constitutive consciousness. Let us look more closely at the theory. The phenomenon of the self-presence of an object (and, through generalization, of the world) is motivated and sustained by the fulfillment, in certain ways, of anticipations inherent in perceptual experience. This means that these anticipations *anticipate* in "certain ways," *ways in conformity with the intentional object.* If I am perceiving my house, these anticipations "anticipate" that this or that will be given as I move toward and into it. If I am only perceiving "a" house, then they are different, they are in conformity with "house" as an intentional object, not "my" house or some other particular house − just "house," or perhaps, "house of this or that particular type." Here one could surely point to the "matter" of a perceptual experience as the correlate of these intentional objects. But how do I come to intend houses? How do I come to have experiences containing this or that "matter?" The answer at this point seems to be, or rather, seems to *have* to be: *because there are houses and I have encountered them.* The same can be said in the case of any object. Houses, etc., are still thought of, and need to be thought of, as being there independently of consciousness. I my encounters of them, I come to "learn" how to perceive houses, how to have them as intentional objects and to have experiences of them in which they are themselves present to me. Likewise, the anticipations which structure my perceptual experiences of them, and which motivate and sustain the experience of their self-presence, are derived from encounters with them. In this connection, Husserl writes of "rules" which prescribe what the appearances should be like in the course of experience if the consciousness of the same individual thing or kind of thing is to be sustained.[373] We can give this idea an empirical interpretation and say that these rules are just those factors which unify and regulate anticipations so that they will be in the "certain ways" which are in conformity with the self-presence of a particular object or a particular kind of object. Although these rules may be within consciousness, nothing has been forthcoming within the development of the psychological theory to prevent understanding these rules and the "matter" of intentional experience as being derived from the world itself, the world itself, then, being thought of as being there independently of these factors of consciousness.

Let us look at the issue from the point of view of the idea of world-constitutive consciousness and the two criteria which a conception of consciousness must meet if it is to be world-constitutive.[374] The basic idea is that the world (i.e., the world of everyday life and not some theoretical world) is present and available through consciousness. The criterion of "scope" was set up to ensure that what a particular theory showed to be present and available through consciousness was indeed the world, and not some impoverished version of it which would only be a "representation" of the world. The scope criterion has two aspects, "spread" and "depth." The "spread" aspect requires that there be correlates in consciousness to the extent of what is on hand as world. The concern here was that a theory must not only show how consciousness achieves the presence and availability of objects right before us, but also, for instance, of our surroundings, both near and remote. One might say that the concept of horizon-consciousness, suitably developed, could satisfy this aspect of the criterion. The "depth" aspect concerned the "richness" of the world, for instance, the individual and generic features of objects. Here one might point to the concept of the "matter" of intentional experiences, and their sensory content as satisfying this part of the criterion. The "availability" aspect of the idea of world-constitutive consciousness would seem to correspond to the non-attentional moments of consciousness and to the non-intuitive (or "empty") nature of some intentional moments, and the "present" aspect would have as its correlate the factors which were found to be the correlate of the self-presence phenomenon (these being conceived as operative also in horizon-consciousness), as well as the syntheses of consciousness which motivate and sustain that phenomenon. From among all these factors and dimensions of consciousness which concern the scope criterion, the deficiency of the psychological theory was said to concern the concept of the "matter" of an intentional experience. How this deficiency relates to a failure to meet the scope criterion can only be appreciated once the "reality" criterion is discussed.

The reality criterion also has two aspects, the "transcendence" or "being-on-hand" of the world, and the world's "actuality." The concept of transcendence expresses the naive sense that "the world" is precisely that which is on hand to us independently of consciousness. In a sense, then, it expresses the very opposite of what a theory of consciousness as world-constitutive wishes to establish. Moreover, it is the world as actuality which is to be shown to be on hand through consciousness. Thus, any theory which claims that consciousness is world-constitutive must also show that the naive sense of the transcendence of the world, and the world's actuality, is an achievement of consciousness. Although a certain "positing" has been mentioned as the correlate of the latter, nothing has been said about the former, and it is in this respect that the psychological theory is most fundamentally deficient.

This problem can be seen in the following way. A theory which claims that consciousness is world-constitutive must not be grounded in the naive concept of transcendence. In a sense, of course, the theory must not deny the legitimacy of that concept, for it is precisely the legitimacy of that concept which it seeks to explain. Thus the theory is in the peculiar position of having to establish something which in a way is antithetical to its own idea, to its own conception of consciousness and world. But there will be no formal contradiction in this as long as the theory shows its own conception to be theoretically prior to, and the foundation for, the naive conception. To put it in another way, the theory must provide a way for the theorizer to "overcome" the naive concept of transcendence, and any concepts of consciousness compatible with and requiring it, as a fundamental conceptual attitude towards consciousness and world. This, of course, is what Husserl refers to as overcoming the natural attitude through the methods of transcendental reduction and epoche. But the psychological theory elaborated here is quite compatible with the natural attitude as a fundamental attitude for theorizing, and, in fact, seems to require the naive concept of transcendence. How else can it explain how I can intend the objects I do, how the phenomenon of the self-presence *of* this or that object can arise, and how the actuality of that phenomenon can be confirmed *or* disconfirmed, except by postulating a world being on hand independently of consciousness, a world which is both the source of the "what" and the "how" of the intentionality of my consciousness and the measure of the genuineness and veridicality of that intentionality.

The presupposition of the psychological theory, that the world is already there prior to the functioning of consciousness (as psychologically conceived), is not an invention of that theory; rather, it comes from the experience of life itself. The psychological theory develops from a type of reflection that life affords. The critique of the presupposition of that theory reveals a new sense of the idea of the pregivenness of the world, namely, the world as substrate for the *development* of consciousness, a substrate for the enrichment of and changes in our intending a world. As we grow from infancy to maturity and into old age, "our world" changes, even "perceptually," and in a sense we already "know" this before we become "psychologists." When we read Husserl's observation that "in infancy we had to learn to see physical things,"[375] and having acquired that ability, we had to learn to see a particular physical object "as sissors,"[376] we may find Husserl articulating something that we have, in a general way, known all along, namely, that the changes in "our world" are changes in us and not in the world itself. This "knowledge" is part of our natural attitude, part of the sense of the transcendence of the world. The "matter" of our intentionality is a developing "matter," the rules which govern our anticipations change, what *of* the world that is able to come to self-presence broadens and deepens, realities are replaced by "truer" realities, or perhaps just different ones. We acquire discriminating tastes in foods and other things whereby aspects of them never experienced before come to self-presence — but as having been there all along.[377] This is true in every aspect of life, although we may not always note its happening, and sometimes do not let it happen, which is itself a form of acknowledgement of something else being there which is not yet part of "our world." Given this additional sense of the concept of transcendence, we can see that if "the world" were limited to what is or can become itself-present to a subject by virtue of the matter of that subject's intentionality, even throughout that subject's lifetime, this would be only an impoverished version of the world. The psychological conception of consciousness, then, is not the world-constitutive conception, but a world-representational conception. It fails to meet both the scope and reality criteria.

Perhaps the most significant way for us to evaluate the psychological theory is from the point of view of the problem of cognition. We recall that it is for the sake of a solution to this problem that Husserl developed the theory that consciousness constitutes the world. The question is: How is cognition of transcendent objects possible? We have seen that the psychological conception of consciousness provides an answer to the "psychological problem of cognition." The psychological version of the problem arose as a challenge to an already developed intentional theory of consciousness, but it was shown to have a validity independently of that theory. In terms of the metaphor used previously, the problem concerns the correctness of the "aim" of perceptual consciousness. In intending an object, perceptual consciousness "aims" at it in the sense of claiming to be consciousness of the bodily self-presence of the object. This cognitive claim resides in the belief that the object intended is itself present. The permanent possibility of empirical illusion posed a challenge to the theory to explain how perceptual consciousness "hits the mark," how it does not merely intend worldly objects, but has them in its grasp. This problem of "evidence" was solved by showing how consciousness brings objects to self-presence, and how it confirms the validity of the self-presence phenomenon. However, in a certain sense the problem of cognition is still not solved, or perhaps it is better to say that in the solving of the psychological problem of cognition a new, more serious problem of cognition has arisen.

The theory explains how perceptual consciousness can hit or miss "marks," and through the concept of the intrinsic intentionality of perception, it can even explain how perception can aim at "marks" in the first place, which it can then hit or miss. But what are those "marks?" What I am conscious of in perception is determined by the "matter" of my experience. To pick an arbitrary example, let us say I am having a perceptual experience of a house. It may be that there is, in fact, no house there. Then, I am suffering an empirical illusion, my perception has missed the mark. I intended a house, but that house is not really present. If I intended "my house," then I know that it is somewhere else; if I intended a house I never saw before, perhaps the house I intended does not exist at all. Now if we deprive the psychological theory of its fundamental assumption, which in this case is "the fact: that there is a house which is my house," and we have remaining only the intrinsic factors of experience, the theory only has me intending my "idea" (representation), "house" (or my idea, "my house"), an idea about whose origin and validity the theory can have nothing to say.[378] Even if we assume that the anticipations become fulfilled in a subsequent course of perception, and that there is indeed a "house" itself present, this confirms nothing about the validity of *intending houses*.

To be sure, my experience "posits" its object to be an actuality. What does this mean? One way of understanding it refers us back to certain cases of empirical illusion. I have a perceptual experience of a house I have never seen before. It turns out that no house is itself-present. On such occasions one usually comes to believe not only that the particular house which was intended is not itself present, but also that it does not exist in reality. It is possible to be right in the former case, but wrong in the latter. Perhaps there is such a thing as prevision. At any rate, the mistake of intending the particular house was an "honest" one, since to intend a house is a perfectly legitimate intending, *provided there are houses*. Thus, "knowledge" of the fact that there are houses makes possible the unquestionedness of the initial house-intention, an unquestionedness (or naiveté) without which the experience of error could not arise. It can be said, then, that the "positing of the actuality" of the house involves this unquestionedness of the house-intention. Thus, to posit the actuality of a particular house is at the same time to posit that there are houses, and, in general, to posit the actuality of an intentional object is at the same time to posit that there are those sorts of objects. Even more generally, this is the positing of a world of individual instances of kinds. Let us simply call this the "positing of the world."

The positing which provides the basis for the unquestionedness of the intending of objects in perception (i.e., for the positing of the actuality of particular intentional objects) constitutes the new problem of cognition. I will call this the "transcendental problem of cognition." Taken generally, this positing is what Husserl calls the "general thesis" of the natural attitude. This "aiming" claims to bring within the scope of consciousness precisely that transcendence which is excluded from it in the psychological theory, namely, the world as the source and measure of our "ideas" of it. As Husserl says, "We must therefore not let ourselves be deceived by any talk about the transcendence of the thing over against consciousness or about its 'being in itself'. The genuine concept of thing-transcendence, which is the standard whereby all rational statements about transcendence are measured, cannot be extracted from any other source other than the perception's own essential content.... An object that has being in itself is never such as to be out of relation to consciousness and its Ego."[379] Why should the positing of the world be called an "aiming" and a "claim?" Because according to Husserl, there exists the permanent possibility of *transcendental* illusion. The assertion of this possibility is the crucial item in Husserl's argument as "transcendentally" interpreted.

*c. The "Transcendental" Interpretation.* Husserl's argument, interpreted "empirically," does not establish that consciousness is world-constitutive. It is just this which it claims to do under the "transcendental" interpretation. Interpreted transcendentally, the argument goes as follows:

1. Thing-perception is necessarily inadequate since it is perception through appearances.
2. Because of this inadequacy, the things which we perceive could be inactual, which means that our perceptual consciousness of them (and our consciousness of them in general) is a believing or doxic consciousness.
3. Whatever could be inactual and is on hand, is on hand through consciousness.
4. Therefore, the things we perceive are on hand through consciousness, and,
5. The world is on hand through consciousness.

This is the argument which Husserl puts forth in the "psychological" sections of *Ideas*. Thus, the central purpose of the second part of what I have called the "schema" of Husserl's "introductions to phenomenology," the part I have entitled "the acquisition of the idea of transcendental consciousness," and whose elaboration is now coming to a close, is to establish the premises of this argument and to draw its conclusions.[380].

The first statement of the argument as formulated above is essentially unchanged from the original version, as are the third and fifth.[381] Our extensive discussion of the first statement applies as well to the argument as interpreted here as it did to its empirical interpretation.[382] The second and fourth statements are slightly changed in comparison with the original versions. One of these changes is common to both statements, the changing of the expression "any perceived thing" to read "the things which we perceive." This change is made in order to emphasize that it is *that which* we perceive which the argument claims could be inactual and claims to be on hand through consciousness, i.e., the intentional objects of our perceptions. This is done to stress the difference between this interpretation and the previous one. The other notable change is in the addition of the phrase "and our consciousness of them in general" to the second statement. The purpose in doing this is the same as the one just stated. It emphasizes the fact that what is being discussed is not just something that manifests itself through a perception, but is the very same object which we might intend in a variety of modes of consciousness. This is to stress that it is not the self-presence phenomenon which is at issue, but rather the intentional objects of perception. Once again, the second statement of the argument, and the coherence-thesis which elaborates it, is crucial for the soundness of the argument. The previous general discussion of the second statement and of the coherence-thesis is especially relevent to the present interpretation.[383] There is no need to reformulate the coherence-thesis.[384] One should simply keep in mind that, under the transcendental interpretation, one is not to take its various propositions as referring to the self-presence phenomenon. As before, it is the fourth proposition of the coherence-thesis which is the key to Husserl's entire argument, and to it we now turn.

The coherence-thesis basically states that our experience of objects and of the world in general as actual is motivated and sustained by the fulfillment of anticipations "in certain ways." However, according to the fourth proposition, it is always possible that anticipations could be disappointed along the lines of those "certain ways," and thus our consciousness of objects and of the world as actual is basically belief. Consequently, as we have seen Husserl claim, the world is a "presumptive actuality."[385] Thus, the fourth proposition of the coherence-thesis and the second statement of the argument claim the existence of the permanent possibility of transcendental illusion. How does Husserl validate this claim? He attemps to tell "stories" in which the world turns out to be and to have been a transcendental illusion. We will not examine these stories now, that is reserved for later. For the moment, we will simply assume that such stories can be told, and that the permanent possibility of transcendental illusion exists.

I will now bring my discussion of this part of Husserl's introductions to a close by reviewing what it is supposed to accomplish. We recall that the second part of the schema has two main sections.[386] In the first, the "natural attitude" is disclosed to have a "general thesis," namely, the positing of the actuality of the world and of the world as being-on-hand independently of consciousness. Once this thesis is uncovered, Husserl raises the possibility of suspending it, a procedure which is called the transcendental phenomenological epoche or reduction. The purpose of this procedure is to reveal "pure transcendental consciousness," which is said to include "within it" the world as a being-for-consciousness. In my interpretation, this is world-constitutive consciousness, where the world is the intentional correlate of consciousness. However, before actually suspending the thesis, and then entering into the constitutive analyses that would form the basis of a new theory of knowledge aimed at solving the problem of cognition (this problem being the motive for turning to consciousness),[387] Husserl embarks on a "psychological investigation" of consciousness, an investigation carried out in the natural attitude. The purpose of this investigation, in Husserl's words, "is to see upon evidence that the phenomenological reduction, as a means of disconnecting us from the natural attitude and its general thesis is possible, and that, when carried out, the absolute or pure transcendental consciousness is left over as a residuum...."[388] These two purposes are carried out through Husserl's argument and the analyses which support it.

The general thesis of the natural attitude is a double positing: it posits the world as actual and as being-on-hand (independently of consciousness). It was remarked above that Husserl often seems to use the words "*wirklich*" (actual) and "*vorhanden*" (on hand) synonymously.[389] Our analysis showed them to refer to distinct features of the world, a fact which, as observed above, makes Husserl's tying them to the same subjective correlate noteworthy.[390] In our development of the psychological conception of consciousness, we saw the intimate association of these two features. Every time something became linked to a subjective correlate, it was something either inactual or non-actual (we can count the "representation" of the world discussed above as also being an appearance and therefore something non-actual). Furthermore, the crucial step in Husserl's argument to demonstrate that the being-on-hand of the world is an achievement of consciousness consists in showing that the world's actuality is the correlate of a thesis, a belief. It would seem quite plausible that the same thesis is also that which "achieves" the sense of the world's being-on-hand independently of consciousness. The naiveté of the natural attitude in regard to the being-on-hand of the world would then be identical to the positing which is the ground of the unquestionedness of the intending of worldly objects. How this positing remains undisclosed in life, and how it produces a double effect, the naiveté and the unquestionedness, would still have to be accounted for. The important role of the third statement of Husserl's argument (whatever could be inactual and is on hand, is on hand through consciousness) should also not be overlooked in a critical appraisal of the argument.

My own critical focus, however, will concern another aspect of Husserl's demonstration. It was said above that Husserl's purpose in this part of his "introductions" was to show that the suspension of the general thesis of the natural attitude is possible, and that once done, in our terms, world-constitutive consciousness would remain as a residuum for analysis. We can now understand what Husserl may have meant by showing the "possibility" of the suspension of the thesis (of the epoche). The pre-psychological analysis of consciousness and world, operating in naive reflection, disclosed a general thesis, but it was the psychological analysis which determined that this thesis is a *belief*. This determination rests on the validity of the coherence-thesis and its crucial fourth proposition (which asserts the permanent possibility of transcendental illusion). The suspension of the thesis becomes "possible" in the sense of being a *rationally motivated* procedure. We may suppose any thesis to be able to be suspended, even one which is a knowing. But to suspend a thesis which is inherently incapable of cancellation could be looked upon as an irrational performance. Thus the coherence-thesis justifies the epoche as a rational procedure, and Husserl's argument as a whole shows that the desired residuum, world-constitutive consciousness and its correlate, the world as a being-for-consciousness, does indeed remain as a field for phenomenological work.

Or so it seems. Before critically examining these claims, I will fill out the rest of the schema of Husserl's "introductions" with a brief discussion of the epoche (and reduction) and the idea of "constitution."

## NOTES

1. *Ideas,* sections 27-49, pp. 101-53.
2. For example, *CM,* sections 7-15; *Crisis,* sections 28-42.
3. *Ideas,* section 46, p. 146 (last paragraph).

132

4. Ibid., section 55, pp. 169-70—translation modified, see *Ideen I*, p. 136. I have not translated Husserl's emendations, which appear in the body of Biemel's edition of the *Ideen* I text, but have used the text as published by Husserl, as did Gibson. For the original text, see Edmund Husserl, *Ideen zu einer reinen Phänomenologie und phänomenologischen Philosophie,* first book, *Husserliana* III, 1, ed. Karl Schuhmann (The Hague: Martinus Nijhoff, 1976), p. 121.

5. *Ideas,* section 27, p. 101—translation mine, see *Ideen* I, p. 57. This section is entitled "The World of the Natural Attitude: I and my Surrounding World."

6. Ibid., section 30, p. 105.

7. Concerning "awake," see ibid., section 27, last paragraph, p. 103 and Husserl's emendation to the text he published which is included in Biemel's edition of *Ideen* I, p. 63, lines 6 and 8. See also *Beilage* VII in that edition.

8. One must consult the German text of sections 27-30 to see the consistency with which the word *"vorhanden"* is used, for it is rendered in many ways in the English translation.

9. *Ideas*, section 29, p. 105.

10. Ibid., section 31. p. 107. See *Ideen* I, p. 64.

11. Ibid., section 30, pp. 105-6.

12. Ibid., p. 106—translation modified, see *Ideen* I, p. 63.

13. Ibid., section 31, p. 107.

14. See ibid., section 50, p. 154, second paragraph, and section 1, p. 51 first paragraph. Husserl indicated an emendation to the former paragraph which is included in Biemel's *Husserliana* edition (p. 118). There, instead of *"naturlichen theoretischen Einstellung,"* the text reads *"naturlichen erfahrenden und theoretischen Einstellung."*

15. Ibid., section 50, p. 155.

16. Edmund Husserl, *Logical Investigations,* 2 vols., trans. J.N. Findlay (New York: Humanities Press, 1970), 2: 624-27 (hearafter cited as *LI*). It should be pointed out that "positionality," "thetic," and "thesis" do not refer to a moment of judgment in experience. Judgments, like other acts of consciousness may or may not posit their objects as existing.

17. *Ideas,* section 117, p. 329. On what is posited in cases of non-doxic positings, see *Crisis,* p. 237 and Edmund Husserl, *Experience and Judgement*, trans. James S. Churchill and Karl Ameriks (Evanston: Northwestern University Press, 1973), p. 80 (hereafter cited as *EJ*).

18. Ibid., section 103, p. 297. Gibson's translation of the first paragraph of section 103 is seriously defective. The German edition should be consulted. See also *Ding und Raum,* p. 151.

19. *Ideas,* section 113.

20. Ibid., section 103, p. 297: "That which appears perceptually or memorially had, in the previously considered sphere, the character of 'actually' [*wirklich*] being pure and simple — of 'certainly' [*gewiss*] being...." (My translation, see *Ideen* I, p. 256). See also section 104, p. 298.

21. Ibid., section 31, p. 108—translation mine, see *Ideen* I, p. 64. See also *EJ,* p. 93 for a highly similar passage.

22. *Ideas*, section 50, p. 155—translation mine, see *Ideen* I, p. 119. The translation was based on the original text, for which see the Schuhmann edition, p. 107.

23. For explicit statements that the thesis is doxic, see *CM*, pp. 18-20.

24. See above, p. 6.

25. See above, pp. 11-14.

26. See above, pp. 8-9.

27. *Ideen* I, p. 57 (*Ideas,* section 27, p. 102, Emphasis mine.

28. Husserl, *Cartesianische Meditationen*, p. 124 (*CM*, p. 92).

29. *Ideas,* section 27, pp. 102, 103; *Crisis,* p. 142.

30. It is unfortunate that we must translate *"Einstellung"* as "attitude" (as in "natural attitude"). Although not incorrect, it does not express as literally as does the German word *"ein-stellen"* the idea of being set-into. For an explication of this important concept of *"Einstellung"* and the correlative idea of a "province of meaning," see Alfred Schutz, "On Multiple Realities," in his *Collected Papers,* 3 vols. (The Hague: Martinus Nijhoff, 1962-66), 1: 207-259. For a critical discussion of Schutz's theory, see Gurwitsch, *The Field of Consciousness,* part. 6, pp. 379-413. For Husserl's discussion, see *EP* II, pp. 98-100, *EJ,* pp. 81-83, and *Ideen* II, pp. 11-13.

31. *Ideas,* section 28, pp. 103-4; *Ideen* I, Beilage VII.

32. Ibid., section 27, p. 102.

33. Ibid., sections 27-28.

34. See ibid.

35. See Gurwitsch, *The Field of Consciousness,* p. 406; *EJ,* sections 7-9.

36. Husserl, *Cartesianische Meditationen,* p. 179 (*CM,* p. 153).

37. *Crisis,* p. 145.

38. This characterization derives from Husserl's own reference to this type of reflection as "naive." See *IP,* pp. 9, 30 and *Ideas,* section 39, p. 127. With respect to this latter citation, Gibson has incorrectly rendered the first sentence of the last paragraph by translating *"Ich meditiere zunachst als 'naiver' Mensch"* as "I meditate first as would the man 'in the street'." See *Ideen* I, p. 89.

39. For example, in *EJ,* p. 30.

40. For examples of these, see Edmund Husserl, *Die Krisis der europäischen Wissenschaften und die transzendentale Phänomenologie, Husserliana* VI, ed. Walter Biemel (The Hague: Martinus Nijhoff, 1962), p. 145 (hereafter cited as *Krisis*). See *Crisis,* p. 142.

41. *APS,* p. 203.

42. *IP,* p. 9. In naive reflection, attentional consciousness is considered to be transparent. Thus, differences in ways of attending, such as looking and listening, are not differences in consciousness, but in *what* is attended to. In looking, one attends to a sight; in listening, to a sound. Strictly as consciousness, looking and listening are qualitatively undifferentiated. Objects are considered to manifest themselves as sights and sounds, and to be on hand as such, whether I, or anyone, attend to them or not. Of course the differences in ways of attending also involve differences in bodily comportment. Thus, we look with our eyes and listen with our ears, but these are not differences in consciousness according to naive reflection.

43. *FTL,* pp. 225-26.

44. *IP,* pp. 9-19.

45. *FTL,* pp. 232.

46. Ibid., p. 230.

47. Ibid., p. 233.

48. *Crisis,* p. 175.

49. *CM,* pp. 152-53.

50. *Crisis,* pp. 175-76.

51. *Ding und Raum,* p. 151.

52. *APS,* p. 28.

53. *Crisis,* p. 145 (*Krisis,* p. 148).

54. Ideas, section 30, p. 106—translation modified, see *Ideen* I, p. 63.

134

55. *Krisis,* p. 148.
56. *APS,* p. 28.
57. *EP* II, p. 55.
58. *APS,* p. 23.
59. See above, p. 42.
60. Above, p. 40.
61. See Dorion Cairns, "The Many Senses and Denotations of the Word *Bewusstsein* ('Consciousness') in Edmund Husserl's Writings," in *Life World and Consiousness,* ed. Lester E. Embree (Evanston: Northwestern University Press, 1972), pp. 22-23. Emphasis mine.
62. See Gurwitsch, *The Field of Consciousness,* p. 166.
63. *Ideas,* section 34, p. 114 – translation modified, see *Ideen* I, p. 74. This psychological investigation extends from section 34 through at least section 46 and perhaps through section 49.
64. Ibid., section 33, pp. 112-13. The wider investigation extends from section 33 through section 55.
65. Ibid., "Introduction," pp. 41-47.
66. Ibid., section 32, p. 110.
67. *CM,* p. 18.
68. *Ideas,* section 33, p. 112. The word "pure" here is used to mark these entities as non-realties – see section 55, p. 170.
69. See ibid., section 76, p. 212.
70. Ibid., section 50, pp. 154-55.
71. Above, pp. 6-7.
72. Above, pp. 11-12.
73. Above, pp. 9-10.
74. *Crisis,* p. 160 – translation modified, see *Krisis,* p. 163.
75. *Ideas,* section 135, p. 374 – translation modified, see *Ideen* I, p. 329. "Senses and positions" refer to aspects of the "intentional content" of consciousness which was mentioned earlier (above, pp. 9-10).
76. Ibid., section 49, p. 153 – translation modified, see *Ideen* I, p. 117. The text of the Biemel edition of *Husserliana* III has an error on line 33, p. 117: *"Erfahrungsmannigfaltigkeiten"* should be *"Erscheinungsmannigfaltigkeiten."* See the original text in the Schuhmann edition, p. 106.
77. See above, p. 13.
78. *CM,* p. 42.
79. *Ideas,* section 39, pp. 126-27.
80. Ibid., p. 127.
81. *Ideen* I, p. 100 – translation mine, see *Ideas,* section 43, p. 137.
82. Our discussion here begins with section 34 of *Ideas.*
83. See our previous discussion, p. 34 above.
84. *Ideas,* section 35, p. 118.
85. Ibid., p. 117.
86. Ibid.
87. See pp. 47-48 above.
88. Above, p. 48.
89. *Ideen* I, p. 80 – translation mine, see *Ideas,* section 36, p. 120.
90. For the example of psychophysical connection, see Husserl's emandation to the original text incorporated in the Biemel edition of *Ideen* I, p. 80, line 11.

91.  *Ideas,* section 41, p. 129.
92.  Ibid., section 40, pp. 128-29.
93.  See *Crisis,* sections 33-35, pp. 121-37.
94.  *Ideas*, section 41, p. 130.
95.  Ibid., p. 135. There are of course differences in the treatment of the same aspect of the schema of Husserl's introductions in each of *his* "introductions," which reflect differences in emphasis as well as his philosophical development. In terms of the logical order of the schema, this step should come right at the beginning of the aspect being developed in this chapter, i.e., just after the "motivating problem." In this regard the order of the textual development of *Crisis* is more explicitly logical than *Ideas*. It should be clear, however, that the "perceived thing" is what Husserl has been talking about in *Ideas* all along and that this step only makes that explicit.
96.  For instance, on p. 126 of *Crisis.*
97.  *Ideas,* section 44, p. 137.
98.  Ibid., section 42, p. 135.
99.  Ibid., section 88, pp. 257-60. Husserl says here that this distinction was already touched on in section 41, which tends to confirm this conjecture. The intentional or noematic components are sometimes referred to by Husserl as "ideal" (*ideell*) components – see *PP*, p. 179 and *Ideas*, section 99, p. 291.
100. *Ideas*, section 42, p. 135 – translation modified, see *Ideen* I, p. 97. Here, the word "orientation," I believe, should be taken noematically, while "modes of appearing" should be understood to refer to the correlative really intrinsic components of an experience.
101. Ibid., section 41, p. 131 (*Ideen* I, p. 94).
102. Ibid., section 85, p. 248.
103. See ibid., sections 41, 85 and 98, and *PP*, pp. 163, 165.
104. *Ideas*, section 41, p. 132.
105. Ibid., section 85, p. 247.
106. Ibid., p. 246-47.
107. Ibid., section 41, p. 132 and section 98, p. 289. In section 98, a transcendental section of *Ideas,* the latter two are said to pertain to the noematic side of consciousness.
108. Ibid., section 98, p. 288.
109. Ibid., section 41, p. 132.
110. Quoted above, p. 51. See also *CM*, p. 40.
111. *Ideas,* section 95, p. 277. See also section 94, p. 273.
112. Gurwitsch, *The Field of Consciousness,* p. 273.
113. For the distinction between these components of the noema, see *Ideas,* section 129, p. 361.
114. In one place Husserl distinguishes these as the ontic and perspectival dimensions respectively – see *PP*, pp. 317-18.
115. *Ideas,* section 88, p. 258.
116. Ibid., section 131, p. 367.
117. See ibid., section 88, pp. 258-60.
118. *PP*, pp. 316-17.
119. *Ideas*, section 90, p. 261.
120. Ibid., section 89, p. 260.
121. *APS*, p. 229.
122. *Ideas*, section 129, p. 361.
123. Ibid., section 90, p. 262.
124. Ibid., section 129, p. 363.

125. Ibid., section 131, p. 267.

126. Ibid., section 131, pp. 365-66. As analytic concepts, the "pure X" mentioned here is not the same as the "empty X" mentioned above as the substrate of purely mathemetical predicates (above, p. 52). Husserl is referring here to perceived objects and perceived predicates. In terms of the intentionality of scientific thought, however, Husserl's analysis finds them to have the same referent – see *Ideas*, section 40, p. 129 and section 52, pp. 159-61. In later works Husserl uses the phrases "noematic pole" (*PP*, p. 136) and "object-pole" (Crisis, p. 170) instead of "pure X."

127. *Ideas*, section 130, p. 364.

128. Ibid., section 99, p. 290.

129. Ibid., section 130, p. 364.

130. *CM*, p. 44.

131. Ibid., p. 45.

132. See *Ideen* I, p. 323.

133. *Ideas*, section 132, p. 368. "Saturation-differences in clearness" is Gibson's translation of "Klarheitsfülle" – see *Ideen*, p. 323.

134. See ibid., section 136, p. 380. It is possible that something else is meant by this, namely what Husserl calls "*Sättigungsunterschiede*" (saturation differences) in *Ding und Raum* (p. 132). As an example of this, he mentions the differences in the *appearance* of a thing depending on whether we are near or far from it. *LI*, p. 591 may be helpful in clarifying this issue. See also *APS*, p. 332.

135. *APS*, pp. 321-22.

136. *Ideen* I, Beilage XXIV, pp. 411-12.

137. I cannot go into all the subtleties involved here, but one must be mentioned. The following analysis is confined to that level in the analysis of the constituttion of a thing which is reached by abstraction from its causal properties, i.e., its capacity to act upon other things and to be acted upon by them. This is the level of the "phantom," i.e., a thing considered purely as a *res extensa* and not as *res materialis*. We will further be concerned only with the visual phantom. For a fuller account of these subtilties, see Robert Sokolowski, *Husserlian Meditations*, chapter 4; Ulrich Cleasges, *Edmund Husserls Theorie der Raumkonstitution* (The Hague: Martinus Nijhoff, 1964); and Husserl's *Ideen* II, especially sections 12-17 and 32. In *Ideen* II (p. 36), Husserl mentions what one sees in a stereoscope as an example of a pure phantom. A more contemporary and even better example is the hologram.

138. Later, in Chapter 6, I will show that this procedure of performing the epoche is questionable, if it is to be a suspension of the belief in the "actuality" of the object as "actuality" is explained there. The epoche that we imagine ourselves to perform here is possible as the interpretive procedure explained in Chapter 7.

139. *Ideas*, section 98, p. 289; section 150, p. 418; *PP*, p. 157.

140. *Ideen* I, Beilage XXIV, p. 411.

141. Claesges, *Raumkonstitution*, p. 59, n. 5; Husserl, MS D 13 I (1921), p. 2 (this manuscript, which is in the Husserl Archive, contains the clearest presentation of the distinctions being made here).

142. Cleasges, *Raumkonstitution*, p. 59; MS D 13 I, pp. 2-3.

143. *PP*, p. 158; *APS*, p. 296; *Crisis*, p. 158; MS D 13 I, p. 5.

144. *APS*, pp. 5, 295-99; *Ideen* II, p. 130; *PP*, p. 318.

145. Claesges, *Raumkonstitution*, p. 64. As Claesges reports, the *flow* of aspects is correlative to the kinaesthetic flow (p. 65). See also *Ideen* I, Beilage XXIV, pp. 411-12 and *Ideen* II, p. 127-30 on all of this.

146. *Ideas*, p. 418. It is difficult to tell if Husserl's comment about perspectives here in *Ideas* is in-

tended noetically or noematically, but it surely holds either way. See also *PP,* pp. 157-58 and MS D 13 I, p. 6.

147. *PP,* p. 159.

148. For Husserl's use of "appearance" in this way, see *Ideen* II, p. 128, line 37 and p. 129, line 17. For the equation of aspect and appearance, see *APS,* p. 6, lines 33-35.

149. MS D 13 I, pp. 3-5.

150. See especially *Ideen* II, p. 130, where Husserl discusses an ambiguity in the expression *"Abschattung"* (adumbration). There he says it can mean an aspect or the sensory data which are in immanent time.

151. *Ideen* I, Beilage XXIV, p. 412. Gurwitsch, in his critique of Husserl's theory of perception, presents Husserl's theory as saying that "interpreted and apperceived, sense-data enter as *components* or *constituents* into the perceptual sense or noema..." (*Field of Consciousness,* p. 269). I do not find that Husserl says this anywhere, but rather maintains the opposite. Gurwitsch cites the apparent color of an object, i.e., the color as it appears under certain conditions, as an example. But in the texts of Husserl *that Gurwitsch cites,* it is the one *unchanging* color, and not its perspectival adumbrations that Husserl finds to be a constituent of the noema. Husserl does not, *in these texts,* cite the apparent color as a *noematic* constituent, but as a noetic one. In another text, however, Husserl does seem to cite the apparent color as a noematic constituent (see *EJ,* p. 73). In *Logical Investigations* (p. 861), however, Husserl emphasizes the distinction between the apparent color of an object (and the apparent features generally) and sensory data.

152. *Ideas,* section 90, p. 262.

153. Ibid., section 97, p. 283.

154. Ibid., section 89, p. 260—translation modified, see *Ideen* I, p. 222.

155. An ideal object is one which is not spatially or temporally individuated (i.e., is not real), yet is observable, distinguishable and repeatedly identifiable. See *Ideas,* section 99, p. 291; *EJ,* p. 265; and Dorion Cairns, "The Ideality of Verbal Expressions," in *Phenomenology: Continuation and Criticism,* ed. F. Kersten and R. Zaner (The Hague: Martinus Nijhoff, 1973), p. 240.

156. *APS,* p. 394.

157. *Ding und Raum,* p. 49. *"Perzeption"* is *Wahrnehmung* minus belief (p. 16).

158. Ibid., p. 17.

159. Ibid., p. 62.

160. *Ideas,* section 98, pp. 288-89; section 41, pp. 130-31; section 97, pp. 283-84.

161. See also *EJ,* p. 73.

162. *Ideas,* section 44, p. 137-38.

163. See ibid., section 44 and *APS,* pp. 3-7.

164. *Ideas,* section 149, p. 414.

165. See ibid., section 143, pp. 397-98.

166. *Ideas,* section 44, p. 139. In a commentary on this section of *Ideas* written in 1922, Husserl says that the definition of "absolute" given here is false. The question of absoluteness or non-absoluteness of givenness does not just concern whether or not the givenness is through adumbrations, but whether it is or is not "presumptive" givenness. The givenness of things is presumptive givenness in the sense that the actual being of the thing is not guaranteed by its givenness in a perception (see *Ideen* I, Beilage XII, p. 398). Of course this sense of absoluteness is brought out in the second statement of Husserl's argument. Our concern here, however, is with the sense Husserl *did* give to "absoluteness" in the edition of *Ideas* he published and which served as the basis for the English translation. One note of caution: the

Biemel edition of the *Husserliana* text has incorporated many of Husserl's emandations which are in accordance with the "correct" sense of "absolute."

167. Ibid., p. 140.

168. In *APS* (p. 16), Husserl calls these temporal modes of givenness "appearances" also, but he distinguishes this sense of appearance from that which specifically has to do with the spatiality of objects.

169. *Ideas,* section 44, p. 139 – translation slightly modified, see *Ideen* I, p. 102. Emphasis mine.

170. Ibid.

171. Ibid. See *Ideen* II, pp. 59-60, and *Ding und Raum,* pp. 106, 124 on "secondary objectification."

172. *Ideas,* section 44, p. 139 – translation slightly modified, see *Ideen* I, p. 102. Husserl probably means by this remark that if there were only the normal form of appearance we could never experience a thing being at different distances from us, or in different orientations. Hence, being capable of movement in space could not be part of the sense of a thing.

173. Ibid., section 42, pp. 134-35.

174. Ibid., section 43, p. 135 – translation modified, see *Ideen* I, p. 98.

175. Ibid., p. 137.

176. Ibid., section 44, p. 139.

177. The following summary is taken from *Ding und Raum,* pp. 106-35. Specific references are given where possible. This book contains lectures which Husserl gave in 1907, six years prior to the publication of *Ideas.*

178. *Ding und Raum,* p. 123.

179. See ibid., pp. 130-35.

180. Ibid., p. 128.

181. Neither appearential inadequacy nor the above considerations supporting it as something distinct from epistemic inadequacy are meant to replace epistemic inadequacy and Husserl's analysis *in general.* Rather, the intention is to show that they account for different things.

182. Above, pp. 42-45.

183. *Ideen* II, p. 59.

184. Above, p. 45.

185. Above, p. 12.

186. The divergence intended here is a noticeable divergence. This would be a rather strange pair of tracks, of course.

187. See above, p. 43, for the previous discussion of this type of appearance.

188. *Ideas,* section 77, p. 215. See also section 45, p. 142.

189. Quoted above, p. 51.

190. As Dorion Cairns puts it, they are "sensuously perceived," but they are not "terminal objects" of sensuous perceivings. See his essay "Perceiving, Remembering, Image-awareness, Feigning Awareness" in *Phenomenology: Continuation and Criticism,* ed. F. Kersten and R. Zaner.

191. This point relates to the second sense of "absolute" mentioned in n.166 above (p. 137). Thus we have shown in our discussion here how the two senses of "absolute" are related.

192. *Ideas,* section 46, p. 144.

193. Ibid. – translation slightly modified, see *Ideen* I, p. 108.

194. See *APS,* p.16.

195. On the concept of "open possibility," see *EJ,* pp. 98, 306; and Gurwitsch, *The Field of Consciousness,* pp. 246-47. Open possibilities are such that nothing "speaks for" any of the alternatives which are possible, i.e., one cannot assign degrees of likelihood to them, not

even to say that they are equally likely. In the case here, the open possibility of disharmony is one which may in no way be probable on the basis of past experience, nor for that matter improbable. The possibility rests on the *structure* of perceptual experience and not on its content.

196. Among other places, see *EJ*, pp. 92-93, 101.

197. *APS*, p. 26; *Ideen* II, p. 20.

198. *APS*, pp. 5-6.

199. Gurwitsch, *The Field of Consciousness*, p. 290; *CM*, pp. 41-42.

200. *Ideas*, section 46, p. 145.

201. *Ideen* I, p. 108, this phrase having been added to the previous one in the Biemel edition of the *Husserliana* text. See also *APS*, p. 211.

202. *EP* II, Beilage XIII, p. 406. See also *CM*, pp. 61-62 and *FTL*, p. 281.

203. *EP* II, pp. 53-54.

204. Ibid., p. 54. See *EJ*, p. 306.

205. Ibid., pp. 54-55. On the compatibility of open possibility with certainty, see *EJ*, p. 98 and *FTL*, p. 235.

206. *Ideas*, section 49, p. 152 – translation modified, see *Ideen* I, p. 116.

207. Ibid., section 46, p. 146.

208. *CM*, section 7, p. 17.

209. Above, p. 13.

210. *CM*, p. 44.

211. Ibid.; *EJ*, p. 87.

212. *APS*, pp. 12-13.

213. Ibid., p. 26 and Beilage XXV, pp. 428-29; *EJ*, pp. 84-87.

214. *Ideas*, section 44, p. 137; section 142, p. 417; sections 149-50.

215. *CM*, p. 45. See also *APS*, p. 22 and *EJ*, p. 96.

216. See above, p. 57. See *EJ*, p. 96 and Gurwitsch, *The Field of Consciousness*, p. 280.

217. *APS*, p. 25; *EJ*, p. 87.

218. *APS*, p. 26; *EJ*, pp. 88-91.

219. *APS*, pp. 26-27.

220. *EJ*, p. 88.

221. Ibid., p. 89; *APS*, pp. 27-31.

222. *EJ*, p. 89.

223. See, for instance, *Ideas*, section 46, p. 145 and *FTL*, pp. 251-52.

224. *FTL*, p. 282.

225. *Ideas*, section 46, p. 145; section 138, pp. 384-85.

226. *EJ*, pp. 53, 59-62.

227. Ibid., pp. 306-7. See *CM*, p. 17. Presumptive certainty is also to be distinguished from that *modalization* of simple belief which Husserl calls "presumption of belief." The latter arises in situations of perceptual conflict, such as the manniquin/person conflict, where two alternatives present themselves and where there is not yet a resolution of the conflict. The former, however, is an unmodalized form of belief. See *EJ*, p. 95.

228. *CM*, pp. 22-23; *Ideas*, section 46. In one place in *Ideas*, Husserl uses the term "apodictic" in regard to "evidence," i.e., the consciousness of something itself, and particularly to consciousness of essential *relationships* (section 137, p. 383). In this sense, the relationship grasped in such evidence would be said to be "necessary." But in section 46, the notion of necessity and thereby of apodictic evidence is also used by Husserl in connection with the "thesis of my pure Ego," by which we can presume he means the positing included in the re-

flective grasp of the pure ego. In contrast to the "thesis of my pure Ego," the "thesis of the world" is said to be "contigent."

229. *FTL,* p. 251.
230. Ibid.
231. *Ding und Raum,* p. 22.
232. Ibid., p. 24; Emphasis mine.
233. See *Ideas,* sections 103-106, especially section 103, p. 297. See also APS, p. 28. In *EJ,* Husserl says: "Normal original consciousness has the primal mode of being existent, of being simply valid: such is naive certainty pure and simple. The object which appears is there in indisputable and unbroken certainty. The undisputed refers to possible manners of dispute or even to outright breaks..." (pp. 93-94).
234. Above, pp. 34-36.
235. See pp. 50, 81 above.
236. Above, pp. 76-77.
237. See pp. 75-76, above.
238. The permanent possibility of *empirical* illusion is posed by Descartes in his *first* discussion of the inability to distinguish dream from wakefulness in the first Meditation (E.S. Haldane and G.R.T. Ross, *The Philosophical Works of Descartes,* 2 vols. [Cambridge: Cambridge University Press, 1967], 1: 146). When Descartes then proceeds to envision the possibility that "these general things, to wit, a body, eyes, a head, hands, and such like, may be imaginary" and even further that other objects "yet more simple and more universal" such as "corporeal nature in general" and its determinations, from which other objects are formed, also may not exist (pp. 146-47), he is posing the possibility of *transcendental* illusion.
239. See Paul Edwards, ed., *The Encyclopedia of Philosophy* (New York: Macmillan, 1967), vol.I, p. 137.
240. See our previous discussion of "decidability" on pp. 79-80 above. It may be that the proposal is compatible with transcendental illusion, where decidability is not an issue. Husserl's statement, quoted above (p. 79), that "everything which appears in the mode of being through appearances is undecided between being and not being," reinforces this suggestion.
241. See H. Poincaré, *Science and Hypothesis* (New York: Dover Publications, 1952), pp. 51ff, and H. von Helmholtz, *Popular Scientific Lectures* (New York: Dover Publications, 1962), pp. 223ff.
242. See above, p. 67.
243. See, for instance, *APS,* pp. 16-19, 291-93; and *Ideas,* section 138, pp. 384-85. The concept of appearance in section 138 of *Ideas* is not the one which has been developed here.
244. *Ideas,* section 38, p. 124—translation slightly modified, and Husserl's emphasis omitted, see *Ideen* I, p. 86 (On the basis of a correction indicated by Husserl, the Biemel edition has "only as a dependent moment" as the final clause). The references of the ambiguous pronouns have been supplied on the basis of the next sentence in Husserl's text.
245. Ibid., section 45, p. 141.
246. Ibid., section 46, p. 143.
247. Ibid., – translation slightly modified, see *Ideen* I, p. 106.
248. See ibid., section 77, p. 216 for the use of these terms in place of "exists."
249. Ibid., section 42, p. 134. It is best to consult the German text when reading this last paragraph of section 42, as the English translation is somewhat misleading in places. That will not help, however, to overcome the misleading way in which Husserl expresses himself here. He says that one way the two types of perception differ is that in immanent perception the object is really (reell) immanent in the perceiving, but in transcendent perception it is not.

He then says that they differ "much more" in the way their objects are given. But, as Boehm points out, the preceeding analyses in the chapter have shown that the distinction between immanence and transcendence is *grounded in* the distinction of modes of givenness. See *Ideen* I, p. 98 and Rudolf Boehm, "Immanenz und Transzendenz," in his book *Vom Gesichtspunkt der Phänomenologie* (The Hague: Martinus Nijhoff, 1963), p. 157.

250. *Ideas*, section 42, p. 134 and section 44, p. 140.

251. See above, p. 64.

252. *APS*, p. 16. Cf. *Ideas*, section 44, p. 140.

253. *APS*, pp. 16-17.

254. On this "coinciding," see p. 67 above.

255. Husserl uses the words *"Gegenwartserscheinung"* and *"Leibhaftigkeits-Erscheinung"* to refer to what I have called the "phenomenon of self-presence." See Edmund Husserl, *Phantasie, Bildbewusstsein, Erinnerung: Zur Phänomenologie der anschaulichen Vergegenwärtigungen, Husserliana*XXIII, ed. Eduard Marbach (The Hague: Martinus Nijhoff, 1980), pp. 241, 580 (hereafter cited as *PBE*).

256. *PP*, p. 261. The draft in question was worked on by both Husserl and Heidegger. The editor of *PP*, Walter Biemel, tells us that the section from which this passage is taken was edited by Heidegger (see p. 590). Judging by their style, it is clear that the lines quoted here were not written by Husserl.

257. *LI*, p. 761.

258. See pp. 49-50 above for the complete argument. The third statement expresses something that Husserl leaves implicit in his presentation of the argument. For this reason I cannot, as in the case of the other statements, provide a reference to a place in one of his texts where the statement is affirmed. There is another idea that is implicit in Husserl's argument: Whatever *is* inactual or non-actual is on hand through consciousness. This idea resembles the one which is expressed in the third statement. Through that resemblance and through the greater credence which no doubt is given to it, it lends a persuasive force to the third statement. The backing for the idea that whatever is inactual or non-actual is on hand through consciousness comes from the ontological presupposition of psychological reflection that the inactual and non-actual are "subjective." This presupposition has been implicitly operative in the entire psychological reflection above.

259. See p. 48 above for "achievement."

260. *PBE*, p. 222.

261. Ibid., n. 4.

262. See *LI*, p. 869, where Husserl says that hallucinatory objects "exist only in a phenomenal and intentional manner." On p. 596 he explains that the expression "the object is merely intentional" does not mean that the objects exists as a really intrinsic part of consciousness, rather it means that the intention, the reference to the object, so exists.

263. Above, p. 96.

264. Edmund Husserl, *Zur Phänomenologie des inneren Zeitbewusstseins, Husserliana* X, ed. Rudolf Boehm (The Hague: Martinus Nijhoff, 1966), p. 179, n.l (hereafter cited as *ZB*).

265. Ibid. – translation mine. Cf. Edmund Husserl, *The Phenomenology of Inner Time-Consciousness*, trans. James S. Churchill (Bloomington: Indiana University Press, 1964), p.63. This book, which is the English translation of the main text of *ZB*, will be cited as *PITC* hereafter. The English translation is in error in translating "als es selbst" as "other than itself."

266. *APS*, p. 96.

267. There is, of course, a spatial connotation in the expression "here, in the present." We will

not consider that aspect separately in what follows. It can be thought of as the *form* of distinctness-within-simultaneity.

268.  *PITC*, p. 63 (*ZB*, p. 40).
269.  *APS*, p. 96.
270.  *PITC*, pp. 61, 64 (written in 1905). See also pp. 53-54 (1909). In an earlier text (*ZB*, pp. 211-13, from 1904) Husserl says that the "Now" and the "Self-there" coincide. He seems to conclude from this that primary memory is not perceptual. The later texts cited here indicate that he abandoned this view. Another later text (*ZB*, pp. 342-44, from 1909) confirms this. It is known that Husserl's conception of time-consciousness underwent many changes during the first decade of this century. Concerning this, see John Brough, "The Emergence of an Absolute Consciousness in Husserl's Early Writings on Time-Consciousness," in *Man and World* 5 (1972): 298-326. This article also appears in Elliston and McCormick, *Husserl: Expositions and Appraisals,* pp. 83-100. On this topic, see also the "Editor's Introduction" to *ZB*, and Sokolowski, *Husserlian Meditations,* chapter 6.
271.  *ZB*, pp. 417-18 (1905).
272.  *PITC*, p. 64. In one place, Husserl calls primary memory *"Erinnerungs-Wahrnehmung"* (*ZB*, p. 310).
273.  *PITC*, pp. 63-64.
274.  Ibid., p. 64.
275.  See pp. 71-75 above.
276.  *LI*, pp. 740-41. Another, three-fold, way in which Husserl distinguishes the components of a "representation" will be discussed later.
277.  *LI*, pp. 712-14, 741, 785-86.
278.  See *Ideas,* section 99, p. 291 for the distinction between the "painted picture" as image or likeness, and the painting as a physical thing.
279.  The concept of phantasy, for Husserl, encompasses not only consciousness of fictitious objects, but also of objects known to be actual. This is not always obvious from his examples, which, most of the time, are of presentifications of fictitious objects (centaurs, fairies, etc.). In one text, however, he writes of phantasizing *himself* in a certain situation (*EP*, p. 114). See his discussion of the different senses of phantasy in *PBE*, pp. 1-6.
280.  See Sokolowski, *Husserlian Meditations,* pp. 24, 147. We shall see later that Husserl comes to abandon this view, in a sense.
281.  See *LI*, p. 712.
282.  Ibid., p 589.
283.  Ibid., p. 648.
284.  *LI*, p. 741. See Edmund Husserl, *Logische Untersuchungen,* vol. 2, part 2 (Tubingen: Max Niemeyer, 1968), sixth investigation, section 26, p. 91. Hereafter, this work will be cited as *LU,* followed by a roman numeral and an arabic numeral designating the particular investigation and the section of that investigation, respectively, to which reference is made, and then the page reference of the edition cited here. Thus, the reference just given would be *LU,* VI/26, p. 91. See also *LI*, pp. 589, 652.
285.  *LI*, p. 589.
286.  This is the way some commentators, for instance Sokolowski (*The Formation of Husserl's Concept of Constitution,* pp. 47, 93), seem to understand quality.
287.  See *LI*, pp. 624-27, 638. In *Ideas,* Husserl explicitly abandons the term "quality" in favor of terms more clearly expressive of positionality. Thus, an act's quality is referred to as its "thesis" (section 133, p. 369, especially n.l, and section 129, p. 362). He then speaks of "pleasure-theses," "wish-theses" (section 114, p. 320), and "belief-theses" (section 117, p. 329).

288. See *LI*, p. 743.
289. Ibid., p. 646.
290. Ibid., pp. 638-39, 625-26.
291. Ibid., pp. 646, 740, 786.
292. See *Ideas*, section 112, p. 313, n.l.
293. *LI*, pp. 638, 642-47 (esp. 643). See *Ideas*, sections 109-114 and section 117, for Husserl's improvements on the analysis in *LI*.
294. *LI*, p. 646. See also p. 740.
295. Ibid., pp. 646-47 – translation modified. Findlay's translation does not quite bring out the fact that Husserl is here saying that these *are* the relevant factors (see LU, V/40, p. 492). See also LI. p. 652.
296. *LI*, p. 731 (*LU*, VI/22, p. 79). Husserl notes that one could call both "sensations," and then distinguish between "impressional" and "reproductive" sensations (*LI*, p. 655). I use the word "phantasma" here for Husserl's "*Phantasma*" in order to distinguish this concept from the concept of phantasm discussed above.
297. Ibid., p. 730 (*LU*, VII/22, p. 78).
298. Ibid., p. 655 (*LU*, V/44, pp. 503-4). See also *PBE*, p. 13.
299. This point is clarified in *Ideas* (section 112, pp. 312-13) where Husserl says that phantasmata are phantasies *of* a corresponding sense datum, and that the "of" here cannot be accounted for through any thinning of the intensity, fullness, etc., of the sense datum.
300. *LU*, VI/27, p. 94. "*Auffassungsform*" is translated as interpretive form" by Findlay (*LI*, p. 743).
301. *LU*, VI/26, p. 91. "*Auffassungssinn*" is rendered "interpretive sense" by Findlay (*LI*, p. 741).
302. Ibid. Findlay's translation leaves out the all-important clause beginning with "as representing..." (*LI*, p. 741).
303. *LI*, p. 743.
304. In Sokolowski's words, the theory presented in *LI* is in terms of the "matter-form schema of constitution." See his presentations and analyses of this schema as applied by Husserl to the constitution of sensations and phantasmata in *The Formation of Husserl's Concept of Constitution*, pp. 92-98, 177-80, and in his *Husserlian Meditations*, pp. 145-46.
305. *LI*, p. 646 – translation modified and bracketed material supplied by me (see *LU*, V/40, p. 491). This passage from the later, revised edition of *LI* (1913) is in essence the same as that in the first edition of 1900-1. The relevance of this remark will become evident shortly.
306. *Ideas*, section 111, p. 311.
307. Ibid., and *PBE*, p. 40.
308. *PBE*, p. 575.
309. *Ideas*, section 111, p. 311. As Husserl notes (p. 312), one should not identify the idea of neutrality-modification with a transforming operation carried out on a previous position, although it can be this at times. In our example it is not, for there was no previous positing of the picture-object as being actual.
310. *LI*, p. 646 – translation slightly modified, see *LU*, V/40, p. 491.
311. *Ideas*, section 113, p. 315 – translation modified. I have taken the liberty of changing the emphasis of this sentence by not italicizing the words "appears" and "aware" which are italicized in the English translation on the basis of Husserl's emphasis. I feel justified in doing this because in this whole section 113, the choice of words in many places in the text which Husserl published runs counter to and obstructs understanding of, the distinctions Husserl is making in the section. My rendering is more in line with the understanding of the

144

whole section one obtains by reading Biemel's *Husserliana* edition, which has incorporated certain crucial changes in phrasing which Husserl indicated in the margins of his personal copies of the text. See *Ideen* I, pp. 271-76 and the *"Textkritische Anmerkungen"* for those pages. See also Beilage XX and XXI where Husserl explicitly refers to his presentation as confusing and corrects his terminology.

312. Ibid., section 111, p. 309 – translation modified, see *Ideen* I, p. 268. In the sense in which Husserl uses *"Erinnerung"* here, the concept of memory is coextensive with the concept of positing, intuitive presentification ("intuitive," here, meaning the actual having of the presentified itself, as opposed to empty presentification, where the object is intended, but not yet itself presentified). Thus, in *APS,* he calls the act of recollection *"Vergangenheits-erinnerung"* (p. 70) and *"Ruckerinnerung"* (p. 74); he terms the act of anticipation *"Zukunftserinnerung"* (p. 74) and *"Vorerinnerung"* (p. 74).

313. See *PITC,* section 43, pp. 115-17; *Ideas,* section 78, p. 221. and section 118, p. 333.

314. See *PITC,* section 43, pp. 117-22; section 44, pp. 122-23; and pp. 175-81.

315. *Ideas,* section 81, p. 237.

316. Ibid.

317. See Brough, "The Emergence," p. 93, and *ZB,* p. 326.

318. See *APS,* pp. 324-25, and *ZB,* p. 291.

319. *Ideas,* section 111, p. 310; *EJ,* p. 168; *PITC,* p. 116.

320. See *ZB,* pp. 289-91, and *PITC,* pp. 116, 176-78. In my discussion of presentification I will omit consideration of the ego, i.e., the presentified ego as the subject of the presentified experiences. On this, see *APS,* pp. 306-11. Also, a complete account of presentification would discuss how the retentions, protentions and impressional aspect "originally" constituting the presentified experiences are also presentified. On this, see *APS,* pp. 325-26.

321. *PITC,* p. 77; *APS,* p. 68.

322. See *Ideas,* section 77, p. 216 and *APS,* p. 97.

323. *EJ,* p. 254.

324. *PITC,* pp. 118-22, 173, 164.

325. *EJ,* p. 254.

326. Ibid., pp. 175-76, 256-57.

327. *ZB,* p. 274.

328. See *PITC,* p. 164. Cf. Husserl's discussion of the perception of a star (p. 146).

329. See *ZB,* p. 181.

330. *APS,* p. 74. See also pp. 69-70, 239-41, 310. I cannot think of an adequate translation of *"Gegenwartserinnerung."* On the basis of Husserl's explanation of how it can be based on a recollection (p. 69 and also *ZB,* p. 309), one might call it "remembering into the present." According to Husserl, *Gegenwartserinnerung* is the intuitive mode of consciousness of the psychic life of another person (pp. 70 and 240), although this term seems not to be used in *Cartesianische Meditationen* (see sections 50-52). But it is quite understanable that Husserl should say this, because, as he analyzes it, a crucial aspect of the constitution of an alter ego is the positing of a stream of consciousness whose Now is the same as my own. See Klaus Held, *Lebendige Gegenwart* (The Hague: Martinus Nijhoff, 1966), p. 157, on this.

331. *APS,* p. 69; *ZB,* pp. 308, 310. Co-presentation can also be based on a description (*PITC,* p. 84 and *ZB,* p. 309).

332. *ZB,* pp. 307-8. Cf. *ZB* pp. 59-60 and *PITC,* pp. 83-84.

333. *ZB,* p. 51 – translation mine, see *PITC,* p. 74. See also *ZB,* pp. 186, 306-7.

334. *APS,* p. 97; *ZB,* pp. 306-7.

335. *ZB,* p. 307.

336. This is especially evident in the case of a co-presentation based on a description provided by someone else.

337. See *PITC*, p. 85.

338. This conditionality is important for understanding the constitution of the spatiality of objects and of the world, because an empty, non-intuitive form of co-presentation makes up part of the horizon-consciousness of a perception. Through this we are conscious of those parts of objects and sectors of our environment which are not strictly perceived, and conscious of them as being simultaneously present with what we do perceive (*APS*, p. 75). These emptily intending moments of co-presentation are what was referred to above as that aspect of horizon-consciousness which lies in "dead" potentiality (p. 82).

339. *ZB*, p. 310.

340. Of course in some sense we "know" that our picture may not be completely accurate. But we do not know in what ways it is inaccurate. The case of going to see an old friend whom one has not seen for a long time may be helpful to analyze what is involved here. Before meeting the friend we presentify him. We "know" he has grown older, but when we actually meet him there is the experience of disappointment of expectations. Whatever positings are affected here would also have been contained in the co-presentation.

341. The object as that which is identical in and which endures through time is Husserl's "pure X" which was discussed earlier (p. 56 above).

342. *APS*, p. 97, 188, 211; *PITC*, p. 137; *EP* II, p. 113; *ZB*, p. 182.

343. See above, p. 84

344. *ZB*, p. 186.

345. See *APS*, pp. 114-16, 192-211.

346. Ibid., p. 500.

347. See ibid., pp. 211-12, 323-24.

348. See *PBE*, p. 217.

349. See *ZB*, p. 291.

350. Thus Husserl often calls the purely presentifying factor in recollection "phantasy." This is what is left over after abstracting from the seriousness of the positing (see *ZB*, pp. 394, 418).

351. *Ideas*, p. 316. Here it is best to consult the Biemel edition of *Ideen* I (p. 274). As mentioned before (n. 311 above), Husserl's terminology in the text he published prevents a proper understanding of a distinction he wishes to make. His indicated corrections are incorporated in Biemel's edition. The distinction in question is that between not "actually" carrying out a positing in the same sense in which moments of a non-attentional consciousness are not "actually" engaged in by an ego, and not "actually" carrying out the positing in the sense of remaining neutral. Husserl usually uses the word *"aktuell"* for the former "actual" and *"wirklich"* for the latter. His published text did not make this verbal distinction, which the Biemel edition of *Ideen* I corrects.

352. *EJ*, p. 169 – emphasis deleted.

353. In *Ideas*, (section 112, p. 313), Husserl indicates that the transformation of a phantasy into a perception is one way in which hallucination can come about. We can understand the hallucination used in the earlier example to illustrate empirical illusion as having come about in this way.

354. Ibid., section 111, pp. 310-11.

355. A less dramatic form of this experience is often had by petrified speakers in front of large audiences. I once had the very strange experience of looking at a reflection of myself in a full-length mirror and then coming to perceive myself from the point of view of the "me" in the mirror. A study of such phenomena could be important for understanding how we experience ourselves as being an Other to an Other.

356. Husserl gives an example somewhat similar to ours in *ZB* (p. 182), the transformation of a

recollection into a (hallucinatory) perception. Here the recollected object becomes itself given, but, Husserl notes, "not as past." In his thought-experiment, the time of the object is also altered, whereas I have controlled for this variable by using the case of a co-presentation.

357. All presentification involves the reproduction of another experience intact. See Husserl's analysis of recollection in this respect, in *ZB*, p. 181.

358. *PBE* p. 592 (written in 1921 or 1924).

359. In *PBE* (p. 580), Husserl uses consciousness of the picture object *(Bildobjekt)* to illustrate perceptive phantasy, and in *Ideas* (section 111, p. 311), he uses the same to illustrate neutralized perception. Again in *PBE* (ibid.), he uses the experience of an object in a stereoscope to illustrate perceptive phantasy, and in *LI* (p. 646), he uses this to illustrate neutralized perception. In *EP* II (pp. 112-13), the picture object is called a "fiction" *(Fiktum)*, it is "not believed to be there, but only appears as if it were there."

360. *Ding und Raum,* p. 16.

361. Ibid., p. 15.

362. Ibid.

363. Ibid.

364. *"Dastehen,"* figuratively, can mean *"Geltung haben"* (to be valid). See *Wahrig Deutsches Wörterbuch* (Gütersloh: Bertelsmann Lexikon-Verlag, 1978). Husserl often uses *"Geltung haben"* to express that something is believed to be actual.

365. Later in the text of *Ding und Raum* (pp. 151-52) Husserl seems to recognize this problem, but says that "perhaps" there is an identical appearance *(Erscheinung)* in an abstract sense.

366. In *Ding aund Raum,* as in *Logical Investigations* and *Ideas,* Husserl presents a three-fold structural analysis of perception: sensory contents, apprehension, and positionality (see *Ding und Raum,* pp. 45-46).

367. See above, p. 78

368. Cf. the original version of the argument on pp. 49-50 above.

369. See p. 49 above.

370. See p. 81 above for the original version.

371. See pp. 84-85 above.

372. See p. 76 above for the statement of this problem.

373. *APS*, p. 6; *CM*, pp. 53-54.

374. See above, pp. 11-14 for the discussion of these criteria.

375. *CM*, p. 79.

376. Ibid., p. 111.

377. In this connection, it has been noted that in blind tastings, even experts in certain foods or types of drink are often unable to discriminate between, and correctly identify, samples of even the commonest items, which, when they know what they are tasting, they find to have strikingly different qualities. In the media, such results are often presented in a way to imply that the "experts" are not so expert after all. Others find in this evidence that the characteristic taste of something is not an objective property of it, and that taste is purely "psychological" (a "secondary" quality in older parlance). But neither of these inferences may be correct. The characteristic taste of a substance may be an objective quality of it, only in order to have that quality itself given, one may have to be conscious in a "certain way." Being conscious in a certain way allows access to the self-presence of the taste, and knowing what one is tasting may be important in some cases for that way of being conscious to come about. When Gurwitsch describes consciousness as a "medium of access to whatever exist and is valid," he may be understood to be expressing the point made here (see *The Field of*

*Consciousness,* p. 166). Gurwitsch's remark is made during the course of elucidating the *transcendental* conception of consciousness. As it is interpreted here, the idea he expresses forms part of a psychological-phenomenological theory. It seems to me that his characterization of consciousness is more suited to the psychological context. It should also be noted that when Carr interprets Husserl's notion that "consciousness is constitutive of the world" as meaning that consciousness is responsible for the *givenness* of objects (see p. 8 above), Carr may be expressing the same idea as Gurwitsch does, and thus also may be taken to be interpreting Husserl's theory psychologically.

378. See *CM,* pp. 76, 90 for Husserl's use of the term "idea" (*Vorstellung*) in a context similar to the one here.
379. *Ideas,* section 47, p. 148 – emphasis deleted.
380. See p. 2 above on the schema.
381. See pp. 49-50 above for the original version.
382. See pp. 51-76 above for this discussion.
383. See pp. 81-88 above.
384. The coherence-thesis is formulated on p. 81 above.
385. Above, p. 83
386. See p. 32 above.
387. See the first part of the schema, the "motivating problem," pp. 18-29 above.
388. Quoted above, p. 33
389. Above, p. 36.
390. Ibid.

## 5. THE ENTRY INTO THE TRANSCENDENTAL REALM

### A. THE PHENOMENOLOGICAL EPOCHE AND REDUCTION[1]

The purpose of Husserl's argument is to demonstrate *that* consciousness constitutes the world. The purpose of the transcendental-phenomenological epoche is to bring the world-constitutive function of consciousness into the purview of reflective intuition, so that the manner of this functioning can be elucidated through constitutive analysis.[2] There has been considerable discussion in the literature on Husserl concerning whether the epoche and the reduction are the same.[3] Some seem to hold that for Husserl the words "epoche" and "reduction" are synonyms, others that they refer to distinguishable aspects of the same operation, and still others that they refer to distinct operations. My understanding of the matter is based on a certain way Husserl often describes the relationship between epoche and reduction. In one place Husserl states that the transcendental reduction is the "accomplishment of a reduction of 'the' world to the transcendental phenomenon 'world,' a reduction thus also to its correlate, transcendental subjectivity, in and through whose 'conscious life' the world, valid for us straight forwardly and naively prior to all science, attains and always has attained its whole content and ontic validity."[4] In this context, Husserl indicates that the transcendental epoche makes this reduction "possible."[5] Elsewhere, he writes that the "method of transcendental epoche, because it leads back to this realm [of transcendental being], is called transcendental-phenomenological reduction."[6] I interpret these remarks as saying that the epoche is *a* method for bringing world-constitutive consciousness into view intuitively. Thus, I would say that any method which would do this could be called a "reduction" (Latin: *reducere*), a "leading back,"[7] and I would leave it entirely open whether or not there might be some other way besides the epoche of doing this. Later, I will discuss further the relationship between epoche and reduction. For the present, I wish to give an exposition of the transcendental epoche, and also show that there can be a "psychological epoche." The account of the transcendental epoche will be an account of what I understand that procedure is supposed to be. Later I will provide an account of what I think it really is. For the purpose of the present exposition, it will be assumed that we have "acquired the idea of pure transcendental consciousness," i.e., world-constitutive consciousness. This means that at this point in the path of being "introduced" to phenomenology, we are convinced that consciousness constitutes the world, and that the thesis we will suspend is a belief.

In section 109 of *Ideas*, entitled "The Neutrality-Modification," Husserl discusses a modification of consciousness which "relates to the sphere of belief," but which is unique in that it is not only a way in which every modality of belief-consciousness can be modified, but also a way in which any positional modality of consciousness whatsoever can be modified.[8] Describing the neutrality modification as it relates to belief, Husserl says, "We are dealing now with a modification which in a certain sense completely removes and renders powerless every doxic modality to which it is relates." Unlike negation, which has a positive positional effect, Husserl continues, "it 'performs' nothing, it is the conscious counterpart of all performance."[9] Some lines later Husserl says that through this modification "(e)verything has the modifying 'suspensory bracket', *closely related* to that of which we have previously spoken so much, which is also so important for preparing the way into phenomenology" (emphasis mine).[10]

Taking the phrase "that of which we have previously spoken so much" as referring to the epoche, which Husserl did elaborate at some length in previous sections, it can be asked: Why "closely related?" Is it not the case that the epoche *is* the neutralization of an act, and one like the neutralization of any other act, except for being the neutralization of a certain kind of *reflective* act? Does this difference make it such that we do not have a single essence here, be two belonging to the same family?

The following reflections are an attempt to clarify this puzzling remark of Husserl's by showing that the epoche is not *simply* the neutralization of a reflective act and in what way it is not. My point will be basically this: although the reflective acts involved in phenomenological research are positionally neutral in the same sense as any other neutral act, because of the way in which their neutrality *must* be brought about, these acts contain a component which is unique to them and which amounts, in a sense, to a "performance." This component, noetically speaking is variously expressed by Husserl as refraining, inhibiting, or abstaining; I will use the word "refraining." The correlative noematic component is the qualification of the intentional object of the reflective act as having a *claim*. In addition, I will point to a wider sense of epoche which goes beyond what is involved in the neutralization of reflective acts. This concerns the total attitude of research of the phenomenologist and especially any judgements made about the objects of research. I will show how this is related to epoche in the narrower sense having to do with reflective acts.

As we have seen, according to Husserl, our straight-forward consciousness of the world is positional, and specifically, it is a doxically positional or believing consciousness. This doxic modality characterizes not only our consciousness of the world in general, but as well, it characterizes any single act of consciousness in which we are directed towards specific worldly objects. But when we are conscious of objects we are also aware, however dimly, *that* we are conscious of something and this awareness can be transformed at will into an explicit act of reflection *on* our being conscious of an object.[11] This reflection can be either noetic, where the focus is on the straight-forward experience as a temporally extended phase of our mental lives, or noematic, i.e., directed towards the object of the straight-forward experience as it is present to us in that experience.[12] We will be concerned primarily with noematic reflection here.

Perhaps the easiest way to perform a reflection is "in memory," i.e., by reflecting upon an act just carried out and retained by us or upon one performed in the more distant past which is explicitly recollected. Reflection is not restricted to this mode of performance, as it can, for instance, also be carried out "in phantasy," on a phantasized act,[13] and perhaps it can be a reflection on an act which is simultaneous with the reflective act. Let us use an example from memory, specifically a judging just performed by us, say, in a classroom before our students: "... and Husserl was the greatest philosopher since Leibniz" we say to them, recalling and affirming for ourselves the judgement of our own teacher. We pause, reflecting on our judgement, perhaps in appreciation of ourselves for having uttered so audacious a statement, and at the same time being caught up in the splendor of its evident truth and thus participating in the certainty with which we just uttered it. Suddenly Immanual Kant comes to mind. Our judging, still lingering on in our memory, begins to turn sour and we begin to feel a little embarassed. The judging is still with us, with its judged as judged, but we are no longer regarding it with such favor. We no longer share in the certainty of the judging. Its continued presence to us, along with our present disbelieving, has evoked a consciousness of the contrast and motivates our embarassment. Likewise the judgement as judged still stands before our reflective gaze, still radiant with certainty, that radiance now a hurtful glare in the dim of our new appraisal of it.

We observe that during the entire course of the reflection, our judging and the judgement meant in it stood before our reflective gaze; we maintained it in grasp as it gradually moved further into our past. At no time did we perform a new judging, either with the same or contradictory content. To be sure, we were engaged in a new act, the reflection, but its object was that very past act and its objective content. The certainty of the judging and of the judgement made in it remained throughout, even as our reflective act altered its doxic modality from the positive appraisal, which shared the certainty, to negative appraisal. This alteration did not result in the judgement's certainty being no longer present to us, although it did alter its mode of appearance, from "splendor" to "glare." The negative appraisal phase did not represent a new judging, neither a judging of the contradictory of the first judgment, nor one of the same judgement with the provisio "except for Kant," although such would soon follow. Thus, a reflective act can be directed to a straight-forward act and present that act and its objective content without altering the doxic modality of the act, whether the modality of the reflecting act is the same or different from that of the act being reflected on. It goes without saying that re-flection can make an act and its objective content as present in it an object of study. it should be noted that we have not yet spoken of any epoche, but have simply drawn out a possibility of reflection as such.

It is Husserl's contention that a reflecting act can be neutralized, i.e., in reflection one can refrain from taking a position with regard to the object of the act being reflected upon, be it the same position as the underlying act or some modality of it. Such a procedure is called epoche (from the Greek ἐποχή, a check or cessation).[14] Neutral consciousness is often attained in straight-forward acts, for instance, when, uncritically listening to a lecture, we merely grasp the thoughts of a speaker for the purpose of taking notes. We neither agree nor disagree, but merely understand what is being said. But the neutralization of a straight-forward act is not quite the same as what is achieved by the epoche, although it is "closely related" to it. First of all, the epoche is the neutralization of a *reflective* act, and although a neutralized reflection is neutral in the same sense that a straight-forward act is, i.e., it lacks a certain position-taking, the effect of the neutralization on that which appears is different in the two cases due to the way the reflective neutralization must be brought about. Second, the epoche occupies a central role within a total attitude of research and has, through its central role, a certain effect on the non-reflective acts which help make up the total research performance. It is in this respect that the epoche takes on a wider and even different sense than neutralization. In order to explicate these points it is first necessary to distinguish two senses of reflection that are involved here.

Phenomenology is carried out "in reflection."[15] But this "in reflection' is ambiguous. Taken in its narrow sense, reflection is the intuitive grasp of one's own mental process, i.e., reflective *acts*. But the phenomenologist is a scientist and thus makes judgements about what is intuitively grasped. Such judgings are straight-forward acts and not reflective acts. In addition, the phenomenologist may perform other types of straight-forward acts. Thus, the phenomenologist does not always live in reflective *acts*. But in a sense one could say that the phenomenologist always lives "in reflection" and that the judgements are made within a cognitive orientation which has, as a whole, a reflective style. An endeavor has a reflective style whenever the objects about which the judgements are made are made available exclusively through acts of reflection, in other words, whenever the objects to be judged about are given for immediate judgement only in acts of reflection, and whenever acts of reflection are resorted to for the ultimate verification of mediate judgements. Thus an endeavor has a reflective style whenever its evidential phases consist of reflective acts.

We are now in a position to describe the phenomenological epoche and to distinguish it from the neutralization of straight-forward acts. First, in connection with the first sense of reflection, the epoche is the neutralization of all the reflective *acts* making up the evidential phases of that cognitive endeavor called Husserlian phenomenology. Assuming that a straight-forward act being reflected upon is positional, and, let us say, specifically, contains a doxic moment which is a believing in the actuality of its object or some modality of that belief, the epoche involves refraining from performing *that* position-taking or any modalization of it. But is should be emphasized that the epoche is not a modification of the straight-forward position; it is not a modification affecting the straight-forward act. It is not a neutralization of that act. However, the epoche does involve the neutralization, i.e., a neutrality-modification, of some act. What act? Any neutral act is a neutrality-modification with respect to a *corresponding* positional act, an act which, among other things, has the same object as the neutral act. A neutral reflection, then, is a neutrality-modification with respect to a non-neutral or doxically positing *reflection* which grasps the same mental process. Thus the epoche brings about a neutral reflection which lacks the specific doxic positing contained in its non-neutral reflective counterpart. But it has also been said that the epoche involves refraining from performing the position-taking of the underlying grasped act. Let us now see how these three acts, the mental process being reflected upon, the doxically positional reflection upon it, and the latter's neutral counterpart are related to one another.

The object of a non-neutral reflection in noematic reflection is the object of the straight-forward act as it appears in that act. Let us use straight-forward visual perception and reflection upon it as our example, say my seeing a book before me. When I reflect on this seeing and glance at what appears in it, I find, and have now as the object of my reflecting, that book — more precisely, that book in a certain perspective. As well, my reflecting contains a believing in the actuality of the book and thus has as its object "an actual book in a certain perspective." This reflecting contains that believing by participating in the position-taking of the perception, which perception, then, is the original "source" of the ontic character of actuality.[16] In participating in the position-taking of the perception, the reflecting merely *accepts* the position and does not "constitute" it originally. The reflecting, of course, need not so assent, but could take on an opposing or other modal varient of the postion. it could, for instance, disbelieve in the actuality of the book, as a skeptic would.[17] If it did this, that would not alter the ontic character with which the reflected upon "book in a certain perspective" appears to the reflecting act and which continues to be in force since the originally constituting perception has not altered *its* positional modality. Rather, there is a certain overlapping of the two senses, actual and inactual, where the former because of its greater "force" (due to its originariness) "shines through" the latter, but which, because it appears through this medium, appears to the reflecting act as a *mere* claim to actuality. When the reflecting act does participate in the position-taking of the perception, there is also an overlapping of the ontic characters, but because of the coincidence of the two this is not apparent at first glance. Such an overlapping would become apparent in the case of a disbelieving perception being reflected upon by a believing reflection, if such a thing could ever come about. Thus, the modality of being which the object of a non-neutral reflecting has in and through the reflective positing is a completely transparent duplicate of the original positing.

Now it is precisely this which is lacking in a corresponding neutralized reflection. The neutral reflective act does not contain the same positing as its non-neutral counterpart, hence, it does not contain the same positing as the act reflected upon nor any of the possible positings that are modalizations of the original positing. It has no *such* positionality and thus lays down no *such* overlapping character. This does not mean that it is not positional in *any* sense. It is lacking only the positing of the underlying act or any of its varients. However, a neutralized reflection does not merely *not* so posit, it precisely *refrains* from so positing, and it is for this reason that an epoche is involved. This refraining has its "effect," but its effect is not the same as that achieved by the overlappings that have just been discussed. The effect is that the ontic character correlative to the positing of the act reflected upon appears to the reflecting act as a *claim*, but not as a *mere* claim as in the case of a disbelieving reflection.[18] Thus, if the straight-forward act is a perception, and its object appears in it as something actual, that object appears in the reflecting act as one which *claims* to be actual.

If it is to serve a cognitive interest, a reflection on a non-neutral straight-forward act can become neutralized *only* by refraining from positing whenever the underlying act continues to posit an ontic character. This is clear from the following considerations: A reflective act is parasitic, it depends on another act to give it its object. Thus the underlying positing is the relatively original source of the ontic character of the object being reflected upon. Due to the relative originariness of the underlying positing and the necessarily non-originality of the giving of the object in reflection, the intrinsically first mode of reflection is one which 1) contains a positing, and 2) contains one which is in agreement with the original positing. This means that neither neutral reflection nor reflection which contains some modal varient of the positing of the underlying act is the intrinsically first mode of reflection. This is not a matter of a temporal sequence of events, so that "first" is not to be taken in the temporal sense of "first in time." Thus, it is not a matter of psychological necessity. It is entirely possible for a doxic perceiving to be going on and then, while it continues, for there to be, as a first in time, a disbelieving reflection — as a matter of psychological fact. Rather, what is meant is a kind of logical priority. Where the reflective act contains a positing, any difference in its mode of positing from that of the underlying act *which is epistemically justified* requires a counter epistemic *motive* based on a counter *evidence*, whereas *no* motive or evidence other than that involved in the underlying act is required where there is no difference in positionality. Of course, no such requirements govern differing positionalities as psychological facts. Neutral reflection also requires epistemic motivation. Where neutralization is only a step toward positional modalization, such as doubt or disbelief, the motivation is the same as that governing the positional modalization. According to Husserl, any modalization of a reflective positing involves a prior neutral having of the object in question,[19] and it is for this, plus the following reason, that the intrinsically second mode of reflection is neutrality. Neutralization is not only justified as a step toward modalization, for there are possible motivations for neutralized reflection other than those involved in modalization.[20] It is the clarification of these motivations, I believe, which is the subject of what Husserl calls "ways into transcendental phenomenology."[21] But unlike motivations which lead to modalization of the positionality of the reflecting act, these motivations are not properly called "counter motives." They aim at neutralization, pure and simple. They are not based on any evidence running *counter* to the evidence of perception. Rather, they stem from the interest of the phenomenologist to ground the evidence of perception.

The neutralization of reflective acts in pursuit of this interest requires a refraining. As with talk of "first" and "motivation," the necessity for refraining is not to be taken in a psychological sense. Rather, it is connected with the epistemic goal of the phenomenologist. The "pull" of the doxic positionality of straight-forward acts which the reflective refraining resists is not one derived from a natural impulse or habit, but from the *evidence* of perception. To be sure, such natural factors are present and play a role in our tendency to co-posit the actuality of objects in reflection. But it is quite possible for a neutral reflection to come about, as a matter of psychological fact, without any refraining in a psychological sense or, for that matter, in the epistemic sense of refraining. Refraining in the epistemic sense is one which is brought about in conscious awareness and acknowledgment of the evidence of perception and is precisely a refraining from taking a position with respect to that evidence. A neutral reflection is surely possible as a fact of mental life which is not brought about through refraining in this sense, but such a reflection would not serve the interest of the phenomenologist. The intrinsically first mode of reflection with its co-positing must have its right of primacy acknowledged by the phenomenologist so that the neutral reflection *can be* animated by an epistemic refraining. Such a refraining must be an ingredient of the reflection because it is through that refraining that the phenomenologist's interest enters into the reflective act and comes to bear on the object reflected upon instead of just remaining in the background of consciousness. The phenomenologist's reflective act is to be neutral, but it is not to be disinterested. We must not be misled by Husserl's talk of a "disinterested onlooker."[22] In a neutral reflection that is aware of itself *as* a second mode of reflection (and that is what it means to contain a refraining), two fundamental features of the attitude of a phenomenologist enter into the reflective act: 1) its profound *respect* for the evidence of perception, and 2) its interest in seeking the grounds of that evidence, of its validity, and of the natural acceptance of its validity in sources which do not presuppose any of these.

Before discussing the noematic correlate of this refraining it is appropriate here to indicate how this relates to the second sense of "in reflection" mentioned before, and thus how it points to a broader sense of epoche. Phenomenology is a reflective enterprise because its evidential phases consist of reflective acts. Other kinds of acts involved in phenomenology can be said to be performed "in reflection" in the sense that they either yield material to or are epistemically oriented towards these reflective acts. Of special concern in the latter case are the judgements which the phenomenologist makes about the objects given for judgement through neutralized reflective acts. These judgements, we may say, cristalize the results of reflective intuition so that they may enter into the body of phenomenological theory. Since this theory is the realization of an interest, these judgements must also be executed so that they participate in the phenomenological attitude. But here, this cannot be achieved only by refraining, in immediate judgement (judgement of reflective intuition), from performing the position-taking of the act being reflected upon, for in the process of building a theory judgements enter into a context of their own. Detached from the immediacy of intuition, they combine with one another in various logical relationships which yield further mediate judgements. During this process they invariably come under the influence of other modes of thinking and other sciences, if only in the very language they employ. There is ample opportunity here for ideas to become part of phenomenological theory which are based on the very positionality which the reflective intuitions must refrain from, thus violating the very spirit of the enterprise. Hence, care must be taken in the judgemental phase of phenomenology to exclude such thoughts and the judgements absorbing them from entering into the body of phenomenological theory. This excluding can also be called an epoche.[23]

As has been said, during a neutralized reflection the object of the underlying act continues to be present to that act with the ontic character correlative to that act's positionality. The character is present, then, also to the reflecting act, but now as an ontic *claim*. This "as a claim" is due not to the mere *neutrality* of the reflecting act, but to the refraining necessary to bring that neutrality about. Let us have in mind straight-forward perception which posits its object as actual as our example. We recall that the epistemic refraining from co-positing the ontic character on the part of the reflective act involves, on the one hand, and acknowledgement of, and a respect for, the evidence of the underlying perception, and, on the other hand, an interest to remain free from that evidence so as to seek its grounds in something that does not presuppose it. This refraining, then, involves a doing, it does "perform" something. I have called the noematic correlate of this performance "presence of the ontic character as a claim." What is meant by this is that the object as it is present in the act being reflected upon is seen through the reflection not merely as *appearing* to be actual, not only as an actuality-phenomenon, as would be the case if the reflecting were neutral without involving a refraining, but as presenting a *legitimate claim* to so appear, a legitimate claim to actuality. The perception of the object, when it too becomes considered, claims to be a cognition and is seen to harbor a belief in the mode of presumptive certainty.[24] The phenomenologist is interested precisely in these claims, for he seeks the conditions of the possibility of cognition.

Let us try to see this more clearly by comparing the three possible reflections that have been discussed. In a positing reflection, the actuality character is posited just as it is in the underlying perception. The object appears in the reflective act as simply actual. There is no "claim" or even "appearance" of being here; the thing simply *is*. Perception does not *claim* to be a cognition, it needs no grounds of legitimation. In a neutral reflection which just happens to come about as a matter of psychological fact, but which contains no refraining, the object merely appears as phenomenon of "simply being actual," the perception merely appears as the phenomenon of a cognition, and no stand is taken one way or the other towards these manners of appearing. Here is the truly "disinterested spectator." But here perception is not seen as *claiming* to be a cognition, nor the object as claiming to be actual, for perception and perceived present themselves precisely as they did in the positing reflection, as "simply a cognition," "simply actual," except for the added index "phenomenon of." But in a neutral reflection which contains a refraining, something new enters in. To be sure, here also there is no stand taken with regard to the actuality of the object, but this neutrality is for the sake of a motive which brings into the reflection the recognition of something, or perhaps we might say the uncovering of something: that perception as cognition is in need of grounding, beings are not "simply beings," but are grounded beings. It is this which "appears" to the refraining reflection and which is its "performance."

This account of the epoche shows it to be the way the phenomenologist's interest enters into the reflective act. This interest is the problem of cognition. However, we can see that the method of epoche embodies a certain interpretation of that problem. Through its refraining, the epoche as applied to a perception gives intuitive access to a perceptual belief in the mode of presumptive certainty, and to the object of perception as a presumptive actuality.[25] The word "presumptive" expresses, on the one hand, the correlate of the respect of the evidence of perception that is brought into the reflective act by the refraining; on the other hand, it expresses the correlate of the interest to ground that evidence, an interest which is motivated by the idea that there is a *problem* of cognition. In addition, we saw earlier in the discussion of the coherence-thesis that the word "presumptive" also expresses the idea that the actuality of an object and of the world in general is one "until further notice."[26] Thus the method of epoche stems from an interpretation of the problem of cognition which specifies the problem to be the need for a *legitimating* grounding of the evidence of perception, for a grounding of the right of perception's claim to be cognition despite its own inherent openness to the delivery of the "notice." It can be said, then, that the idea of a phenomenological reduction stems from the *general* interest in grounding cognition, while the method of epoche implies a specification of that interest.

From where does this specification come? It comes from the way in which the idea of transcendental consciousness was "acquired" in the psychological analysis. It was that analysis which determined the thesis of the natural attitude, which was disclosed in a "naive," non-psychological analysis merely as a thesis, to be a belief. The problem of cognition which emerged at the end of the psychological analysis and in Husserl's argument as transcendentally interpreted is essentially determined by the "disclosure" of the permanent possibility of transcendental illusion. We saw that the coherence-thesis, by determining that the positing contained in perceptual consciousness of the world is doxic, provides a rational motivation for performing the epoche. Now we can see that it does much more than this. As a refraining from belief, the epoche is not simply a method originating outside the context of the coherence-thesis, which merely sanctions that method as a rational practice. Rather, the epoche is precisely the methodological embodiment of the interpretation of the problem of cognition to which the coherence-thesis gives rise. The refraining of the epoche is the way in which this interpretation is transformed from a thought into a way of "seeing." Once this transformation is achieved, the work of phenomenology can begin, namely, the work of showing concretely how consciousness achieves the ongoing validity of world-experience and thus the being-on-hand of the world. This is the task of "constitutive analysis," a subject we will turn to next, after having discussed the possibility of a "psychological epoche."

The transcendental phenomenological epoche, which has just been discussed, is a neutralization of the positing of the *actuality* of an object (and of the world in general). Earlier, another positing contained in perceptual experience was disclosed, namely the positing of the self-presence of an object. This positing was also said to be doxic. Clearly, this positing can be "suspended" in reflection to reveal the phenomenon of the self-presence of the intentional object of a perception (and generally, the phenomenon of the self-presence of the world) along with its correlate. I will call this procedure the "psychological phenomenological epoche." This does not seem to be the same operation as the one to which Husserl gives the same name.[27] The procedure I am discussing would also have an interest, an interest in grasping and studying how consciousness functions to make the world itself-present to us, and how, through syntheses of consciousness, the self-presence phenomenon is motivated and sustained. In light of the psychological problem of cognition, which would be the motivating problem behind this procedure, perceptual consciousness would be seen as claiming to give an intentional object itself, and the self-presence phenomenon would be viewed as a claim. Here too there would be a task of "constitutive analysis," about which I will say a few words in the sequal. What is most important to realize is that this psychological epoche does not give access to world-constitutive consciousness. It should be clear from all that has been said concerning the difference between the positing that it suspends and the positing that the transcendental epoche suspends, and the difference between the psychological and world-constitutive conceptions of consciousness, that the performance of the psychological epoche would not leave world-constitutive consciousness and its correlate, the world as a being-for-consciousness, as a phenomenological residuum, as a field for study.

## B. CONSTITUTION AND CONSTITUTIVE ANALYSIS

The epoche brings about intuitive access to the world as a being-for-conscious-ness and to consciousness in its functioning to constitute the world. Describing the epoche as a "liberation" from the natural attitude, Husserl writes, "Given in and through this liberation is the discovery of the universal, absolutely self-enclosed and absolutely self-sufficient correlation between the world itself and world-consciousness."[28] The epoche creates an attitude of focusing on this cor-relation and in this attitude "the world...becomes itself something subjective," a "transcendental phenomenon."[29] As remarked earlier, the reduction of the world to a subjective transcendental phenomenon does not imply that the world is seen as a really intrinsic part of consciousness. The world is immanent in consciousness "ideally," it is an immanent "objective sense" of conscious-ness.[30] Stated generally, the problem of the "constitution" of the world and of mundane objects concerns the disclosure of how an "actually existing world" and "actually existing worldly objects" arise for us as noematic senses and are maintained as valid through a correlative constitutive intentionality. Let us examine how the concept of "noematic sense" figures into the issue of constitution.

Earlier, two dimensions of the noema were distinguished, the object-dimen-sion and the appearance-dimension.[31] The noematic sense pertains to the ob-ject-dimension. The noematic sense of a perception was defined as the object of a perception (whether or not that object exists in actuality) taken exactly as it presents itself in the perception, i.e., taken in light of the determinations which it is experienced to have in that particular perception.

The concept of noematic sense serves the same theoretical function in *Ideas* as does the concept of the "matter" of an intentional experience in *Logical Investigations*.[32] These two concepts are not exactly the same, however. At the time of the writing of the first edition of *Logical Investigations,* Husserl had not yet formulated the concepts of transcendental epoche and reduction, al-though it may be that these procedures were implicitly operative in Husserl's thinking at that time.[33] One major difference between the two concepts, which, as Husserl himself points out, reflects the different orientations of *Logical Investigations* and *Ideas*, is that "matter" is a noetic concept, while "sense," as it is conceived in *Ideas,* is a noematic concept.[34] In spite of this, and of whatever other differences there may be between the way in which Husserl conceived these concepts, they both designate something "in" an intentional experience which has at least these two characteristics: 1) it is that by virtue of which consciousness is related to (or refers to, is directed to) an object, and, 2) it relates consciousness to an object in a circumscribed and therefore *epistemically* inadequate way.[35] These two characteristics are intimately associated. Let us see how.

Earlier it was said that the noematic sense of a perception is in a certain respect identical to the perceived object.[36] This identity was said to be an identity which is experienced when one makes the transition from straight-forward perception in the natural attitude to reflection on the perceived object in the transcendental attitude. Due to this identity, the noematic sense can be defined as "the object of the perception taken exactly as it presents itself in that particular perception." However, the phrase "taken exactly as it presents itself in that particular perception" expresses the awareness which one has as one reflects upon the noematic sense of a perception that, in that particular perception, the object is experienced to have a delimited set of features or "predicates," and that in other perceptions one could experience the object to have features which did not figure into the particular perception. Since this circumstance is repeated no matter what perception or series of perceptions of the same object is considered, perception was said to be epistemically inadequate.

As we thematize this inadequacy, we occupy the position of someone who knows from experience that objects always have more to offer us than we have learned of them up to any given point, and who brings this knowledge to bear on the theoretical appraisal of the epistemic status of the noematic sense. From this theoretical posture, despite the experienced identity between the object perceived and the noematic sense, a critical appraisal of the latter shows it to be in some way different from the object perceived, namely, to be something less than object in the "completeness of its actual being," the concept of which Husserl calls the "Idea" of the object.[37] Thus we may say that the noematic sense, like the "matter" of an intentional experience,[38] is a necessary but insufficient basis of the world-constitutive function of consciousness

In this connection, we recall that the meaning of "world-constitutive" consiousness is that "through" consciousness of a "specified sort" the world is on hand. The expression "specified sort" refers to the requirement, stemming from the idea of world-constitutive consciousness as an intentional achievement, that for every moment on the side of the world (as it is there for us in the natural attitude), there must be a moment on the side of consciousness (as conceived by phenomenological theory) that corresponds to it.[39] One way that the noematic sense falls short of corresponding to a worldly object is expressed in the concept of epistemic inadequacy. Yet the noema does account for the "through" mentioned above, i.e., for the intentionality of consciousness, since it is by virtue of the noematic sense that consciousness refers to an object. Having disclosed the concept of "object" which determines the meaning of the epistemic inadequacy of the noematic sense, and which specifies the nature of the object referred to through the noematic sense, we can see the connection of the intentionality of perception with its epistemic inadequacy. By being nonidentical with the object in the completeness of its actual being, the noematic sense *can be* the vehicle of reference to it.

From our present point of view (of straddling the natural and transcendental attitudes), the object perceived, taken as something the completeness of whose actual being transcends the noematic sense, seems to be in some way still outside the transcendental sphere, and thus in some way not to be itself a noematic sense. We have seen that Husserl's argument claims to bring just "this" object into that sphere, and as something noematic. Yet we still lack full insight into the way in which this is to be achieved. We must now see how the intentional object is "represented" in the transcendental sphere and how the intentional reference to it looks from entirely *within* that sphere. In pursuing this, we will come to understand more concretely the problem of the "constitution" of objects in consciousness.

In *Ideas,* Husserl raises the issue of the noematic sense as something different from the object referred to by consciousness in the following way. "Intentional experience...has *'objective reference'*...it is 'consciousness of something'.... If we recall our previous analysis, we find the full noesis related to the full noema as to its full intentional What [*Was*]. But it is then clear that this relation cannot be the same as is meant in the phrase concerning the reference of consciousness to its intentional object."[40] Husserl goes on to say that the phrase concerning the "relation," or, as he adds, "more specifically the 'direction' " of consciousness to its object points to the consciousness of what he calls the "determinable X," the "something" which is the bearer or subject of its possible predicates.[41] Thus, he concludes, "the distinction between 'content' and 'object' must be drawn not only in the case of 'consciousness', of the intentional experience, but also in that of the *noema taken in itself*. Thus the noema also refers to an object and possesses a 'content', 'by means of' which it refers to the object, the object being the same as that of the noesis...."[42] This "content" is the noematic sense.[43]

In another text, Husserl discusses a broader concept of noematic sense which he calls an "objective sense" (*gegenständliche Sinn*), and within which he distinguishes a "flowing [*fliessend*] sense" from an "identical sense." Using the example of the perception of a table, Husserl says that the objective sense is "this thing: the table which is seen."[44] At this point in his discussion, Husserl also seems to be straddling the natural and transcendental attitudes, and has the above-mentioned experience of identity. Then, immersing himself in the transcendental attitude, he makes an observation in connection with another identity. He notes that in a changing perception which takes in different aspects of the same thing, the objective sense in one respect changes and in another remains identically the same.[45] Later in the text, he distinguishes the flowing sense from the identical sense in the following manner. "Here we can observe that in the sense of a harmonious and synthetically progressing perception we can always distinguish the ceaselessly changing sense from the throughly identical sense. Each phase of the perception has its sense in so far as it has the object both in the manner [*Wie*] in which it has been determined through the originally presentative moments and those of the horizon. This sense is flowing, it is new in every phase. But through this flowing sense, through all the modes [which we call] 'object in the How [*Wie*] of determination', the unity of the substrate X, of the object itself, is maintained in the continual overlapping as it becomes more and more extensively determined. This substrate, this object, consists of all that which the process of perception determines it to be and which all further possible perceptual processes would determine it to be. Thus an Idea, lying in infinity, belongs to every outer perception, the Idea of a completely determined object, of an object which would be completely determined and known...."[46] This Idea of the "absolute self of the object" is an "unreachable" Idea.[47] In contrast to this, "every object of perception, [as given] in the process of becoming cognizant of it, is a flowing approximation. We always have the outer object bodily (we see, grasp and comprehend it), and nevertheless it lies in an infinite mental distance."[48] From the point of view of the concept of evidence, Husserl explains the approximation in the following way. "This imperfect evidence becomes more nearly perfect in the actualizing synthetic transitions from evidence to evidence, but necessarily in such a manner that no imaginable synthesis of this kind is completed as an adequate evidence: any such synthesis must always involve unfulfilled, expectant and accompanying meanings."[49] Thus, Husserl concludes, "an actual object belonging to a world or, all the more so, a world itself, is an infinite idea, related to infinities of harmoniously combinable experiences — an idea that is the correlate of the idea of a perfect experiential evidence, a complete synthesis of possible experience."[50]

The concept of perception which is formulated in these quotations is an epis-temological concept. The individual perceptions which connect with one an-other to form a synthesis are not just those which merely present the same ob-ject again, i.e., merely enter into a "synthesis of indentification,"[51] although that is presupposed. Rather, and more importantly, the synthesis contains perceptions which progressively contribute to our (prepredicative) knowledge of the object and to what it will be pregiven to be for us in further perceptions. Thus, although the synthesis pertaining to the same object comprises all the perceptions one has ever had of that object, and beyond that, all the experiences of it in general, in its most significant aspect the synthesis is a process of "taking cognizance" (*Kenntnisnahme*), i.e., of "explication."[52] Every perception belonging to the synthesis in which we are mindful of a new determination of the object institutes an "abiding possession."[53] On the one hand, every such original experience, although it passes and is forgotten, be-comes a "possession in the form of a *habitus.*"[54] This means that its con-stitutive achievement persists in a latent form, ready to be activated through associative processes whenever the same object is perceived again. On such an occasion this dormant "knowledge" is awakened and becomes implicitly operative as part of the horizon-consciousness of the new perception.[55] On the other hand, and precisely by virtue of this *habitus*, each new acquisition has a lasting result with respect to the object. In every subsequent perception, the object will be pregiven as having the determination in question.[56] Thus each new acquisition enriches the noematic sense.[57] We could say, then, that any phase of the synthesis, where the synthesis is taken as a process spread over a "life time," embodies the accumulated acquisitions of the preceeding phase and points to ever more possible acquisitions. Thus the "flowing sense" is to be understood not only as a *changing* sense, but as a *developing* sense, a parallel to the "developing matter" discussed earlier.[58] The noematic sense (or matter) of a particular perception can be thought of as the present phase of the developing sense (or matter). It contains all the sediments of past acquisitions, but raises some to prominance and relegates others to relative obscurity as it determines the specificity of the intentional reference of that particular perception.

The object *which* is intended by means of the flowing sense is "represented" in the transcendental sphere by the identical objective sense. This identical sense, or "pole of identity," as Husserl sometimes refers to it,[59] is not to be understood merely as an X of *identity,* but as a *determinable* X, as a substrate for indefinite *determination,* and thus as the "Idea of the absolute self of the object." Thus understood, a "worldly object" is the intentional correlate of certain noetic-noematic multiplicities within the overall synthesis which pertains to it, namely, of those multiplicities which form the process of taking cognizance within that synthesis. These multiplicities "combine to make up one (though perhaps infinite) *total evidence...* which would finally present the object itself in respect of all it is."[60] In this connection, Husserl defines the task of the transcendental constitution of an existing object to be the task of clearing up the essential structure of this evidence, "or to clear up, in respect of all internal structures, the essential structure of the dimensions of infinity that make up systematically the ideal infinite synthesis of this evidence."[61]

Earlier, the concept of "noematic sense" was said to be an insufficient basis for the world-constitutive concept of intentionality. This critique focussed on what we now call the "flowing sense" and considered it in isolation from the larger synthetic nexus to which it belongs. We can now see that the idea of world-constitutive intentionality is realized in the concept of intentional synthesis. As Husserl writes, "Only elucidation of the peculiarity we call synthesis makes fruitful the exhibition of the cogito (the intentional subjective process) as consciousness-of — that is to say, Franz Brentano's significant discovery that 'intentionality' is the fundamental characteristic of 'psychic phenomena' — and actually lays open the method for a descriptive transcendental-phenomenological theory of consciousness...."[62] A mundane object is actually the correlate of an intentional synthesis. Thus, seen from within the transcendental sphere, the intentional reference to such an object in a perception is achieved by that perception implicitly containing the synthesis within itself in the form of its own horizon-intentionality. The intentional reference consists partly in that perception pointing beyond itself and its own determinate content to other possible perceptions of the "same object," possible perceptions which will not merely bring to intuitive givenness what *is* intended, yet not actually perceived, in the given perception, but also perceptions which will fill out the indeterminacy and openness of the present perceptual intention with further new determinings.[63] As well, this horizon of possibility contains pointings to possible recollections of all the past perceivings of the same object,[64] and thus implicitly contains the past synthetic course within itself. It is in this manner of intending that the "transcendence" or "existence in itself" of a thing is constituted.[65]

The phenomenological method that Husserl refers to above as being "layed open" by the concepts of synthesis is the method of "intentional analysis." This method is used to show *how* worldly objects and the world in general are constituted in consciousness. It is a method of explicating the horizon-intentionality of an experience in order to disclose the intentional synthesis correlative to the experience's intentional object and thus to "clarify" what is meant in the experience. Employing this method, one uncovers "the definite synthetic courses of the manyfold modes of consciousness and, further back, the modes of Ego-comportment, which make understandable the objective affair's simple meantness for the Ego....Or, stated more precisely, they make it understandable how, in itself and by virtue of its current intentional structure, consciousness makes possible and necessary the fact that such an 'existing' and 'thus determined' Object is intended in it, occurs in it as such a sense."[66] The method makes it understandable "*how,* within the immanency of conscious life and in thus and so determined modes of consciousness belonging to this incessant flux, anything like *fixed and abiding objective unities* can be intended and, in particular, how this marvelous work of 'constituting' identical objects is done *in the case of each category of objects* — that is to say, how, in the case of each category, the constitutive life looks, and must look, in respect of the correlative noetic and noematic variants pertaining to the same object."[67] Expressed in this way, the method of intentional analysis is clearly a method for solving the problem of cognition interpreted as the problem of understanding how consciousness, in so far as it is cognition, "can accomplish a certain task attributed to it, namely, the task of reaching the object."[68]

Constitutive intentional analysis can be "static" or genetic." Static analysis deals with intentional objects and with their correlative noetic-noematic multiplicities as already formed, and inquires into their types, structures, and relationships, while genetic analysis concerns their "history," i.e., their origin and development.[69] One task of static analysis is to disclose the "synthetic style" of the on-going experience of objects with respect to the sorts of objects that they are.[70] This is the disclosure of the parameters of predeliniation or the "rules" mentioned before which unify and guide anticipations and structure the horizon-intentionality of a perception.[71] Intentional objects in their generic nature, and this means in regard to all the "categories" (kinds or types) which they exemplify, through all levels of generality, both formal and material (for instance, considered simply as an object, and then as a spatial object, material thing, cultural object, a chair), are taken as "transcendental clues"[72] for the uncovering of the rules which shape the parameters of the courses of experience of things which have been determinative of their having been and their continuing to be experienced as being of this or that sort.[73] As Husserl says, "any straightforwardly constituted objectivity (for example: an Object belonging to Nature) points back, according to its *essential sort* (for example: physical thing *in specie*), to a correlative *essential form* of manifold, actual and possible, intentionality (in our example, an infinite intentionality), which is constitutive for that objectivity."[74] This "essential form" of intentionality (i.e., rule governed intentionality) Husserl entitles a "constitutional Apriori."[75] Thus, constitutive intentional analysis studies the correlation of constitutive Apriori and objective Eidos (which at the primary level of analysis is a life-world kind).[76] In this way, intentional analysis contributes to the fulfillment of phenomenology's program of providing a "definitive criticism of every fundamentally distinct science, and in particular therewith the final determination of the sense in which their objects can be said 'to be'."[77]

Genetic analysis is concerned with the temporal "becoming" of conscious life.[78] One of the major concerns of genetic analysis is to show how one's consciousness of the world has developed into its present form by disclosing the decisive stages of that development. These stages consist of the formation of those primordial experiences by virtue of which worldly objects are experienced to be *what* they are for us, i.e., to have the generic determinations that they are experienced to have.[79] This inquiry is not an inquiry into the history of one's experience of this or that *particular* object. As part of a phenomenology of knowledge which aims to provide a criticism of, and a foundation for the sciences, especially the formal and material ontologies, genetic analysis is concerned with the sedimented history of the various *generic* features (which I will henceforth call "object-senses") which qualify particular intentional objects,[80] and with the origin and development of the correlative constitutive Apriori. Thus the interest is not to disclose that experience in which any given particular object was first intended with this or that object-sense, but the nature of the experiences in which the sense *itself* first became constituted.

One can conceive of one's conscious life as containing a multiplicity of lines of intentional synthesis correlative to each individual object one has ever intended perceptually. Included in each synthesis would be those experiences in which the object was first intended to have each of its various determinations. But in the case of most objects, the primordial experiences constitutive of its various generic determinations themselves are not to be found in the synthesis correlative to that object. In fact, most objects are "pregiven" as having a multiplicity of generic determinations. This means that even on the first perception of them, the objects are already formed along generic lines, and are intended to have determinations which have not yet actually been perceived, much less primordially constituted in that initial intending. This is due to prior experience with similar objects. Thus, the lines of synthesis are not separate strands running parallel to one another; rather, they cross at various points where they influence one another. Only certain strands contain the truly "primally institutive" modes of consciousness constitutive of the various "categories" of objects and hence of the diverse generic object-determinations. In such a primordial experience, a *type* of experience first becomes formed, for instance, the type "experience of a physical thing."[81] Then, by means of what Husserl calls an "apperceptional genetic after-effect," the object-sense "physical thing" becomes transferred to other objects.[82] "This makes possible a consciousness of objects that have never themselves been *given* in a consciousness, and a consciousness of objects as having determinations that they were never given as having — but precisely on the basis of the givenness of similar objects, or similar determinations, in similar situations."[83]

Husserl emphasizes that the study of the "history" of consciousness with respect to the type of experiences in which object-senses are constituted (i.e., with respect to what he calls "apperceptions"), and especially the manner in which they develop from one another "does not concern the exhibition of a de facto genesis of de facto apperceptions or de facto types in a de facto stream of consciousness or even in the stream of consciousness of all de facto persons. It is not similar to the development of the species of plants and animals. Rather, each form of apperception is an essential structure and has its genesis according to essential laws, and thus included in the idea of such an apperception is the possibility of its being subjected to a 'genetic analysis'."[84] This lack of concern for the de facto does not imply that the phenomenologist is not concerned with examining his or her own conscious life and the experiences which actually occur in it. Rather, Husserl is saying that what is found in that conscious life, as an already developed consciousness, in its very sense points back to an essential and necessary genesis of the types of apperceptions. The course of an individual conscious life involves many accidental and contingent factors; however, *given* that at a certain stage it has a world which is articulated and determinded in a particular way, the course of that conscious life displays a certain ordering of apperceptions which *any* conscious life (human or otherwise) would also *have to* display. In this respect, the development of conscious life is different from the evolution of animal species where it would be conceivable that the various forms could have evolved in an entirely different way than they in fact did, or even that they did not "evolve" at all. But the forms of apperceptions found in "our" conscious lives by their very nature necessarily point back to an emergence from more primitive forms of consciousness, and thus, the possibility of a genetic analysis is indicated by their very essence.

It is really in genetic transcendental phenomenology that the idea of world-constitutive consciousness becomes fully realized. In this connection, Iso Kern writes that "(i)f intentionality or constitution is interpreted merely as *static*, world-experience cannot be said to be 'productive', since experience by means of 'already formed habitualities', which static phenomenology exclusively considers, is no 'producing'. On the basis of static phenomenology it can only be said that the real world is *relative* to subjectivity.... In order to be able to see the world as a formation produced by subjectivity, constitution or intentionality must be grasped as *genetic*."[85] As Kern points out, static phenomenology considers the world as a being-for-consciousness. Thus we can say that static analysis is guided by the idea of world-constitutive consciousness, as the idea of a correlation between world and world-consciousness, to inquire concretely into the manner in which world-consciousness corresponds to the particularity of the world, and into the intentionalities the experiencing of which are the necessary and sufficient conditions for the being-on-hand of the world.[86]

However we must remember that the theory of world-constitutive consciousness is put forth to solve the problem of cognition. As Husserl says, "Now that the problems of phenomenology have been reduced to the unitary comprehensive title 'the (static and genetic) constitution of objectivities of possible consciousness', phenomenology seems to be rightly characterized also as *transcendental theory of knowledge*."[87] We have seen that the problem of cognition concerns the grounding of the *validity* of individual objective senses and of generic object-senses. The inquiry into these grounds becomes understandable as a search for intrinsic factors in subjectivity only if these senses are seen as being *formed* intrinsically, i.e., as having a genesis in subjectivity. This point can best be seen against the background of our previous critique of the psychological conception of consciousness.

In the psychological theory, the meaning of the concept of the "developing matter" of intentional experiences, and the concept of "rules" that structure and guide anticipations, presuppose a world independent of consciousness as the ultimate source of such matter and rules. Thus the intending of a tree, for example, is possible on the basis of the fact that there are trees and we have learned how to see them and to intend them generally. A phenomenological psychology can be envisioned which analyzes both statically and genetically the entire range of intentionality. One task would be to study how certain perspectival appearances come to be regarded as the "optimal" appearances of objects or classes of objects (a genetic problem), and then how the various other appearances of the object are oriented toward this "normal" form of appearance and derive their perceptual significance from that orientation (a static problem). This is the study of what is known as "object constancy." In general, the development and structure of our individual and common "interpretations" of the world could be examined.

But no matter how close such investigations may seem at times to be to transcendental phenomenology, no matter how far they may determine the world to be a "product" of human thought and action, questions which arise within such investigations about the validity of the world- and object-interpretations are not questions about the world and objects themselves. A perceptual tree-intention may be found to be laden with subjective factors, perhaps through a comparison of what it presents with the tree "in itself" as determinded scientifically. But the scientific determination only gives us the true reality of the tree *which* is intended in everyday life. Whether it considers the tree as it is intended in everyday life or as it is intended in objective science, psychology, if it remains on its own grounds, does not consider the issue of the validity of intending trees as such. It is simply considered to be a fact that there are trees and that our nature as beings-in-the-world is such that we should become aware of that fact. Transcendental phenomenological analysis seeks to give the *grounds* for the factuality of such facts. It seeks to show how it is that a person in everyday life or in the context of positive scientific endeavors has a world of such facts and the fact of a world at all. In our example, it is a question of the grounds of validity of tree-intentions. This is not a matter of whether or not a given object is a tree, nor of how, given that there are trees, we come to perceive and conceive them as we do. It is a question of the grounds of validity of the object-sense "tree" and thus of the grounds, purely within subjectivity, of a world in which something like a tree can be on hand. This issue becomes meaningful only if the sense "tree" is considered as having a purely subjective origin. Then the issue of how the sense can have objective significance as opposed to being merely a product of "transcendental phantasy," as it were, can arise. "Neither the world nor any other existent of any conceivable sort comes 'from outdoors' into my ego, my life of consciousness. Everything outside is what it is in this inside, and gets its *true being* from the givings of it itself, and from the verifications, within this inside...."[88]

The issue of the validity of sense brings us to the problems of "reason and reality [*Wirklichkeit*],"[89] and to what Husserl terms the "more pregnant concept of constitution,"[90] namely, the constitution not of objects simply, not of mere unities of identification, but of *actually existing* objects and of an *actually existing* world. Although this concept was implicit in the previous discussion, it was not sufficiently emphasized. "(T)he world constituted in me," Husserl writes, "though it always exists for me in the stream of my harmonious experience, and exists quite without doubt (I could never summon up such a doubt, where every new experience confirms existence), —this world, I say, has and, by essential necessity, retains the sense of only a *presumptive existence*. The real world exists, only on the continually delineated presumption that experience will go on continually in the same constitutional style."[91] We have encountered these ideas before in our discussion of the coherence-thesis. The "presumption" concerning "constitutional style" points to a projection, within the intending of any worldly actuality, that the synthesis of future experiences of the object, especially the perceptions, will display a certain *coherence*, an agreement or consistency along certain lines which (if the object has been experienced before) has already been exhibited in the past course of the experiences of the object.[92]

It can be said that this projection of coherence provides the criterion for the rationality of the doxic positing of the object. In so far as the ongoing synthesis of perceptual experience of the object exhibits the requisite coherence, this belief will continue to be "motivated," "fulfilled," and "strengthened,"[93] and, in the opposite case, it will be annulled. In this respect, the synthesis correlative to the object can be considered to be a "verifying synthesis," one guided by a "norm of verification," i.e., a rule which prescribes the specific nature of the coherence which is projected and which must be displayed if the intentional object is to be and continue to be experienced as something actual.[94] I will call the process by means of which such norms of verification inherent in our perceptual consciousness of the world originate, and by means of which world-experience functions (or does not function) in conformity with these norms, the process of the "verifying-constitution" of the world. I take this to be what Husserl means by the "more pregnant concept of constitution" in the case of perceptual experience. Accordingly, I understand the problem of "reason and reality" as it manifests itself at this level of experience to be: 1) the general task of determining what a norm of verification as such is, and of analyzing and describing those functions of consciousness by virtue of which perceptual experience can proceed (or not proceed) in conformity with such norms; and 2) the concrete task of identifying and describing the norms of verification that are actually operative in our world-consciousness, of accounting for their origin, and of describing in each case the sorts of experiences which are and would be in conformity with them so that there is and continues to be an actual world for us.[95]

It is important to realize that the norms of verification discussed here are rules which prescribe what the perceptions of an object must be like in order for that object to be and continue to be experienced as something *actual*. They are not rules which prescribe what perception must be like if an object is to be and continue to be experienced to be *itself present*. We have seen before that, although there are times when, as a matter of psychological fact, the cancellation of the self-presence of an intentional object leads to the cancellation of that object's actuality (the case of empirical illusion in connection with an unfamiliar object), these two issues are distinct in principle, and the one need not necessarily lead to the other. This was clear in the case of the hallucination of a familiar object. The norms of verification we are discussing would be, for instance, rules which prescribe what experience must be like in order for the familiar object itself to be and continue to be experienced to be actual. Conformity on the part of ongoing world-experience to the rules discussed here is what makes empirical illusion (illusion concerning self-presence) possible. It is what constitutes a world in which there are certain particular objects or kinds of objects so that experiences of them as themselves present *can be* illusory. It establishes their being-on-hand as such, so that their being right before me can be completely unquestioned state of affairs.

Verifying-constitution has been discussed thus far in connection with the actuality of *particular* intentional objects. Husserl's concrete investigations in this area, guided by his interest in grounding the sciences, have been concerned more with the actuality of object-senses which qualify intentional objects. Thus, instead of investigating the norm of verification which prescribes what experience must be like in order for some particular person to be and continue to be actual for him, say Martin Heidegger, Husserl investigates the norm which prescribes experiences pertaining to the sense "other ego" (or "someone else"). Even more than this, Husserl was concerned with whole strata of sense which qualify the world. His investigations into the constitution of the sense "other ego" as a valid sense was only one part of a wider investigation which attempts to show how the world in general is and continues to be valid for each of us as an *objective* world, i.e., a world which is valid not just for a single ego, but for a plurality of egos, each of which has its own perspective on that world.[96] This study, in turn, contributes to the phenomenological foundations of objective science, of a science like physics which claims to discover truths concerning just such an intersubjectively objective world, and of a science like psychology which, among other things, claims to disclose the processes which operate to shape individual perceptions of "the world."

If we take questions concerning processes involved in constituting valid object-senses into account, questions posed for intentional analysis can be put in the following form: What must consciousness be like in order for there to be a world in which there is (or are)_____? The blank space is to be filled in with the names (or equivalent designations) of individual objects, kinds of objects (of any level of generality, formal or material), properties of objects, etc. An example of such a question is: What must consciousness be like in order for there to be a world in which there are people of two genders, specifically, men and women?[97] Another is: What must consciousness be like in order for there to be a world in which there are "other egos?"[98]

Husserl devotes many analyses to the latter question. One of these, in *Cartesian Meditations,* is a particularly good example to use in order to convey a more concrete idea of what an intentional analysis is like which seeks to display a verifying-constitution. The overall analysis seeks to "discover in what intentionalities, syntheses, motivations, the sense 'other ego' becomes fashioned in me and, under the title, harmonious experience of someone else, becomes verified as existing and even as itself there in its own manner."[99] We will focus on one aspect of Husserl's analysis, namely that part in which he tries to show how a physical body *(Körper)* comes to be experienced as the animate organism

*(Leib)* of another (ultimately human) ego, i.e., how the sense "animate organism of another ego" is constituted and verified as a sense which actually pertains to objects in the world.

The first step in the constitutive analysis is to describe how a sense is fashioned as a sense of an intuitive experience (all other modes of experience being considered as epistemically derivative). This includes describing the sort of experiential situation within which the sense is constituted and analyzing the intentional process which achieves that constitution. This step can be first carried out as a static analysis and then supplemented by a genetic analysis. A static analysis starts with the intentionality constituting objects having the sense as an already formed intentionality. It proceeds by abstractively isolating those moments (if there are any) within the overall intentionality which are constitutionally prior to the moments which are correlated with the sense proper and which serve as a foundation for the constitution of the sense. The specific contribution of these founding moments to the overall intentionality is determined. Then, the manner in which the founded intentionality functions in ongoing experience on the basis of this founding intentionality is described. Finally, the nature of the founded moment is analyzed along with its constitutive effect on the overall intentionality.[100] In *Cartesian Meditations,* Husserl's analysis of the founding level begins by assuming that the sense "animate organism" has already been constituted, but as a sense pertaining only to one's own body.[101] The experience of a body as one's own animate organism is in principle different from that of experiencing another body as the animate organism of another ego because the inward consciousness of "governing" or being able to govern that body is not available to one as an original experience, as it is in the case of one's own body. This is not a deficiency in our experience of another, rather it is a crucial item in the constitution of the otherness of the other. Thus, in the constituting situation, another body becomes perceptually apprehended as being psychically "governed from within," a body which somehow "invites" (motivates) and "accepts" that apprehension, but the apprehension must be through an intention which in principle precludes an original experience of that governance from within.[102] How this can happen is the problem for the constitutive analysis to solve.

According to Husserl's analysis, the apprehension takes place by means of a form of "passive synthesis of association," namely "pairing," in which there is a transfer of the sense "animate organism" from one's own to another body which appears in one's field of perception and which is experienced to be "similar" to one's own.[103] However, since the experience must come about in such a way that the other body is originally perceived to *manifest* an inward governing which is itself intended as something incapable of being originally experienced except by the other, the inward governing is to remain always ap-presented or co-presentified. The further details of this process need not con-cern us here, for it is in the second step of the constitutive analysis where the issue of verification comes to the fore.

One remark does need to be added, however. The static analysis sketched above explicates an intentionality which originated at some point in a con-scious life, a point where the sense was primally instituted. Although it may be the case that the primal institution of a sense takes place in connection with one particular object, a "world in which there are objects having that sense" has al-ready become constituted in the primal situation. The primal institution sets down a habituality, a disposition not just to experience that first object on each subsequent occasion as having the sense, but to so experience any object similar to that object. The habituality is a *way* of being conscious of objects. It is no more specific to one object than is the ability to drive an automobile specif-ic to the vehicle with which one learned to drive. The sense has a tendency to be transferred to other objects. Thus, even if only one object has actually been ex-perienced as having the sense, we may say that the sense already determines the one object to have a certain typicality which is the noematic correlate of the tendency of the sense to be transferred.[104] The intentionality which the static analysis is concerned with, then, is this *way* of being conscious. The static anal-ysis seeks to disclose that manner of intentionality through which we have, in ongoing experience, a world in which there are objects having a certain sense.

The intending of a worldly object to have any given object-sense always con-tains moments of appresentation (co-presentification). As a "spatial" object, for example, there are co-presentations through which its "other sides" are there for me. In the case of most object-senses, the appresentations point to-ward their possible fulfillment through original self-presenting experiences (perceptions). "Every experience," Husserl notes, "points to further experi-ences that would fulfill and verify the appresented horizons, which include, in the form of non-intuitive anticipations, potentially verifiable syntheses of harmonious further experience."[105] In our example, however, the appresented inward governing cannot become itself lived through, i.e., originally made conscious in inner time-consciousness. So, the fulfilling experiences are new apperceptions that proceed harmoniously and which arise in connection with harmoniously proceeding perceptions in which outward manifestations of an appresented governance are originally given.[106]

The continued being-on-hand of objects having a certain sense depends upon experience being and continuing to be harmonious along certain lines. These "certain lines" are those prescribed by the norm (or norms) of verifica-tion for that sense, a norm which is inherent in the intentionality which constitutes the sense. The disclosure of this norm is the second stage of the analysis of a verifying-constitution. For our example, Husserl gives the following "suggestive clue." "The experienced animate organism of another continues to prove itself as actually and animate organism, solely in its changing but incessantly *harmonious 'behavior'*. Such *harmonious* behavior (as having a physical side that indicates something psychic appresentatively) must present itself fulfillingly in original experience, and do so throughout the continuous change in behavior from phase to phase. The organism becomes experienced as a pseudo-organism, precisely if there is something discordant about its behavior."[107] An "organismal conduct" must be displayed. This involves "the understanding of the members as hands groping or functioning in pushing, as feet functioning in walking, as eyes functioning in seeing, and so forth."[108]

Husserl does not give us much beyond these "suggestive clues" in *Cartesian Meditations*. Such details are not our concern anyway. What we must do is correctly grasp what the *kind* of analysis which Husserl indicates seeks to achieve. The issue which the analysis addresses is not that of how a certain sort of object which is experienced to be itself-present is confirmed as indeed being itself-present. In our example, the analysis does not seek to disclose the experiential conditions under which the intending of an animate organism of another ego to be itself-present is validated. As we saw before, this issue presupposes that the intending of objects having a certain sense as such, here "animate organisms of other egos," is a valid mode of intending for us. But it is just this latter validity which an analysis of a verifying-constitution addresses. Let us first see how these issues are distinct in the case of our example. Then it will be shown that the analysis which Husserl indicates concerns disclosing the norm of verification for the object-sense itself, and not simply for the self-presence of objects having that object-sense.

One way of seeking a norm of verification is to analyze the experiential conditions under which the norm is violated and the experience of illusion arises. Such a procedure would disclose the boundaries which define the "certain ways" in which experience must be harmonious in order for a certain phenomenon to remain valid. In the case of the self-presence phenomenon, two kinds of illusion are relevant to our present concern, empirical illusion, as it was defined earlier, and the related illusion of "misapprehension." Seeing what turns out to actually be a wax figure as a human being (i.e., as the animate organism of another ego) is an example of the latter, and hallucinating a person is an example of the former. In both cases, as pointed out before, the *illusoriness* of such experiences is possible only because of the unquestionedness of intending something as the "animate organism of another ego," i.e., only on the basis of that way of experiencing something being a valid mode of intending. Although it may be that the cancellation of the phenomenon of the self-presence of what was intended involves discordance along certain lines of anticipation which are determined by the nature of the sense intended, it is perfectly obvious that such cancellation poses no challenge to the validity of the sense itself.

Nonetheless, it might be thought that an analysis of such illusions does contribute to the showing of the verifying-constitution of the sense. In particular, it might be thought that the norm of verification for the self-presence of an object having a certain sense is the only norm of verification pertaining to the sense, and that the cancellation of the sense itself comes about through repeated frustration, from any given point in a life time onward, of all intentions embodying that norm. In other words, if, from any point onward, all intendings of objects as having the sense turn out to be either empirical illusions or misapprehensions, the sense itself would become invalidated. But suppose, starting now, all my intendings of animate organisms of other egos to be themselves present turn out to be *these sorts* of illusions. Should this mean to me that there is not and never was a world in which there are such objects? Would this undo the work of primal institution and the effect of whatever validation had already occured? Or would it rather lead to a new constitution, namely of myself as having gone "insane," of no longer having an experiencing function which provides me with access to what is, in itself, still there as part of reality? It seems to me that this is what probably would, in fact, happen, but even if it did not happen, it is what ought to happen on the basis of the evidence of such experiences. Thus I believe that norms of verification for senses themselves, if there are such norms, are different from norms concerning self-presence. I will discuss my reasons for thinking this in the next chapter, since they concern the issue of transcendental illusion.

Let us return to Husserl's analysis in *Cartesian Meditations*. Does this analysis concern the self-presence of an animate organism of another ego? I do not believe this would be a correct interpretation of what Husserl says there. He writes: "The experienced animate organism of another continues to prove itself as actually an animate organism, solely in its changing but incessantly *harmonious 'behavior'*....The organism becomes experienced as a pseudo-organism, precisely if there is something discordant about its behavior."[109] Should we take this to mean that the experienced self-presence of an animate organism of another continues to prove to actually be the self-presence of the animate organism of another..., as opposed to being an empirical illusion or the result of a misapprehension...? I think we should not. One clue to the incorrectness of this interpretation is the word "pseudo-organism." When we misapprehend an object to be a person, and then discover the eror, we do not then experience an "pseudo-organism." We experience a wax figure, a bush moving in the breeze, etc. Nor do we perceive a pseudo-organism when a hallucination of a person is uncovered. We either perceive nothing to be there or we perceive a phantasm. As I interpret what Husserl means, a pseudo-organism would be something actual, not a phantasm. But unlike the actualities which are experienced when misapprehension in the usual sense is corrected, a pseudo-organism would be an object which *actually does* have characteristics and display "behavior" similar to my own body. These characteristics and this behavior *are* sufficiently similar to my own to initially motivate the apprehension "animate organism of another ego." However, even as it continues to be experienced to be similar to my body in these ways which initially motivate the apprehension, at some point it begins to display *other* behavior or reveal other characteristics which are inconsistent with the norm of verification embodied in the apprehension. It is precisely in its continuing to display behavior which is in some respects consistent and in others inconsistent with the norm of verification that the object becomes experienced as a pseudo-organism. A wax figure is either misperceived as a person or is correctly perceived as a wax figure; it does not become perceived as something "in between." In general, when such a misapprehension changes into a correct perception, the very similarity to our own body which was initially perceived and *as* it was initially perceived is no longer given, showing that the perceived similarity itself was part of the misapprehension. (Of course we may subsequently perceive the basis for that part of the misapprehension, such as the skin-like looking wax.) But a pseudo-organism would continue to display that initial similarity, and it is this which contributes to its "pseudo" character. A pseudo-organism is an object which probably none of us has ever experienced. It is for us a phantasy-possibility which can aid us in explicating the boundaries which define the norm of verification for the sense "animate organism of another ego."

There is another possible interpretation of Husserl's remarks which I believe is also incorrect. While granting that Husserl is not referring to empirical illusion or misapprehension in the usual sense, but to some very unusual experience of something at first experienced to be the animate organism of another ego and then to be a pseudo-organism, this interpretation would then go on to maintain that Husserl is merely expanding the set of possible ways in which an intended "animate organism of another ego" may turn out not to be itself present, or, more radically, suggesting how some *particular* object, which may have been experienced by us for a long time as "someone else," say an old friend, may turn out not to be "someone else" after all, but to be, in reality, some sort of robot. In either case, in this interpretation the uncovering of the "misapprehension" would not affect the validity of the sense "animate organism of another ego" itself. This interpretation can be shown to be incorrect by considering the context of Husserl's discussion, which is the constitution of the *sense* "animate organism of another ego." The problem which he addresses in the passage about the pseudo-organism is "the difficult problem of making it understandable *that such an apperception* [namely of something as the animate organism of another ego] *is possible* and need not be annulled forthwith."[110] The problem is to explain how an apperception *of this sort* can succeed. It concerns the validity of a *way* of experiencing objects and not how, given that it is a valid way of intending objects, it proves to be a correct intention on some occasion or with respect to some particular object. The exploration of the pseudo-organism possibility, then, aims to reveal how a certain type of experience may prove to be illusory such that there is no longer a world for us in which there are animate organisms of other egos. This inquiry, in turn, is to reveal how this does not happen, and thus, how the type of experience succeeds in being the valid type of experience which it is. In a world in which the sense "animate organism of another ego" is no longer valid, there could be no empirical illusions or misapprehensions in connection with that sense, for the grounds of the acceptance which makes possible the illusoriness of such illusions would no longer be operative. The investigation of such grounds of acceptance is the task of transcendental phenomenology. To explore the pseudo-organism possibility is to explore a possible transcendental illusion. It is such exploration which Husserl has in mind, I believe, when he says "for a phenomenology of 'true reality' the phenomenology of 'vain illusion' is wholly indispensable."[111]

This completes the discussion of the third part of the schema of Husserl's "introductions to phenomenology," the part I have entitled "The Entry into the Transcendental Realm." It also completes the discussion of the schema as a whole. Before entering upon the critical phase of this work, which will begin with a discussion of transcendental illusion, I will bring together the results obtained thus far as they bear on the question of the intended accomplishment of Husserl's "introductions."

## C. SUMMARY

An examination of certain works that Husserl designated as "introductions to phenomenology" reveals a line of thought running through them all which I have called the "schema of Husserl's introductions to phenomenology." Since each of Husserl's "introductions" emphasizes certain parts of the schema over others, I have attempted to fill out the schema by drawing from them all, adding supplementary clarifications from other works wherever necessary. In this way I have composed one "introduction to phenomenology" which is more logically complete than any single "introduction" which Husserl offered us.

The first part of the schema, entitled "Motivating Problem" sets out the problem which Husserl wished to solve with his phenomenology: the problem of how knowledge, especially scientific knowledge, is possible. The second part, called "Acquiring the Idea of Pure Transcendental Consciousness," seeks to establish and define a conception of consciousness whereby consciousness becomes the domain of research for the solution to the problem of cognition. I have called this the "world-constitutive" conception of consciousness. The third part of the schema, "The Entry into the Transcendental Realm," explains the phenomenological methods which are to be used in solving the problem of cognition. These are chiefly the method for gaining intuitive access to the domain of research, the phenomenological reduction, and the method for actually doing the research, constitutive intentional analysis.

I have given the second part of the schema the most extensive treatment. I did so because it contains certain ideas which are central to the manner in which Husserl formulates the problem of cognition as a problem of consciousness, ideas which condition the character of the solution and the nature of the methods to be used to arrive at it. These ideas are presented as part of an argument in which Husserl attempts to convince us that consciousness constitutes the world. I have called this group of ideas the "coherence-thesis."

Husserl's argument aims to prove that it is through consciousness, especially perceptual consciousness, that there is a world on hand in the first place, a world that can then be theoretically known through scientific inquiry. In the coherence-thesis, Husserl asserts that perceptual consciousness embodies a cognitive claim, a *belief* that the world is and is so, a claim which could prove to be specious. As a consequence of this, the "general thesis of the natural attitude," which is based on the thesis of perception, but which pervades all forms of consciousness of the world including scientific cognition, is determined to be a doxic thesis in the mode of presumptive certainty. This means that cognitive claims proper to scientific endeavor presuppose this more fundamental cognitive claim. A basic task of a phenomenology of cognition, then, is to investigate how consciousness functions to manifest and maintain this fundamental claim. At the first level of analysis, this is the task of disclosing how perceptual consciousness functions to doxically posit and maintain in validity a world and a world which is so. In accordance with this specification of the task, the method of constitutive intentional analysis is designed to be one which displays what I have called "verifying-constitutions." Also in accordance with the task so specified, the "transcendental phenomenological reduction," taken as the general idea of a method for gaining intuitive access to the world-constituting function of consciousness, is specified as a transcendental phenomenological epoche, which is a means for intuitively grasping consciousness as bearing a claim to have a world.

The interpretation of Husserl's "introductions to phenomenology" which is presented here locates their central "accomplishment" in the pre-transcendental analyses and the argument they support which together attempt to demonstrate *that* consciousness is world-constitutive. However, the interpretation shows that this central accomplishment itself is not merely the "fact" *that* consciousness constitutes the world, but is more decisively the establishment of the "fact" that the basic modality of world-constitutive consciousness is belief. Thus, upon being "introduced" to phenomenology in this manner, we get the impression that Husserl wishes us to believe that these two matters are settled and are not themselves issues *to be* resolved by concrete phenomenological analysis. We are to believe that the issue of "that" is distinct from the issue of "how," and we are to take the concrete analyses only as ways of showing *how* consciousness is world-constitutive, *how* it posits and maintains in validity a world. Furthermore, we are led to believe that the method of epoche and the method of constitutive intentional analysis are distinct methods and that what they aim to disclose is secured in advance as something which is there prior to and independently of their operation. Because it has already been established that world-consciousness is a belief, the epoche is not to be taken as a merely interpretive method about which one could wonder, when beginning to employ it, whether we will truly grasp what is there. Rather, we are to be assured that when it brings us to focus on world-consciousness as a claim, we precisely *intuit* something which is already there in itself and *disclose* it. We are taught that, at least in principle, the epoche can be fully operative at the start of phenomenological inquiry. The constitutive intentional analyses which we subsequently pursue are done *under* the epoche and are not themselves means for bringing about this epoche. What these analyses are to find is likewise known in advance to be there independently of the method, namely, norms of verification for objects, object-senses, and, in general, the world. These analyses only *reveal* these norms and the functions of consciousness which otherwise operate anonymously in accordance with them to "prove" a world. But whether we can indeed be confident about all of this depends on the soundness of Husserl's argument, on the truth of the coherence-thesis, and, most importantly (since the fate of these depend on it), on whether or not the permanent possibility of transcendental illusion can be shown *prior to* the commencement of transcendental phenomenological inquiry. We turn to this latter issue now.

## NOTES

1. In each of Husserl's "introductions," there is a transition from pre-transcendental to transcendental considerations, a transition made through a discussion of the epoche and reduction. In *Ideas*, this transition occurs at section 50, and in *Cartesian Meditations* at section 8. In *Crisis*, the transition begins with section 35. In *Formal and Transcendental Logic*, the transition is not made with an explicit discussion of the epoche and reduction, but with a critique of the insufficientcy of Descartes' "reduction" as a way into transcendental philosophy. Husserl's own concept of reduction is not mentioned by name, but it is implicit in his whole discussion. See *FTL*, sections 93-100.

2. *Ideas*, section 50, pp. 154-55; *CM*,pp. 20-21 and section 15; *Crisis*, section 39, p. 148 and section 41, pp. 151-52.

3. See the discussion between Spiegelberg and Bossert on this issue in the *Journal of the British Society for Phenomenology:* Herbert Spiegelberg, "Is the Reduction Necessary for Phenomenology? Husserl's and Phänder's Replies," 4 (1973): 3-15; Philip Bossert, "The Sense of 'Epoche' and 'Reduction' in Husserl's Philosophy," 5 (1974): 243-55; Herbert Spiegelberg, " 'Epoche' without Reduction: Some Replies to My Critics," 5 (1974): 256-61. See also Richard Schmitt, "Husserl's Transcendental-Phenomenological Reduction," *Philosophy and Phenomenological Research,"* 20 (1959-60): 238-45.

4. *Crisis*, pp. 152-53.

5. Ibid.

6. *CM*, p. 21.

7. Husserl's "reduction" can be compared to Plato's "recollection." Both are the means of being "led back" to the ground of what exists.

8. *Ideas,* section 109, p. 306.

9. Ibid.

10. Ibid., p. 307.

11. Ibid., sections 38, 45, 77 and 78.

12. Ibid., section 77, p. 216.

13. Ibid., section 38, pp. 123-24.

14. See ibid., section 31 and *CM,* section 15.

15. *Ideas,* section 50, p. 155.

16. On this "participating," see *EP* II, p. 91.

17. See Ibid., p 93.

18. On this "claim" character, see *CM,* section 8, pp. 18-19.

19. *Ideas,* section 31, p. 109.

20. Ibid.

21. See above, p. 1 and chapter 3, n. 16.

22. See *CM,* p. 35.

23. See *Ideas,* section 32, pp. 110-11.

24. See p. 83 above.

25. The epoche, of course, is not only applied to perceptions, but to all experiences which derive their positionality from it. See *Ideas,* section 90, p. 264.

26. Above, p. 83

27. For some attempts to grasp what Husserl means by the "psychological phenomenological epoche," see Aron Gurwitsch, "Edmund Husserl's Conception of Phenomenological Psychology," in his *Phenomenology and the Theory of Science,* pp. 77-112; and Joseph

Kockelmans, "Phenomenologico-psychological and Transcendental Reductions in Husserl's 'Crisis'," in *Analecta Husserliana*, 2: 78-89. For Husserl's presentations, see *PP*, especially "Der Encyclopaedia Britannica Artikel" (pp. 237-301), and the "Amsterdamer Vorträge" (pp. 302-49) therein, and part IIIB of *Crisis*.

28. *Crisis*, p. 151.
29. Ibid,. p. 102.
30. See p. 49 above. Husserl sometimes expresses this by saying that the world is an "immanent transcendence," i.e., it is "intentionally immanent," but "really (*reell*) transcendent." See Boehm's essay "Immanenz und Transzendenz," in his book *Vom Gesichtspunkt der Phänomenologie*. Boehm explains how the phenomenological reduction gives new meaning to the concepts of immanence and transcendence so that expressions like "immanent transcendence" can be meaningfully formed.
31. See pp. 55-60 above.
32. See *Ideas*, section 133, p. 369. The English translation renders *"Materie"* (matter) "ideal content." See *Ideen* I, p. 324.
33. Husserl seems to say that the epoche was implicitly operative in the *Logical Investigations* on p. 243 of *Crisis*.
34. See *Ideas*, section 129, p. 362.
35. See pp. 56-57 and p. 104 above.
36. Above, pp. 60-61.
37. See *Ideas*, section 143, p. 397.
38. See our appraisal of "matter" above, pp. 123-26. See also p. 10 above in this connection.
39. Above, pp. 6, 47.
40. *Ideas*, section 129, p. 362 – translation slightly altered, see *Ideen* I, p. 317.
41. *Ideas*, section 129, p. 363 and section 131.
42. Ibid., section 129, p. 363.
43. Ibid., p. 361.
44. *APS*, p. 4.
45. Ibid., p. 5. See also *Ideas*, section 131.
46. *APS*, p. 20. Cf. *Ideas*, section 143, p. 397.
47. *APS*, p. 21.
48. Ibid.
49. *CM*, pp. 61-62.
50. *CM*, p. 62 – Husserl's emphasis omitted.
51. On the concept of synthesis of identification, see *LI*, pp. 694-97, 790; *CM*, pp. 41-42.
52. See *APS*, pp. 7-8; *CM*,p. 68; *EJ*, section 24. As meant here, the process of "taking cognizance" consists of certain functions of consciousness which operate at a "prepredicative" level of experience. As such, it includes ego activities such as turning towards, contemplating and explicating an object, but does not include "higher level" acts, such as predicative judging. At the prepredicative level, objects are "prepared" for the higher level acts (see *EJ*, p. 61, section 8, and the whole of part I). It must not be thought that the prepredicative and the predicative functions are necessarily separate from one another, especially not in time. Rather, they may be intertwined in willful cognitive striving (see *EJ*, pp. 203-4).
53. *CM*, p. 60; *APS*, p. 8.
54. *EJ*, p. 122.
55. *EJ*, pp. 122-23. The idea of *habitus* is to be understood in direct analogy with "habit" in the usual sense, i.e., a tendency which is established by an act and which becomes operative in

circumstances similar to the one in which it was established without requiring explicit recall of the instituting act.

56. Ibid. See also *CM*, pp. 66-68 and section 38.
57. *APS*, p. 12.
58. Above, p. 126.
59. *CM*, pp. 45-46.
60. Ibid., p. 63.
61. Ibid. Husserl usually maintains that material things have the sense of being indefinitely determinable (see *Ideas*, section 143, p. 397 and section 149, pp. 414-15, and *EJ*, p. 32). However in a note on section 143 of *Ideen* I (Beilage XXVIII, p. 417, written in 1914) Husserl wonders whether a perception of a thing is conceivable in which the thing is intended in a completely determinate way, where no possibilities of further determination are left open.
62. *CM*, p. 41.
63. See ibid., sections 19 and 20; *Ding und Raum*, p. 31.
64. See *CM*, pp. 44-45.
65. *Ideas*, section 144, p. 398 and section 149, p. 414; *CM*, section 27 and 28; *FTL*, p. 233; *EJ*, pp. 34-35.
66. *CM*, p. 47.
67. Ibid., p. 48.
68. *IP*, p. 26.
69. See Kern, *Husserl und Kant*, pp. 350-53, and pp. 279-80; *FTL*, pp. 246, 250, 314-19; *CM*, pp. 76-77, 106; *APS*, p. 345.
70. *CM*, pp. 47-54, 76; *Ideas*, section 149.
71. See *CM*, section 22 and *APS*, p. 6.
72. See *CM*, section 21; *Ideas*, sections 150-52; *FTL*, p. 245.
73. See *Ideas*, section 149; *CM*, pp. 52-54 and section 29.
74. *FTL*, p. 246 — some of Husserl's emphasis omitted.
75. Ibid. See also *CM*, section 59.
76. Above, p. 27.
77. Quoted above, p. 19.
78. For an outline of some of the issues involved, see "Statische und Genetische Phänomenologische Methode," in *APS*, pp. 336-45.
79. See *CM*, section 37 and 38; *FTL*, pp. 316-18.
80. *FTL*, p. 250. The expression "object-sense" will be used to denote the generic senses which pertain to individual objects, i.e., to what we have called "objective senses." Husserl sometimes denotes these generic senses with *"gegenständliche Sinn"* (objective sense), for example in the *Husserliana* edition of *CM*, p. 141.
81. *FTL*, p. 317; *CM*, p. 111.
82. *FTL*, p. 317.
83. Ibid. Object-senses, and senses in general, are also acquired from other subjects, either through direct contact with contemporaries or through the mediation of historical-cultural tradition. Here a subject first acquires a sense in a non-original manner, but with the possibility of converting this into an original evidence. Thus an ultimate account of the constitution of the world leads to the problem of intersubjectivity and of world-history (see *Crisis*, Appendix VI, "The Origin of Geometry").
84. *APS*, p. 339.
85. Kern, *Husserl und Kant*, p. 280.

86. See above, p. 48.

87. *CM*, p. 81.

88. *FTL*, p. 250.

89. *Ideas*, section 128, pp. 360-61; section 135, pp. 377-78.

90. *CM*, p. 56. See also *Ideas*, section 128, pp. 360-61 and section 145, pp. 376-77.

91. *FTL*, pp. 251-52. See also pp. 281-82.

92. *CM*, pp. 61-64.

93. *Ding und Raum*, p. 152; *Ideas*, section 136, p. 381 and section 138, pp. 385-86.

94. *APS*, pp. 214-15. See also *Ideas*, section 138, 140 and 145.

95. See *Ideas*, section 144, and section 145, p. 399.

96. See *CM*, p. 92.

97. Husserl indicates this as the constitutional problem of the "sexes" in *Crisis* (p. 188). For an illuminating answer to this question, see Suzanne Kessler and Wendy McKenna, *Gender: An Ethnomethodological Approach* (New York: John Wiley & Sons, 1978).

98. Another question concerning meterial (i.e., substantial, causal) things is dealt with by Husserl in *Ideen* II, sections 15-18.

99. *CM*, p. 90. For other analyses pertaining to the issue of other egos, see Edmund Husserl, *Zur Phänomenologie der Intersubjektivität, Husserliana* XIII, XIV, XI, ed. Iso Kern (The Hague: Martinus Nijhoff, 1973).

100. This is the way Husserl proceeds in *Cartesian* Meditations. As he says, his analysis there is static, not genetic (pp. 106, 121). The founding stratum is abstractively attained through a "reduction to ownness," i.e., the isolation of a stratum of experience which does not contain the constitutive *effects* of the intending of others, although it does contain the intentionality directed to what is other (section 44). Despite whatever questions may be raised about the possibility of this procedure (see pp. 59-60 of Alfred Schutz's "The Problem of Transcendental Intersubjectivity in Husserl," in his *Collected Papers,* vol. 3 [The Hague: Martinus Nijhoff, 1966]), it at least shows that Husserl's analysis is static. If it were genetic, the intentionality directed to what is other would not yet be formed at the *genetically* founding level. A genetic analysis would show how the sense "animate organism of another ego" is "primally instituted," i.e., how it becomes fashioned *for the first time.* In *CM*, Husserl is not describing this; rather, he is analyzing how the sense is continually constituted in the ongoing experience of an ego which already possesses the intentionality in question as a habituality.

101. *CM*, p. 110.

102. *CM*, pp. 110-11. If someone ever came to believe that they were originally experiencing the inward governance of the movements of another body, as we can imagine could occur in certain "abnormal" states of mind, that person would experience the other body as an extension of themselves.

103. *CM*, section 51.

104. See *EJ*, section 26, p. 124.

105. *CM*, p. 114.

106. Ibid.

107. Ibid., p. 114.

108. Ibid., p. 119.

109. Quoted more fully on pp. 174 above.

110. *CM*, pp. 113-14.

111. *Ideas*, section 151, p. 421. See also section 145, pp. 399-400.

## 6. TRANSCENDENTAL ILLUSION

"This world, which I now experience as the present world with a perceptual belief that is continually and doubtlessly being confirmed, and which, on the
basis of harmonious past experience, I experience as the past world with the indubitable empirical belief of memory — this world need not be more than a
transcendental illusion."[1] "In truth, there could be nothing real, no world,
none ever having been or being now, while I nonetheless experience this [world]
with certainty, and completely without doubt."[2] What is the meaning of this
claim? How does Husserl establish the possibility that the world could be a
transcendental illusion? We will consider the question of meaning first.[3]

### A. THE MEANING OF "TRANSCENDENTAL ILLUSION"

The passages quoted above state that the possibility of transcendental illusion
holds for one's present and past experience. Thus Husserl's claim is not that a
world-experience which has been non-illusory up to the present could *become*
illusory at some future time. It is also clear that the possible illusion would not
be that what has always been perceived to be the world is not really the world itself at all, as would be true, for instance, if right now I were to awaken from
"sleep" to find myself in a totally new environment and were to realize that all
of my past life had been some sort of dream and that what I was now perceiving
was the true world. Such an eventuality is contrary to the idea of transcendental illusion, since it would involve a correction in the form of positing something as the true world in place of the non-existing "world."[4] If the world were
a transcendental illusion, this would not mean that what I perceive to be the
world is not the world itself and something else is; rather, it would mean that
there is not and never was a world, despite the fact that the "world itself" is

present to me in perception. As Husserl says, "The possibility is always open that the world, which at this very moment *is* itself given, in fact does not exist."⁵ The "bodily self-givenness [of the world] in principle never excludes its not-being."⁶

If "self-givenness" is taken seriously here, as actual and not just apparent self-givenness, as I think it should, then there seems to be something paradoxical about these statements. How can "existence" be denied to something which appears to be and which indeed is itself given in perception, nothing else being "really" there instead of it? Is not existence precisely established by the actual givenness of something itself in perception? Does not the non-existence of something given perceptually imply that something else is the case instead? Likewise, the illusoriness of transcendental illusion seems incomprehensible, particularly when we attempt to understand it in terms of the type of illusion discussed earlier, the illusion of self-presence, where what appears to be itself present in a perception is not present. But what does it mean to say that the world which is perceived is an illusion if this does not mean that the "world" which is perceived is not the world itself? Similarly, what could constitute the illusoriness of world-experience, if it is not that world-experience fails to give us the world itself, although we think it does?

Transcendental illusion seems to be a fundamentally different *kind* of illusion than any with which we are familiar. Although this point was made earlier,⁷ it needs to be reaffirmed here, since there is a type of illusion which may be mistaken for transcendental illusion and with which we may be familiar, namely, illusions in which the object intended in a perceptual experience is not only not "itself" present, but also turns out not to exist. I will call this type of illusion the "illusion of existence" (or "existence-illusion"). It may be thought that transcendental illusion is simply this kind of illusion, only more comprehensive and lasting, since it concerns the "world" and a lifetime of experience. We will now see that this is not the case, and this will allow us to appreciate even more the novelty of Husserl's idea.

Suppose I perceive a house which, it seems, I have never seen before, and then I discover that I have been hallucinating. I then say, "The house I saw does not exist." If I mean by this that the house which was intended was not, in fact, itself present, then I would be saying that the house-phenomenon which had seemed to fill a portion of space in front of me was not real, since (let us suppose), there was nothing occupying that portion of space, as a veridical, i.e., truly self-giving perception would have shown me. However, let us assume that I was saying more than just this, and meant something which, had it been my own house which I thought I was perceiving, I normally would not have meant, namely, that the house which was intended does not exist. It was noted before that one could be mistaken about the non-existence of the object intended in a hallucination, while being correct about its not being itself present.[8] Indeed, it could be that after a while I remember that some years ago I did see the house which was intended in the hallucination and had forgotten that I did. The house did exist, and as I find out later, still does. Thus, the failure of an object intended in a perception to be itself present is not conclusive evidence of its non-existence, in the case of what seems to be an unfamiliar object, although it is certainly reasonable to believe that the object does not exist on the basis of such evidence. This is because the experience of something as itself present in a perception normally establishes the existence of new objects for us. Thus, if what we take to be our first perception of the object turns out to be an illusion of self-presence, the grounds for the object's existence are withdrawn, and we normally have no reason to continue to think that the object exists.

Illusions of existence are phenomena distinct from illusions of self-presence. Just as there can be an illusion of self-presence which is not an illusion of existence, as we saw in the case of a familiar object, so there can be illusions of existence which do not involve illusion of self-presence. For example, a child may believe and then disbelieve in the existence of the tooth-fairy without ever having perceived it. But although the *illusion* of existence is distinct from the illusion of self-presence, the meaning of "existence" in the existence-illusion refers to *possible* self-presence in perception. We can say, then, that when the child ceases to think that the tooth-fairy exists, he or she in effect comes to believe that there was no such "self" which could have been "itself" present in a perception. Likewise, my belief in the non-existence of the house can be analyzed as meaning that there is no such "self" as that intended in the hallucinatory perception which could have been "itself" present in any perception. To say that there is "no such self" means that there is no object anywhere in the world which satisfies the description of that which was intended.

Let us now examine the case of an illusion of existence in the case of a familiar object, my own house. According to my memory, I have perceived that house on numerous occasions over a period of many years. Indeed, I *lived* in it. Any failure of it to be itself present in a perception which I might now have would certainly not constitute evidence for me that the house does not and never did exist. Although it is extremely difficult for me to imagine myself coming to believe that my house never existed, we will suppose that somehow I do come to that belief. In saying that I have difficulty imagining myself coming to that belief, I do not mean that I have trouble imagining myself believing that my house never existed, as a mere matter of psychological fact, for that is easy. I can imagine having taken a "mind-altering" drug, or having been "brainwashed," and having the experience of believing that the house never existed.

Rather, I mean that I have difficulty imagining what could constitute good *grounds* for the belief. It is this problem which we shall suppose is "somehow" solved. We further suppose that my memories of having "perceived" the house are correct, i.e., that I did have those perceptual experiences at the times I remember having had them.[9]

In believing that my house never "existed," what is it that I believe? As in the case of the unfamiliar house, I believe, in effect, that there was no object in the world satisfying the description of what was intended and which thus could have been itself given in a perception. But there is a factor here which makes the meaning of this more specific than in the case of the unfamiliar object. A certain house, for years, had been *on hand* for me, somehow always there either as present or as available to be present. Such being-on-hand was never established for the unfamiliar object, so that the denial of its existence amounts to the rather general denial of its being "anywhere" in the world. But in the case of my house, and for any familiar object, a belief in its non-existence is not a belief in its not being some indefinite "anywhere," but in the unreality of it as something embedded in a whole nexus of concrete relations, some of them spatial, which constituted its having been on hand. Indeed, the nexus of relations itself comes into question. The illusion of existence in such cases, then, is an illusion concerning the concrete being-on-hand of the object and all that this entails. The disclosure of the illusion would give rise to questions such as the following. Where was I "living" if not "in" my house? What of the events which occured "in" it? Was there something else there each time I perceived my house? Was there empty space there instead of it? And where is the "there" to which these questions refer? Was I indeed "in" that city, "on" that street, where the "house" was supposed to be? Such questions can be answered only in the context of a detailed "story" which would attempt to establish the possibility of the non-existence of my house.[10] The questions pose options whose possible inclusion in such a story cannot be determined in advance of its being worked out. Only this much can be said: a world seemed to exist for me in which ther was such a house, but in reality the world was different. Only a plausible story can tell in what ways it could have been different.

What if the illusion could be expanded into an illusion about the existence of "the world?" In this case, there would have been no "selves" satisfying the descriptions of what was intended in *all* of my worldly-directed intentions, or better, no such objects as those intended would have been truly on hand at all, and the contexts of relations constituing their being-on-hand would have been unreal. Basically, the illusion of the being-on-hand of a world would have been based on the error of accepting the claim of *any* of my perceptual experiences to be self-giving. The distinction which had been made between the self-giving and the non-self-giving perceptions, and correlatively, between reality and illusion within world-experience would prove to have been an erroneous distinction. In a sense, the "natural attitude" would have been an illusion, i.e., if we take its "positing of a world" to be the belief that there are objects on hand which can be given themselves in self-giving perceptions.

Is this what Husserl means by "transcendental illusion?" If it were, Husserl's statement, that the "bodily self-givenness [of the world] in principle never excludes its not-being,"[11] could not be taken to refer to genuine self-givenness, but only to the mere "phenomenon of self-presence."[12] We will turn now to Husserl's description of how transcendental illusion could come about. Then we will see that the world-illusion just discussed is not what Husserl has in mind. If genuine self-givenness is to be preserved, transcendental illusion must involve a different concept of existence than the one just employed.

Basically, there is only one way in which Husserl conceives of the possibility of transcendental illusion becoming realized, namely, as a consequence of the "dissolution" (Auflösung) of the harmonious style of world-perception into a "confusing tumult" (Gewühl) of appearances.[13] The most vivid description of this dissolution is in Ideas:

> It is quite conceivable [denkbar] that it is not only in single instances that experience through conflict dissolves into illusion, and that every illusion does not, as it in fact does, announce a deeper truth, and every conflict, in its place, be precisely what is demanded by more comprehensive interconnections for the harmony of the whole; it is conceivable that experience becomes a swarm of oppositions that cannot be evened out either for us or in themselves, that experience suddenly shows itself obstinately set against the presumption that the things it puts together [ihre Dingsetzungen] should persist harmoniously to the end, and that the connectedness of experience would lack the fixed rule-governed ordering of adumbrations, apprehensions, and appearances—that a world, in short, exists no longer. It might happen that, to a certain extent still, rough unitary formations would be constituted, fleeting concentration centers for intuitions which would be the mere analogues of thing-intuitions, being wholly incapable of constituting self-preserving "realities," unities that endure and "exist in themselves whether perceived or not perceived."[14]

According to this description, the consequence of the dissolution of the harmonious style of world-perception is that there "no longer exists" a world. By its no longer "existing," Husserl seems to mean that the world is no longer on hand. This interpretation is confirmed by Husserl's discussion of transcendental illusion in Erste Philosophie, where he writes that the consequence of the dissolution would be that "there would no longer be things and a world perceptually there for the experiencer, neither as actually experienced nor as ready to be experienced, [i.e.,] as always accessible through a perception which can be freely activated."[15] It is significant that Husserl says here that the world is "no longer" on hand. In none of his discussions of transcendental illusion does Husserl ever say that the experiencer would come to think that the world never really was on hand. Rather, the implication of the phrase "no longer" seems to be quite the opposite. Thus, in contrast to the type of existence-illusion which was discussed before (which will now be called "empirical" existence-illusion), if the world I now experience is a transcendental illusion, the illusoriness of my present world-experience would not consist of my believing that the world is on hand while, in fact, it is not. What then would be the illusion?

One possibility is that the illusion consists of a presumption that the world which *is* on hand will continue to be on hand. This interpretation is suggested by the last passage quoted from *Ideas*, where it is said that experience could suddenly show itself "obstinately set against the presumption that the things it puts together should persist harmoniously to the end."[16] Furthermore, in two other texts Husserl uses the possibility of the dissolution of world-experience precisely to criticize the idea that there must continue to be a world on hand to us.[17] The point of his criticism is to show the "contingency" of the world. "Contingency," in this context, seems to mean two things. On the one hand, the possibility that our experiencing life could continue, even though there ceases to be a world on hand, shows that the "existence" (*Existenz*), or the being-there (*Dasein*) of a world is "contingent on" the temporal course of consciousness proceeding in a certain harmonious way.[18] On the other hand, the world is "contingent" in the sense that there is no necessity that there be a world for us at all. The latter idea is that, since our experiencing life could go on, albeit in a changed form,[19] even though the world ceases to be there for us, we could have had an experiencing life which was different from the one we in fact have had, namely one in which no world was there for us. "All in all," Husserl writes, "the existence and being-so of the world is an irrational fact,"[20] "or rather, the rationality which lies in the actual and possible connections of appearances that makes possible enduring thing- and world-unity, is an irrational fact."[21]

In *Ideas*, conclusions such as these about the contingency of the world form an essential part of what was referred to earlier as the "separating movement" of thought in the psychological sections of the book.[22] These conclusions aim to establish that "no real being [*reales Sein*], none that presents and manifests itself for consciousness through appearances, is necessary for the being of consciousness itself (in the widest sense of a stream of experience [*Erlebnis*])."[23] But they also form part of the "relating movement" mentioned before, and thereby part of Husserl's argument that consciousness is world-constitutive.[24] In this respect, they aim to show that "the world of the transcendent 'res' is entirely dependent on consciousness, and indeed, not on a consciousness which is logically devised, but on an actual one.''[25]

The above interpretation of what constitutes the illusoriness of transcendental illusion is no doubt valid, but it does not extend deeply enough. There is yet another sense to the illusion which seems to be connected with sense just given to it. This concerns the "existential" status of the world which was on hand up to the point of the dissolution. We recall that Husserl says that "this world, which I *now* experience as the present world" and which I remember as the past world, "need not be more than a transcendental illusion," i.e., that "in truth, there could be nothing real, no world, none ever *having been* or being *now*.''[26] This goes beyond merely saying that the being-on-hand of a world is no necessity. The point is not that our experiential life *could have been* different from the way it has been, or could be different in the *future* such that no world is on hand. The being-on-hand of the world is not the issue at all. Rather, the point is that the world which *is* on hand could possibly not have ever "existed."

This seems to be precisely the point of many statements Husserl makes in the context of discussing the possibility of the dissolution of world-experience. For instance, in *Erste Philosophie* he asks, "Is it not already indicated that the presumptive character of outer experience...leaves open for it the permanent possibility that the world, no matter how much it is now given as the experienced world, perhaps does not exist at all?''[27] "Perhaps...I, who am caught up in the harmonious experience of a world and thus live this natural world-life, can imagine [*mir vorstellen*] my experience proceeding such that I would judge on the basis of it that this world does not exist and never has existed — in spite of my harmonious experience.''[28] What is the meaning of the "existence" of the world which is referred to in these statements? What is the relationship of a possible illusion with respect to the presumption that the world will continue to be on hand to a possible illusion concerning the "existence" of the world which is on hand? To answer these questions, we must look at the context within which Husserl raises the possibility of the dissolution of world-experience.

The four texts in which Husserl argues for the possibility of the dissolution of world-experience introduce this issue with a reference to or a discussion of the "corrective style" of world-perception, and they characterize the dissolution as a breakdown of that style.[29] In one of these texts, this style is exemplified as follows:[30] Walking in a fog, one sees a person. However this apprehension does not hold up as perception continues. The harmony of the perceptual process is disturbed by appearances which conflict with the apprehension. Harmony is restored through a new apprehension, and one sees that what is there is a tree stump. In using this to exemplify the corrective style of perception, Husserl's emphasis is not on how apprehensions can fail to be confirmed, i.e., on the possibility of illusion, but on how they always can become *adjusted* so that we can perceive what is truly there. "Correction continually takes place, or at any rate is always possible. Doubt can be resolved, what is correct underlies what has been consciously negated and a new harmony is restored, a unity of throughly confirmed experience containing a unity of unbroken and continually held belief lives on. Correlatively, the world, as it is experienced after each correction, counts as the true world. This truth is and remains forever on the march [*auf dem Marche*]."[31]

The "corrective style" of world-perception manifests itself in a number of ways. There is the correction of misapprehension, as in the above example, as well as the correction of deceptive hallucination. In addition, the way an object or feature of an object is perceived under optimal conditions is said by Husserl to be a "correction" of the way it appears under non-optimal conditions.[32] The correction of intersubjective discrepancies through a comparison of one's own perceptions with those of others is also said to exemplify this style.[33] But regardless of the ways in which our experience can be said to have a corrective style, the operation of a corrective process as such shows that our world-experience contains a presumption, namely, that there is a world "in itself," a world of "true being" which is the ultimate standard against which all mere appearance, error, and illusion are to be measured.[34]

This presupposition can be explicated and thematized in the form of an "Idea" of an "actual and definitively true world."[35] The factual course of our perceptual lives is such that correction always takes place and possibilities always remain open for further correction. The Idea of a definitively true world is the Idea of the world which we perceive as it would be given in an imaginable ideal course of world-perception that would ultimately achieve a final harmony such that no further correction would be required.[36] A reflection on one's factual experience shows that at any stage of one's life perception only gives a "relative truth," i.e., a "perceived world" (*wahrgenommene Welt*) which is only an "approximation" and thus a "mere appearance" of the world as it is in itself.[37] Husserl's statement above that "this truth is and remains forever on the march" refers to a permanent discrepancy between the "perceived world" and the "definitively true world" which our factual experience can never overcome.[38] The Idea of a definitively true world which is implicit in this reflection is itself grasped by imagining one's experiential life proceeding in such a manner that its "perceived world" would continually develop as an ever closer approximation to the world as it is in itself.[39] Husserl seems to be saying that the Idea of a definitively true world would be grasped as the Idea of a perceived world which would be the limit (in a sense analogous to the mathematical sense) of such a process of approximation. The Idea of a definitively true world is the fundamental presupposition of both the physical and human sciences, sciences which attempt to develop methods to at least conceptually determine the world as it is in itself.[40] This presupposition, as such, is not an invention of these sciences, however; rather, it is motivated within the flow of experience itself.[41]

What is this presumption of a "definitively true world?" Clearly, Husserl does not mean it to be the positing of a second, unperceivable reality which underlies the "perceived world."[42] Rather, it is a presumption about the perceived world itself, namely, that it has a complete and determinate "whatness" (*Sosein*), a whatness which has not been and cannot ever be fully brought to appearance as a "perceived world." In the case of a single worldly object, the contrast is between the "object in the How [*Wie*] of determination" (i.e., the object *as* experienced in a perception) and the Idea of the "absolute self" of the object.[43] Husserl refers to the Idea of the absolute self of an object as the Idea of its "individual essence."[44] This is not a second, unperceivable reality, but something which, in its complete actuality, would be gradually approximated by being brought to ever more complete givenness in an ideal perceptual synthesis that is animated by a cognitive, as opposed to a practical, interest.[45] What we grasp of an object, Husserl says, "claims to be its essence; and it is that, but always only an imperfect approximation."[46]

The presumption of a definitively true world, i.e., the presumption that the perceived world is a definitively true world in the form of its approximate sensuous appearance, is the same as what Husserl calls the "thesis of the natural attitude," understood as the positing of the world as "actuality."[47] This positing is the "unity of unbroken and continually held belief" which Husserl refers to above as living on throughout the corrective process of world-experience.[48]

When Husserl says that our consciousness contains the Idea of a definitively true world, he does not offer this as a metaphysical postulate required by his philosophy. Rather, he claims to be explicating the sense of the cognitive dimension of our factual mundane experience.[49] Whatever we come to know or can come to know as part of the world has its being for us as something which possesses a complex, yet determinate whatness, independently of the fact or manner of our consciousness of it. Thus, when, in the process of uncovering an illusion, the conflict of appearances is resolved, or when, upon deeper investigation, the way something merely appears yields to a deeper truth, this does not indicate to us that something has shifted *its* whatness and through itself plays at eluding us or is intrinsically ambiguous; rather, it indicates that our experiencing life generates its own "false being," that mere appearance, illusion and error are "subjective,"[50] and yet our experiencing intrinsically has the capacity to adjust itself, through the correctability of its sense-giving, to what is truly there all along. The Idea of "true being," or of *what* is there in itself emerges in and through a corrective process which understands false being as a "what" which was only for us. Correlatively, we can be said to only become aware of ourselves as *knowing* subjects in that we produce our own false being. If perception never erred, and always gave us actuality, we could not be aware of it as a cognitive function, since perceiving could not then be distinguished from the presence of what is perceived.

The positing of the perceived world as having a true being is sustained by the overall successfulness of the corrective process, whereby, either by bringing to bear the stock of habitual apprehensions or through new creative achievements, a true "what" is thought to be attained, or, at least, the sense of advancing toward some truer "what" is able to be maintained. In everyday experience, the presupposition takes the form of an attitude of taken-for-grantedness which remains so unchallenged by the emergence of illusion that even then it does not become thematized. And this is as it should be, for as we have said before, the illusoriness of the illusions of everyday life presuppose this attitude.[51] But that this attitude might *itself* be an illusion is the very sense of the possibility of transcendental illusion. The meaning of the concept of the "existence" of the world which figures in the idea of transcendental illusion is to be found, then, in the correlate of the natural attitude, i.e., in its presuming that perceived objects and the perceived world in general have a true being, a determinate and complete whatness in themselves. It may be said, then, that for Husserl, "essence" and "existence" cannot be sharply separated.[52]

The possibility of transcendental illusion is the possibility that there is no "definitively true world." If there is not, then the "existence" of the "perceived world," to the extent that the sense of its existence derives from its being the appearance of a definitively true world, is a transcendental illusion.[53] Let us see what this means more concretely by developing further the interpretation of the meaning of transcendental illusion which was put forth earlier, namely the interpretation that the illusion primarily concerns the actuality of "object-senses," as opposed to the actuality of particular intentional objects.[54] In this interpretation the inactuality or "non-existence" of particular worldly objects is a consequence of the inactuality of all generic object-senses which pertain to them, or, equivalently, of the inactuality of all the *kinds* of things that they are.

As a "developed" consciousness, my consciousness has at its disposal numerous habitual ways of perceiving objects. These ways consist of different object-senses which function, on occasions of perception, by means of the sense-giving or apprehending function of perceptual consciousness, to present objects to me. These object-senses correspond to the "whatness" of objects which has just been discussed. When "something" is perceived, a complex intentionality is at play whereby a number of object-senses of various levels of generality come to bear on that something to apprehend it as "what" it is. This apprehension is never epistemically adequate to the complete actuality of worldly objects, although it becomes more adequate as my life of experience progresses.

Each of these habitual ways of perceiving objects has an origin in consciousness. To take one example, there is on hand to me a world in which there are "persons." This can be accounted for in the following way. By means of the object-sense "person," my consciousness gathers together a variety of appearances into a unity such that they become appearances of something identical, a person. This is first achieved through a "primal institution of sense," which is the originally creative process of unification in which the object-sense first arises in consciousness. Through this process, a determinate whatness, "personhood," is attributed to a certain object which is already given to me as having other generic determinations, determinations which point back to other primal institutions of sense. In the primal institution, the whatness is attributed in such a manner as to present me with an object that has "personhood" as an *intrinsic* determination. Accordingly, the intentionality at work has the character of a "transcendent cognition," a consciousness which has come into correspondence with something outside itself. The process of sense-giving lets appear to me something which is there in itself, and makes possible a subsequent being-on-hand to me of a world in which there are persons. In this way, "my world," my "perceived world," comes to better approximate the world as it is in itself.

In addition to forming new object-senses, the process through which "my world" comes to better approximate the world as it is in itself also operates *within* the intentionality related to a new object-sense. This intentionality is complex, containing partial meaning-components which co-determine the total object-sense and thus condition the way in which anything given as having the sense is experienced in perception. Some of these components are anticipatory and go unfulfilled in the course of the initial experience with the object involved in the primal institution. Some of these, in turn, may become fulfilled during the experience of other objects intended to be of the same sort, while others remain only emptily intended. In reference to our example, as experience of persons becomes more varied, some of the partial meanings turn out to only be "contingent," i.e., to only pertain to some of the persons or some of the sorts of persons experienced thus far, and not to be essential to the intending of a person as such. Still other components may become cancelled outright as experience produces counter-evidence as to what can be expected to pertain to persons at all. As well, new meaning-components may enter into the intentionality. These happenings bring about a reorganization, supplementation and refinement of the intentionality containing the object-sense. Thus it can be said that through perceptual experience one comes to "know" better what a person as such is. An ideal course of experience of persons can now be imagined wherein all such corrections have been made and a final harmony is reached. The intentionality would have come into perfect correspondence with the full actuality of personhood. What would be intended at the end of this ideal synthesis would be what was presumed to be there all along in *each* object experienced to be a person—the *determinate* whatness "person" in its complete actuality.

A certain possible counter-evidence has not yet been taken into account. The intentionality of perceiving a person is such as to leave open the possibility that the object-sense itself may be invalid, i.e., that it could become retroactively cancelled. In contrast to the sort of cancellation mentioned above, this invalidation would not bring about a *correction* in the intentionality containing the object-sense, as if the entire sense had been erroneous and required replacement by a new one. It would not be that consciousness had been totally mistaken in the *way* in which it had intended persons, but that it had been mistaken in intending "person" at all. The primal institution of sense would itself become undone and I would no longer perceive persons or have them on hand. This means that the presumption upon which this particular empirical process of correction and ever closer approximation was based, and through which it obtained its very meaning as a corrective process, namely the presumption of a determinate whatness, would become invalidated. The intentionality containing the object-sense would prove to have never been a transcendent cognition, to have never truly served to reveal to me something there is itself. This would entail that all the worldly objects I had perceived as persons, regardless of what they might otherwise validly be, were, as persons, nothing at all in themselves, their personhood having been a mere construction of my consciousness, a mere transcendental illusion.

In its full sense, of course, transcendental illusion concerns the "existence" of the entire world, and not just of an aspect of it. In our interpretation, this means that the illusion concerns the validity of *all* worldly object-senses. However, Husserl assigns a critical foundational role in the constitution of the world to one object-sense, namely "physical thing."[55] For us this means that the invalidation of that object-sense entails the invalidation of all others, and accordingly, we interpret his discussion of the dissolution of world-perception as showing how the invalidation of that object-sense could come about.

Furthermore, transcendental illusion concerns the "existence" of the "perceived world." The "perceived world" is the world which has come to be on hand to each of us by means of the sense-giving function of perceptual consciousness and through other aspects of consciousness that function to maintain a world as present and available. It is called a "perceived" world to contrast it with the "definitively true" world which it is posited as being the sensuous appearance of. If the world is a transcendental illusion, then the perceived world does not "exist" in the sense that it is not the appearance of a definitively true world. Earlier it was stated that transcendental illusion is not the same kind of illusion as empirical illusion; it is not an empirical existence-illusion concerning the "world."[56] Consequently, as was also stated, if the "world" were a transcendental illusion, this would not mean, as it would if transcendental illusion were the same as empirical illusion, that the "world" is not itself given, that it is not on hand, or that the distinction which we make between empirical illusion and reality is an erroneous distinction.[57] It can now be said that these assertions hold of the "perceived world." The "non-existence" of the perceived world, as that is meant in the idea of transcendental illusion, does not affect the validity of those processes of verification which function to distinguish genuine from spurious self-giving perceptions. What it does affect is the status of the "selves" which *are* given in *genuine* self-giving perceptions. Thus, if the world were a transcendental illusion, empirical reality would not become assimilated to empirical illusion; rather, empirical realities would turn out not to be something which only *they,* and not empirical illusions, could possibly be, namely, appearances of "true beings." Let us see how this is so.

Empirical illusions are illusions of self-presence, i.e., illusions in which something intended and believed to be present is not present. An empirical "existence-illusion" concerning a familiar object, where an intended object turns out not to be an object in the world at all, can be understood in terms of the self-presence illusion. It is one where *all* of one's perceptions of the object were illusions of self-presence, and thus where the belief in the object's existence in the world, as motivated by its apparant self-presence, turns out to have been unwarranted. Let us look at one of Husserl's analyses of an illusion of self-presence. His example is that of perceiving an apple tree. "In the natural attitude, the apple tree is something that exists in the transcendent reality of space, and the perception...[is] a psychical state which we enjoy as real human beings. Between the one and the other real being [*Realen*], the real man or the real perception on the one hand, and the real apple tree on the other, there subsist real relations. Now...in certain cases...it may be that the perception is a 'mere hallucination,' and that the perceived, this apple tree that stands there before us, does not exist in 'actual' reality. The real relation which was previously thought of as actually subsisting is now disturbed. Nothing remains but the perception; there is nothing actual there to which it relates."[58]

Husserl's analysis brings out an important point. When we have used the expressions "the self-presence of an object" and the "being-on-hand of an object" we have, of course, meant the self-presence or being-on-hand of an object *to someone,* and particularly, to a human being. A human being, as Husserl reminds us, is also a part of the world. As such, it also is thought to have a "true being," a determinate whatness of its own. I am not simply a consciousness, I am an embodied consciousness, and it is through this relation to a body, according to Husserl's theory, that I am a "real" being, i.e., a being which has a "place in Nature's space and time."[59] Thus, my experiences are states of consciousness of a "real ego-subject," and are real events within the world.[60] Husserl calls such experiences "psychical" (*seelisch*) or "psychological" experiences,[61] to distinguish them from "pure" transcendental experiences. When I am conscious of something as itself-present in a perception, or merely as available in my environment but out of sight, and this consciousness turns out to be illusory, the real relations between myself and the object which constitute the concreteness of the object's being-on-hand are also illusions. In truth, only the psychological state of consciousness was actual, the object and the real relations between myself and it having been "merely intentional." Of course this does not mean that the *sort* of object or the *sorts* of real relations (or the sort "real relation" itself) was an illusion, for, as was indicated before, the actuality of "sorts" is presupposed in the illusoriness of illusory perceptions.[62] If "apple tree" and the relation of "before me," were not accepted by me as valid, I could neither be deceived by the experience of "an apple tree standing there before me," nor uncover the deception.

It can be said, then, that the consciousness of an object to be itself present, or to be on hand in any sense is the consciousness of myself as a real psychic being (an embodied subject in the world) subsisting within concrete real relations with an object, which object is "outside" the immanence of my "mind." Furthermore, this being-in-relation-to-objects, which we have called the "being-on-hand of a world," and which includes the special mode of being-present-to-me, is necessarily a being-on-hand or a being-present to a psychical, i.e., mundane subject. This is so because the relation of the "being-on-hand of a world" is the *same* relation as that of being-in-the-world, only seen from the point of view of the subject as the center of the nexus of the concrete relations involved. The being-on-hand of a room in the concrete sense of its being "around" me, for example, is the same relation as my being "in" the room. The presence of an object to me is the same as my being "before" the object. Thus, the consciousness of something worldly being itself present, or of its being-on-hand in general, whether the consciousness is illusory *or* veridical, necessarily involves a consciousness of oneself as a mundane subject. There can be no self-presence or being-on-hand of a worldly object or world in general to a non-mundane subject.

If the world were a transcendental illusion, this apperception of oneself as a mundane subject would itself be an illusion. This can be seen from Husserl's continuation of his account of the dissolution of the harmonious style of world-perception in *Ideas:*

> Let us suppose that we have been apperceiving in the natural way, but that our appercep-tions have been continually invalid, so that all coherent connections in which empirical unities might take shape have become impossible; in other words, let us imagine [*denken wir uns*] in the spirit of the foregoing exposition that the whole of nature—and the physical in the first instance—has been 'annuled.' There would then be no more bodies [*Leiber*] and therefore no more human beings. I, as a human being, would no longer be, and indeed, there would no longer be any fellow human beings for me. But my consciousness, however its states of experience might vary, would remain an absolute stream of experience with its own distinctive essence.[63]

Husserl continues by saying that a non-embodied and even a non-personal con-sciousness is conceivable, "a stream of experience in which the intentional empirical unities, body, soul, empirical ego-subject do not take shape, in which all these empirical concepts, and therefore that of *experience in the psychologi-cal sense* (as experience of a person, an animal ego), have nothing to support them, and at any rate no validity."[64]

The dissolution of the harmonious style of world-experience would affect the validity of "empirical concepts," such as those mentioned above, and, most importantly, the concept "physical thing." This effect on the validity of *concepts* comes about through a cancellation of the positing of the sheer facticity of the real kinds to which these concepts refer. Such cancellation is just what we have meant by the invalidation of object-senses, for to posit the facticity of real kinds is simply to posit that worldly objects have a determinate whatness in themselves. In that it brings about an *invalidation,* the dissolution of world-perception is not to be understood merely as the *de facto* dissolution of its corrective style because of the inability of the corrective process to achieve results, i.e., to maintain the actual presence of self-identical unities and then to have them as enduring objects available to be perceived as the same. Rather, the dissolution of the corrective process should be understood as the retroactive invalidation of that process as a *cognitive* process, or better, the retroactive invalidation of the presumption from which that process derived its sense as cognitive, namely, the positing of the "true being" which is thought to become known or to be knowable through it. The existance of the *possibility* of this retroactive invalidation proves that this positing is no absolute, uncancellable position;[65] rather, it is a "belief" whose validity is a validity "until further notice."[66] The *realization* of that possibility comes with the actual delivery of the "notice" by a force of counter-evidence which overpowers the merely "inductive" evidence which had maintained the belief. The existence of the world (and we understand by this the "definitively true" world), according to Husserl, is grounded *a posteriori.*[67] Its being is an "acquisition of cognition,"[68] and is the correlate of a belief which requires the sort of confirmation which could maintain the harmonious style of world-perception.[69]

The *possibility* that my own "true being" as a psychological subject may be an illusion shows that my being such to myself does not come about through a transparent apprehension of a sheer fact, but through the sense-giving intentionality of a non-worldly, "transcendental" consciousness. This para-mundane consciousness had mundanized itself through taking on the "natural attitude," that is, through the positing of a definitively true world, a positing which was no mere hypothesis, but which was rationally motivated and legitimated by the style of the flow of its own experience.[70] As affecting the retroactive invalidation discussed above, the *actual occurance* of the dissolution of world-experience would not merely show that my being a psychological subject to myself was a constitutive achievement of a transcendental consciousness, but rather, that my being such to myself was an *illusion,* and it was an illusion I suffered as a *transcendental* ego, which I would still validly be.

It is by being an illusion of a non-mundane consciousness that "transcendental" illusion gets its name. In contrast, "empirical" illusion is so called because it is an illusion of a mundane (or psychological) subject. As is implied by what was said earlier, an illusion of self-presence necessarily presupposes that the subject of the illusion and of its disclosure remains conscious of itself as a being in the world. It can be seen from this that such an illusion concerning the "perceived world" which would entail that nothing exists outside my psychic immanence is impossible in principle. We need only to see how the world's being a transcendental illusion does not entail this impossibility. This will finally allow us to understand how Husserl could say that "the bodily self-givenness [of the world] in principle never excludes its not-being."[71]

To attain this goal, it is sufficient to show how our interpretation gives a meaning to the idea of transcendental illusion which is such that the world could be thought to be a transcendental illusion even if it is *not* thought to be an empirical illusion. It does this by first distinguishing two dimensions of consciousness, one constitutive of the other (following Husserl), and then by assigning to each dimension norms of verification proper to it. The consequence of this is that even if I believe the world is a transcendental illusion, there is a sense in which I can say that I do exist as a mundane being with a perceived world of objects which do exist outside the sphere of my psychic immanence.

A mundane subject, its psychological life, and its world are the constitutive achievements of a more fundamental transcendental life.[72] This constitution is a self-constitution, i.e., the transcendental subject, on the basis of the style of the flow of its own experience, has entered into a state of self-forgetfulness in which it believes itself to be a mundane subject in itself. Consequently, its experiences are apperceived in self-reflection as psychological experiences, and are believed to be that in themselves. The transcendental constitution is subject to norms of verification proper to it. These norms have been called "norms for the verification of object-senses."[73] Should these norms be violated, wordly objects, including the psychological subject itself, would turn out not to have the whatness attributed to them as intrinsic determinations in themselves. *Our* constituted psychological lives, on the other hand, have norms of verification proper only to such lives, although such norms are not necessary to a psychological life as such. This means that given that there is constituted a subject in a world, certain norms of verification *may be,* and, in fact in our case are, implicit in its psychological intending of an "outer" world, namely norms we have called "norms for the self-presence of an object having a given object-sense."[74] These are norms which must be kept to in experience if a particular combination of object-senses within the intentionality of a given perceptual experience is to constitute and continue to constitute an intending of something as actually itself present to the psychological subject. If such norms were not part of a psychological life, the "subject" of that life could not become aware of itself as a "knowing" subject.[75].

These latter norms of verification make it possible for a subject to distinguish genuine from illusory self-giving perceptions. This means that they make it possible for a subject to become aware of some of its perceptual experiences as illusions wherein an object intended to be itself present is not itself present, as well as illusions in which the intended object does not exist in the world at all. It may be possible for a psychological life to be so constituted that all of its perceptual experiences, at least up to some undetermined point, are illusions of self-presence. *If* this were true of our own lives, then in the case of each object I have perceived, let us say, up to now, and for each perceptual encounter of it, courses of experience were realizable by me which were not pursued, but which, if they had been, would have brought forth appearances that would have resulted in a violation of a norm of self-presence and consequently a retroactive cancellation of my belief in the existence of the object in question as a part of empirical reality. What was present to me as the world was not the world itself; it was merely an illusion of self-presence. The disclosure of this illusion would entail a correction, since it occurs through the ascertainment of something else being actually present in place of what was intended to be present. The correction of all previous illusions would institute a new perceived world, which would then be taken to be the self-presence of the world itself. Would this correction have to involve the replacement of the previous *object-senses* with a new set? Clearly at least some of them would have to remain valid if there is to be disclosure and correction of self-presence illusions, for what emerges in the process of correction as correct cannot render something else incorrect without some context of constant validity providing the "issue" about which conflict can occur. Such a context would at least consist of whatever object-senses are necessary for the consciousness of a "perceived world" as such. Whatever object-senses would have to remain valid to provide this context would be a topic for further investigation. Among them would certainly be "psychological subject" and certain object-senses having to do with the constitution of "here" and "now."

In addition to the hypothetical psychological life just discussed, a different one is also possible. It is conceivable that a psychological life becomes constituted in such a way that once experience with particular objects has proceeded far enough and in certain ways, a retroactive cancellation of the existence of such objects is ruled out as a rationally motivated cancellation. This, I would maintain, is true of our own lives, although I do not intend to prove this here. There is a certain point reached in the experience of certain objects which are repeatedly reidentified over time and perceived in "certain ways" (ways which a deeper study would have to specify) beyond which any further perceptions of what is taken to be one of these objects that turn out to be illusions of self-presence would not and should not motivate a retroactive cancellation of the empirical existence of the intended object. Rather, the experience and disclosure of such illusions would (or should) motivate an "identity break," that is, a ceasing to believe that the "object" perceived in the illusory perceptions was in fact the object which was intended.[76] Thus, the repeated disclosure that my perceptions, from this time onward, of an old friend are "hallucinations" would not make me think that my old friend never existed; rather, this would make me believe that I was not perceiving my old friend. It would not make me believe that the world is different than I thought it to be. Rather, it would make me think that there is something wrong with my perceptual functioning.

Let us suppose that our own psychological lives are just of this sort, and that certain objects become constituted and then experienced in such a way that they become immune to retroactive cancellation. Is it still thinkable, without contradiction, that our life and our "empirically real" perceived world is a transcendental illusion? According to our interpretation, this is thinkable. If it were, this would mean that the factual course of our experiencing lives leaves open the possibility of experiences whose actual occurrence would rationally motivate the retroactive invalidation of all object-senses. Whatever these experiences would be like, they would not be such as to bring about the disclosure of empirical existence-illusions, but would be such as to violate an entirely different set of norms than those involved in such illusions.

If it is thinkable that the perceived world is, at least in large measure, empirically real, yet also a transcendental illusion, then it should be possible for a subject to hold these two positions as beliefs without conflict. A moment's reflection will show, however, that this cannot be done if "holding these two positions as beliefs" means having them as "existential beliefs," i.e., not merely as judgements which are transciently entertained in the mind, but as fundamental convictions which pervade and condition all our perceptions. To hold these positions in this way would be to actually withdraw and negate one aspect of the natural attitude, namely the transcendental belief that the perceived world is actual, i.e., has a true being or a determinate whatness in itself, and yet to simultaneously maintain the other aspect of the natural attitude, namely the belief that the perceived world is on hand and is itself present in perception. Our earlier discussion has shown that the latter belief is only possible if the subject experiences itself to be a mundane subject in itself. However, the withdrawal and negation of the transcendental belief would bring it about that the subject no longer has this self-experience.

Although the two positions cannot be held simultaneously as existential beliefs, there is another way in which they can be jointly held. Suppose that the dissolution of the corrective style of my world-perception has taken place and that I become conscious of myself as only validly being a transcendental subject. I "no longer" have a world and "no longer" experience myself to be a mundane subject. I believe that my past life was a transcendental illusion. Suppose also that I can recall my past life with perfect clarity and complete accuracy. I now reflect in memory upon my past experiences to see how the amazing illusion was accomplished. I find that, while I was experiencing myself to be a mundane or psychological subject, I had a "perceived world," a world of objects which "existed" outside of my psychic immanence. At times these objects were themselves present to me in perceptual experiences, and when they were not, they remained on hand to me available to be perceived again as the same. From the perspective of my new attitude, I cannot say that this was not so, and that the experiences reflected upon were *empirical* illusions, although in my survey of my past life I do find instances of such illusory experiences also. Neither can I deny that I was indeed present as a psychological subject to myself in self-reflection, nor that I remained on hand to myself as such through a non-thematic self-awareness. What I do realize now, however, is that the being-on-hand of objects, whether they were actually perceived or not, was not due to any intrinsic "physical thingness" or to anything else which secured for them an enduring through themselves. In truth, these objects had no determinate whatness in themselves of any sort, nor did I, as a psychological subject, have a "true being" which was responsible for my enduring as such. Whatever had been on hand was so only through certain functions of consciousness. A crucial factor in this regard was the "belief" (as I now recognize it to have been) that objects had a "true being," that the object-senses formed in my consciousness gave me access to an intrinsic whatness of perceived things, a belief which I now realize was an illusion. But this realization does not prevent me from affirming that, as a psychological subject, I truly had a perceived "world," a world of "objects" existing outside my "mind." However, "world," a world of "objects," and "mind" were nothing in themselves, they were merely formations constituted within the immanence of my transcendental life which were erroneously constituted as "something in themselves." In truth, my perceptual life was not one of a progressive *discovery* of what "world," "objects," and "minds" were in themselves; rather it was one of a progressive *formation* of a more and more enriched, refined, and harmonious perceived world.

We can now finally understand how Husserl could say that the self-givenness of the world does not exclude its not-being. Even if the world were a transcendental illusion, *while* the transcendental belief is operative I am constituted as a mundane subject with a perceived world. The "objects" formed in my transcendental life do exist outside my psychological immanence and do persist independently of my psychological experiences. They are on hand to my perceptual experiences and, for the most part, are themselves given in those experiences, as is the perceived world in general. That all this is merely a constituted formation of my transcendental life does not make it nothing at all; it is just nothing *in itself*. The perceived world can be empirically real, even if it is a transcendental illusion.

## B. REALISM AND IDEALISM IN HUSSERL'S PHILOSOPHY

At this point a few remarks pertaining to the issue of realism versus idealism in Husserl's philosophy can be made. This is a complex and difficult issue which has generated considerable discussion over the past forty years.[77] Some interpreters of Husserl's philosophy have claimed that it represents a form of realism, while others have maintained that it is idealistic. A third group thinks that it transcends the opposition of realism and idealism and should be interpreted "existentially." In addition to this, we have Husserl's own characterization of this philosophy as a form of idealism.[78] In the remarks below, I wish to indicate how the issue would be understood and dealt with from the point of view of the interpretation I am presenting here.

One way of formulating the issue is to ask where Husserl stood philosophically with respect to the thesis of the natural attitude. Did Husserl endorse the realist thesis of the natural attitude according to which the world "exists" independently of our consciousness or did he not? Within the context of our present discussion, this question becomes: Did Husserl maintain that the world has a determinate whatness in itself (realism) or did he think that this is *merely* an "Idea" posited in consciousness (a form of subjective idealism).[79]

Husserl's position seems to have been that this issue cannot be resolved through philosophical analysis, but only in experience itself. The thesis of the natural attitude only has a "relative" or "empirical apodicticity."[80] This means that while world-experience maintains its harmonious and corrective style, the "existence" of the world cannot be reasonably doubted.[81] The possibility of transcendental illusion shows that the positing of the "existence" of the world, i.e., the positing of the perceived world as having a "true being," is not an absolute, uncancellable position. Of course this does not mean that the positing is erroneous. Upon discovering the existence of this possibility, one cannot say that the "existence" of the world *is* a transcendental illusion, and therefore *merely* constituted in transcendental subjectivity. The issue can only be resolved in experience, and then, only in favor of idealism. This is because Husserl conceives the thesis of the natural attitude as an *inductive* thesis, and thus one which can never be definitively proved. But there can be a decision in favor of idealism, if and when the world should prove to be a transcendental illusion in actual experience.

Since *this* issue of realism versus idealism cannot be resolved through philosophical analysis, Husserl adopts a neutral attitude toward both alternatives, and regards the world as a presumptive actuality. This neutral stance is precisely the neutrality of the transcendental phenomenological epoche. Does Husserl abandon *this* neutrality when he says that "we do not have a world existing in advance, and subsequently a cognition of it (cognition in the widest sense, including experience [*Erfahrung*]),"[82] or when he states that the existence of the world is grounded *a posteriori* and that its being is an acquisition of cognition?[83] Statements such as these express the idealism which Husserl attributes to his philosophy. This idealism is succinctly stated in *Ideas:*

"The whole *spatio-temporal world,* to which man and the human ego attribute themselves as subordinate singular realities, *according to its sense, is merely intentional being,* a being which has the merely secondary, relative sense of a being *for* a consciousness. It is a being which consciousness posits in its experiences which, in principle, is intuitable and determinable only as some thing identical in harmoniously motivated manifolds of appearances — *over and beyond* this, however, it is nothing."[84]

It is quite clear that in statements like these, Husserl does not intend to express an idealism which has the sense of the one discussed above and thereby to abandon the neutrality of the epoche. "Our phenomenological idealism," he says, "does not deny the positive existence of the real world and of nature — in the first place as though it held it to be an illusion."[85] When Husserl states that the world is "merely" intentional being, and that "over and beyond this... it is nothing," he does not mean that the "existence" of the world is "merely" posited in consciousness in the sense that it is an illusion. In what sense, then, is the being of the world "merely" intentional? What is the nature of the idealism which Husserl ascribes to his philosophy, and to what is it opposed?

The nature of Husserl's idealism can be understood in terms of the issue of transcendental illusion. Given the possibility of transcendental illusion, the "existence" of the world for us, in the sense of its having a determinate whatness in itself, can only have the meaning of an "Idea" posited by consciousness, an Idea whose validity is being confirmed or is confirmable in a life of actual or possible experience which progressively "discloses" the world's "true being." Because the validity of the Idea is being confirmed in our actual experience, the world's character of having a true being is not "merely" an Idea in the sense of being an illusion. However, it is "merely" an Idea in contrast to an "absolute being," i.e., one whose existence is apodictically certain and not merely "being confirmed."[86] Thus the word "merely" does not express a metaphysical judgement; it expresses an epistemological judgement. It may be said, then, that Husserl's idealism is an "epistemological" idealism.

The epistemological character of Husserl's idealism becomes apparent when his emandations to the statement of this idealism which was quoted above are taken into consideration. These emandations have been incorporated into Biemel's edition of the text of *Ideen* I. Contrasting the sense of the being of the world with that of the being of consciousness, Husserl writes: "On the other hand, the whole *spatio-temporal world* to which man and the human ego attribute themselves as subordinate singular realities, *according to its sense,* is *merely intentional being,* a being which has the merely secondary, relative sense of a being *for* a consciousness, [as something which is experienceable through appearances by conscious subjects and which is being confirmed, possibly in infinitum, as a confirmed unity of appearances]. It is a being which consciousness posits in its experiences which, in principle, is intuitable and determinable only as something identical in harmoniously motivated manifolds of appearances — over and beyond this, however, it is nothing, [or more precisely, for which an over and beyond is a countersensical thought]."[87]

The countersensical "over and beyond" mentioned here gives a clue to what it would mean for the existence of the world not to be "merely" and idea, and thus to one of the views which Husserl opposes with his idealism. Something "over and beyond" could be an unknowable Kantian "thing-in-itself," and Husserl could be opposing Kantian idealism here as he does elsewhere.[88] However, given the context of Husserl's remarks it is more likely that "over and beyond" refers to an apodictically certain or "absolute" being. To ascribe absolute being to the world as its "being-sense" would be countersensical given Husserl's epistemological analysis and critique of world-experience, especially his "results" concerning the existence of the possibility of transcendental illusion. According to this interpretation, Husserl could be opposing a position which would grant that the "existence" of the world is an "Idea," but would claim that it is not "merely" an Idea. It is not an Idea which is merely "being confirmed;" rather it is an Idea whose positing is uncancellable.[89]

There is also another view which, in a sense, Husserl is opposing with his epistemological idealism, namely, the form of epistemological realism which is represented by the "naive" concept of the relationship of consciousness and world which was discussed earlier as characterizing the natural attitude.[90] According to this view, worldly objects and the world in general are there for us independently of and "in advance" of our consciousness of them, and our perceptual consciousness of an object is a transparent, self-validating experience through which what the object is "in itself" manifests itself to us. Statements of Husserl's like "we do not have a world existing in advance, and subsequently a cognition of it" can be understood as opposing this form of epistemological realism, as the basis for a philosophical theory of cognition. Such statements express Husserl's view that the being-on-hand of the world is the *result* of a cognitive process; it is the changeable sedimentation of sense which is formed and verified in and through consciousness as experience progressively "discloses" the whatness of the world.

Although Husserl finds epistemological realism to be an erroneous position for this theoretical purpose, he seems to have a different view toward it in its role in our non-theoretical, experiential lives. Here, epistemological realism is not so much wrong as it is naive. Yet this naiveté seems necessary for the very constitution of our lives as "everyday lives," and, within the limits of such a life, it finds its validation. In this respect, Husserl's epistemological idealism is not opposed to epistemological realism. Rather, it purports to provide a theoretical basis for understanding how it comes to be. Phenomenology would seek to show how something like "existing in advance" arises as a sense in consciousness and how it is maintained. What seems to be lacking in Husserl's writings in this connection is an account of how the self-forgetfulness of the transcendental subject comes about, i.e., how it becomes naive.

The discovery, through actual experience, that the world is a transcendental illusion would shatter the naiveté of the natural attitude and recall the transcendental subject to its proper self-consciousness. The transcendental epoche, as a means of bringing about the transcendental reduction, is supposed to achieve the same result. However, as discussed earlier, the epoche does not disturb the role of the natural attitude in straight-forward experience.[91] Although the attitude of the epoche is not neutral to the epistemological realism of the natural attitude, it is neutral to its realist thesis concerning the actuality of the world, as it is also to the negation of that position. From the perspective established through the epoche one is able to see how the transcendental constitution is effected, but not as the achievement of an illusion, rather as the achievement of the inductively grounded cognitive acquisition of a perceived world as having a determinate whatness in itself. In this attitude, one views one's psychological being, worldly objects, and the perceived world in general as constituted formations of an intentional life which claims to be a cognitive life, that is, which claims to bring to appearance by means of its sense-giving and sense-verifying functions a definitively true world. The attitude of the epoche is supposed to be rationally motivated by the disclosure of the existence of the possibility of transcendental illusion. But is it? Let us now examine how Husserl establishes the existence of this possibility.

C. HUSSERL'S DEMONSTRATION OF THE EXISTENCE OF THE POSSIBILITY
OF TRANSCENDENTAL ILLUSION

Husserl attempts to establish the existence of the possibility that the world is a transcendental illusion by using the same method which was discussed earlier as a method for establishing the permanent possibility of empirical illusion.[92] In this method, "possibility" is understood as "imaginability," and imaginability is demonstrated by actually imagining the matter in question. That which is claimed to have been imagined is submitted for intersubjective verification through the telling of a "story" which expresses the results of the imagining process in detail. In this way, the private imaginings of the imaginer can be evaluated by others to determine whether what has been imagined is truly that which is claimed to have been imagined, or whether it is not. Husserl's story is that of the "dissolution of the harmonious style of world-perception," one version of which was quoted earlier.[93] The task now is to evaluate the effectiveness of this story.

The claim that the world could be a transcendental illusion concerns the cognitive status of world-experience. The claim is that the experience of the world as having a "true-being," i.e., a determinate whatness in itself, is not an incorrigible experience of an absolute fact. Nor are the particular perceptual experiences which this all-embracing attitude pervades, and which provide its ground, self-validating experiences amounting to the sheer presence to us of the whatness of that which is perceived. Rather, that which is given to us as the world has the epistemic status of an approximation-appearance of a yet to be adequately given true being.

The experience of the perceived world as having a true being is an anticipatory belief, a mode of consciousness whose negation is possible, not just logically, but as an actual experience, and one which is not just an occurrence in consciousness, but which is a correct experience. Although this belief is well-confirmed by the harmonious course of world-perception, in that it validates the sense which consciousness bestows as sense which brings to appearance the intrinsic whatness of the world, the possibility is always open that the belief could be disclosed to be an illusion and become retroactively cancelled on evident grounds. Husserl's story of the dissolution of the harmonious style of world-perception relates how such a disclosure and retroactive cancellation could come about. It is the story of what Husserl calls the "epistemological annihilation" of the world.[94]

The story has me (or any one of us) imagine that my perception of physical things breaks down in such a way that they are no longer on hand to me, neither as actually present nor as available to be perceived. As a consequence of this, I no longer experience the world and I no longer experience myself as being in the world. This breakdown of thing-perception is an epistemic process; it occurs through the systematic absence of any perceptual confirmation of the presence or availability of stable and enduring thing-unities. Thus the significance of this for me, the experiencer undergoing this process, is that the physical things themselves which had formally populated my world and formed my environments persist no longer. The same is true of the former world in general. Furthermore, I realize and come to believe that those things never had the true being which had been attributed to them in my experience of them. This is so because the idea of their true being requires that they should persist indefinitely as objects of actual or possible perception (making allowence, of course, for natural processes of death, decay and annihilation which are not the issue here).[95] I expected the world to last indefinitely. Since it has not, I can no longer believe that it was actual, that it had a true being.

Our perspective in examining Husserl's story is determined by our interest in appraising Husserl's argument that consciousness constitutes the world. We recall that the assertion of the existence of the possibility of transcendental illusion occurs in the fourth proposition of the coherence-thesis, which, in turn, elaborates the second statement of Husserl's argument.[96] The coherence-thesis seeks to satisfy the "reality criterion" which was discussed earlier as one of the two criteria which Husserl's argument must satisfy.[97] We further recall that Husserl's argument plays an important role in the pre-transcendental sections of his "introductions to phenomenology." In this context, the argument aims to convince the reader *that* consciousness is world-constitutive. As such, the argument should be based exclusively on non-transcendental considerations. Thus, in addition to evaluating the effectiveness of Husserl's demonstration of the existence of the possibility of transcendental illusion in general, we will also be concerned with seeing whether this requirement has been satisfied.

There are a number of aspects of Husserl's story which could be examined to appraise its effectiveness. For instance, it could be asked whether there could be a self-conscious subject who remains a self-conscious subject upon the completion of the process of the dissolution of its world-experience, as Husserl presumes,[98] and, if so, whether that remaining subject could identify itself with its former self and remember its former condition, as Husserl also presumes.[99] All this would be required in order for the subject to have the belief that the world had been a transcendental illusion. The ability of a subject to have this belief, in turn, is required by the very meaning of the idea of the possibility of transcendental illusion, for it makes no phenomenological sense to speak of the possibility of an illusion if it is not possible for the subject of the illusion to discover the illusion. Although it may be imaginable that there could exist a self-consious subject who does not have a world, the question of identity here is whether a subject who *does* have one can cease to have one and remain conscious of itself as the same subject. Are a mundane subject and a non-mundane subject compossible within the unity of *one* self-conscious life? This question is similar to the question of whether, presuming one can speak of immortality at all, there can be *personal* immortality after bodily death.[100]

Another possible question concerns the role of thing-perception in Husserl's story. Even presuming that a self-conscious and self-identical subject could endure the dissolution of its perception as Husserl describes it, and that there no longer are physical things on hand to this subject, does this necessarily mean that *nothing* remains for the subject of its former world? Perhaps objective space and time could still remain, and consequently, perhaps the subject could still experience itself as located within that space and time, although without a thing-like body. Perhaps such a subject could still be a psychological subject, one alone in space and time. Is the consciousness of objects *in* space and time necessary for the consciousness of space and time?

One way of answering these questions would be to work out a more detailed version of Husserl's story. The version Husserl gives relies on certain assumptions which need to be made explicit and brought into the story itself, assumptions such as those concerning the constitution of a subject of experience, the constitution of objective space and time, and the role of thing-perception in the experience of the full concrete life-world. Husserl has dealt with these issues in some of his *transcendental* phenomenological investigations. We will soon see that this is no accident, and that an imaginative working out of Husserl's story with respect to these issues amounts to doing constitutive transcendental phenomenological analyses. We will also see that the existence of the possibility of transcendental illusion cannot be established prior to engaging in such analyses, and that such analyses themselves constitute the "story" needed to establish this possibility. This means that there is a certain circularity in Husserl's argument, since the method for establishing one of the premises presupposes its conclusion.

The aspects of Husserl's story which were questioned above will not be discussed any further here. Instead we will focus on the subject's belief that a world of physical things no longer persits. Our question will be whether that belief is *warranted*. This aspect of the story is chosen for examination because Husserl has in effect done so himself in what is called "the objection of insanity" in *Erste Philosophie*. Let us first see how Husserl discusses this problem.

"Certainly the possibility is open that a person's harmonious stream of perception could change into a senseless confusion, into a whurl of appearances. But what does that mean other than that a person, and finally every person, could become insane [*verrückt*]? The possibility of insanity cannot have any bearing on the possibility of the non-existence of the world. On the contrary, we see that precisely in this case we must maintain the world's own, absolutely necessary being. For does not the possibility of the insane already presuppose the existence of the world?"[101]

Husserl finds this to be a weak objection.[102] It assumes that although the perceived world is no longer there for the "insane" subject, it would still be on hand to other subjects.[103] Husserl's reasoning in response to the objection seems to be based on the principle that the ultimate warrant for a subject's beliefs is the evidence of that subject's own experience. Thus, the mediate evidence of the experience of other subjects can count for a subject only if the existence of those other subjects is validated in the subject's own experience. Husserl points out that in the case under consideration just this validation is lacking. He supports this contention by appealing to his theory of the constitution of other subjects.[104] The experience of others is founded on the experience of physical things. But if things are no longer experiencable for a subject, then certain physical bodies cannot be experienced as the animate organisms of other egos. Thus the experiential motive for the continued belief in other subjects would be missing. Others, and their perceived world, would be mere "empty phantasy-possibilities" for the subject, possibilities for which "nothing speaks."[105] With this discussion, Husserl claims that the possibility of the dissolution of world-perception establishes the existence of the possibility of the "absolute non-existence" of the world,[106] and not merely, we can presume him to mean, the possibility of the disappearance of the world to a particular subject.

Although in the main text of *Erste Philosophie* Husserl seems satisfied that he has countered the "objection of insanity," he takes it up again in a manuscript included as an appendix to the volume.[107] This time, the possibility that the world itself may still persist after the dissolution of a subject's world-perception is not based on the assumption that the perceived world may still be on hand to other subjects, but on the possibility that "a world-phenomenon could be constituted again, and in such a way that it connects back with the earlier period of harmonious belief, one and the same world again coming to have a valid status."[108] The intervening period of disharmony would have been an empirical illusion, a period of "insanity."[109] It would have been a disharmony within the factual flow of experience, "which, as factual, had not, so to speak, taken advantage of all the real possibilities which were there for the experiencing ego. That they were real possibilities means that, in the integration of the motivations of both periods of harmony which is established through memory-syntheses, just such possibilities are motivated, namely, in the form such that one and the same world endured in between, but [that world] could not manifest itself to the experiencer in the facticity of his flow [of experience], and thus could not be experienced by him."[110]

In connection with these thoughts, Husserl distinguishes "the possibility of the dissolution of harmonious structure of world-perception" from the possibility itself, that this world and a world in general is a 'nothing'."[111] The latter, in addition to being thought of as the possibility of the onset of a disharmony which distroys the experiential belief, "has the meaning of an Idea, namely the Idea of a disharmony which continues indefinitely, but which ought not to be accidental [*die aber nicht zufällige sein soll*]."[112] Husserl immediately asks what this "ought not to be accidental" means. However, he does not answer this question. Instead, his thought turns in another direction. He affirms that after the dissolution of world-perception it would be a possibility, although an empty one, that a world belief is restored and that a world is constituted. But he questions a previous statement of his own to the effect that such a constitution would necessarily be a reconstitution of the same past world.[113] "Why is it not thinkable that I have different 'worlds', one after the other, which just become 'created' and destroyed?" He concludes this line of thought, which is clearly a "thought experiment" and not a definitive statement, by saying: "It is not a possibility entitled '*nothing*' which stands in contrast to a world..., it is endlessly many *ficta,* which all equally count for nothing, all lacking in validity, each a possibility and the correlate of a possible harmony."[114]

In this discussion of the "objection of insanity" Husserl focuses on a fundamental problem with his story of the dissolution of world-perception. Assuming that a self-conscious subject who once did but no longer experiences a world of things can survive such a dissolution and remain conscious of itself as the same subject, would that subject be warranted in believing that the world no longer persists? Perhaps the subject should believe that the world does persist and understand its own condition as pathological. Should the subject regard itself as having lost a world, or as having become lost to the world?

In the main text of *Erste Philosophie,* Husserl discards this objection. It would assume that the world is still perceivable by other, normal subjects. However, our subject has no more reason to believe in the continued existence of other subjects than it does in the continued existence of things, since the former belief is based on the latter. Husserl's argument here can be questioned. In the section of *Erste Philosophie* under consideration, Husserl is pursuing a critique of mundane experience in order to see if the existence of the world is an apodictic certainty.[115] The possibility of transcendental illusion is raised in order to show that it is not. This critique constitutes a "way" into transcendental phenomenology know as the "Cartesian way."[116] In this respect, *Erste Philosophie* can be considered an "introduction" to phenomenology along with the works cited earlier.[117] To counter the "objection of insanity," Husserl relies on his theory of the constitution of other subjects. This brings a certain circularity into his procedure. The theory of the constitution of other subjects forms part of Husserl's *transcendental* phenomenology. This is so because, as was shown earlier, it is a theory of how the object-sense "other subjects" arises and is *validated* in consciousness.[118] This means that the theory seeks to show how the right to the *claim* of the perceptual experience of others to be a cognition, i.e., to give us access to something "in itself," is grounded in experience. As was also shown earlier, the view that perceptual experience is a claim to cognition, the grounds of whose right need to be displayed, stems from a certain interpretation of the problem of cognition, an interpretation which is based on the existence of the possibility of transcendental illusion.[119] This interpretation conditions the nature of both the method of transcendental epoche and the method of constitutive analysis,[120] methods used to develop the theory of the constitution of other subjects. Thus, the theory which Husserl relies on to support his demonstration of the existence of the possibility of transcendental illusion is a theory developed using methods each of whose sense is conditioned by the assumption that the possibility of transcendental illusion exists. Herein lies the circularity in Husserl's discussion of the "objection of insanity."[121]

The circularity in Husserl's procedure which was just discussed is unavoidable. In order to show how the world could be transcendental illusion, one would have to know how the world is constituted in consciousness as actuality. This involves showing the "verifying constitutions" for the worldly object-senses, which, in turn, involves showing the ways in which perceptual experience must proceed in order for a world in which there are objects having a given object-sense to remain valid. Once the "norms of verification" are disclosed, one could then know how experience could proceed in violation of these norms. On the other hand, it can just as well be said that the task of showing how the world could be a transcendental illusion is part of the task of showing how the world is constituted in consciousness as actuality, for showing how object-senses could fail to be verified is a way of disclosing the norms of verification. Thus, these are really just two sides of the same task, which is the work of transcendental phenomenology. There is indeed a certain circularity within the program of transcendental phenomenology, but it is not, as will be shown in the next chapter, a "vicious" circularity. However, in so far as Husserl's "introductions to phenomenology" proport to demonstrate the existence of the possibility of transcendental illusion, and, more generally, to show that consciousness is world-constitutive prior to engaging in transcendental phenomenology, they are to be criticized for assuming that which is to be proved.

The same criticism just made concerning the circularity in Husserl's discussion of his story about the dissolution of world-perception in the main text of *Erste Philosophie* can be made in the case of the story itself, in that it presupposes his theory of how the object-sense "physical thing" is validated in consciousness. In his discussion of the "objection of insanity" in the text appended to the main text of *Erste Philosophie,* Husserl raises an issue which points to another way in which his story can be said to be inconclusive.

In this discussion Husserl at one point concludes that the possibility that the world is a transcendental illusion "has the meaning of an Idea, namely, the

Idea of a disharmony which continues indefinitely, but which ought not to be accidental."[122] Then he asks what the phrase "ought not to be accidental" means. Let us first come to an understanding of why Husserl added this phrase. Again, the issue is the warrant for a subject's belief that the world no longer persists. Suppose I am experiencing the requisite disharmony, and I no longer have a world on hand. Should I believe that the world itself persists no longer, or that I have fallen into a pathological condition, a pathological condition now defined not by reference to the possible perceptions of other subjects, but by reference to possible perceptions of my own? These would be perceptions of the world which are "real possibilities" for me, but which, due to my merely factual condition, I cannot take advantage of. But in what sense could these be "real possibilities?"

The meaning of Husserl's response to this question seems to be the following. I imagine that at some future time a harmonious world-perception is restored, and in such a way that the world I perceive is identified as the same world which I had previously perceived. Looking back from this future vantage point, I recall my experiences up to the period of disharmony and those after that period. In doing this I find that my experiences prior to the disharmony contained anticipations of future perceptions of a sort more or less predelineated, which were expected to occur during the period of disharmony. I further find that my perceptions after the disharmony in some ways point back to these anticipated, but not experienced, perceptions, point back to them as being the sort of perceptions which would have been experienced as fulfilling the anticipations contained within the non-experienced perceptions, had they been experienced. The anticipations concerning the perceptions which did not occur during the period of disharmony, and the "pointings back" to those perceptions on the part of the perceptions which were experienced after the disharmony constitute, I think, the "motivations of both periods of harmony" which Husserl mentions as being integrated as a result of the memory-syntheses. Their integration, which in turn makes possible an integration of the experiences before and after the disharmony (by mediating the integration of anticipations experienced during the pre-disharmony period which were directed toward the *post*-disharmony period with pointings back experienced during the post-disharmony period to the *pre*-disharmony period), and thus the unity of *one* perceptual life experiencing the same world, can only come about by indicating as possible certain perceptions of the world during the period of disharmony. The sense of these perceptions as being "really" possible derives from their having been actually indicated in the pre- and post-disharmony periods, i.e., it derives from their having been "motivated" as opposed to "empty" possibilities.[123]

If I, the experiencer who no longer experiences a world, now want to make sense of my belief that the world itself does *not* persist, I must imagine the disharmony in my experience to go on indefinitely so that no world-perception is restored. However, this indefinite disharmony "must not be accidental." What does this mean? It means that it must not be thought of as a disharmony which is "merely factual," and thus I must not be thought to have any "real possibility" of perceiving the world. But how can this be thought? To do so would be to deny the open possibility that at any point in the disharmony a harmony could be restored. However there would seem to be no more reason to deny this than there is to deny that while experience is harmonious it could become disharmonious. In another context one could say that there is no real possibility of perceiving the world if and only if there is no world to be perceived. Obviously this approach is not available to us here.

It is perhaps because of having reached an impasse such as this that Husserl goes on in the manuscript appended to the main text to affirm the empty possibility that a world belief could be restored and that a world once again is constituted. Here, we recall, he raises the possibility that the world which becomes constituted need not be the same world which was experienced prior to the period of disharmony. There could be an endless sequence of periods of harmony alternating with periods of disharmony in which different worlds are "created" and distroyed. Although this would seem to finally give a viable meaning to the belief that the world no longer persists, it contradicts an earlier statement of Husserl's that "streams of total experience which are at times harmonious and then at other times are disharmonious cannot bear in themselves temporally separated worlds, but, if at all, only *one* [world], in one world-space and the one world-time."[124]

Thus it seems that once again an impasse is reached. What am I, the imagined subject of Husserl's story, now to be imagined to think? Am I to think that my condition is accidental, pathological, and that the world still persists? Or am I to go on thinking my way through one or the other of these difficulties in the hope of finally giving if not a warrant, at least a *meaning* to my belief that the world persists no longer? Certainly the latter option is open, but that the matter was not resolved by Husserl shows that his demonstration of the existence of the possibility of transcendental illusion is inconclusive. The same is true, then, also of his argument that consciousness constitutes the world. As having been "introduced" to phenomenology through this argument, we do not stand before the portals of the transcendental realm knowing *that* consciousness is world-constitutive, having only to show *how* it is so. Nor do we have a rational motivation for the method of epoche, since we do not *know* that the basic modality of world-constitutive consciousness is belief. What meaning are we even to give to the concepts of "transcendental epoche," "transcendental reduction," and "constitutive intentional analysis," if an understanding of them which is conditioned by Husserl's "introductions" is now in question?[125] How is transcendental phenomenology to begin? I will conclude this work with a discussion of these issues.

## NOTES

1. *EP,* p. 67
2. Ibid., p. 68. See also *Ding und Raum,* p. 270.
3. In at least one place (*FTL,* p. 241), Husserl uses the expression "transcendental illusion" to denote something different from what will be discussed here. There, he uses the expression to refer to the illusion of "transcendental solipsism," i.e., the illusion of thinking that "if everything I can ever accept as existent is constituted in my ego, then everything that exists... [is] ...a mere moment of my own transcendental being." For the connection of transcendental solipsism to the transcendental illusion we are concerned with, see *EP* II, pp. 64-66.
4. See p. 79 above.
5. Quoted above, p. 79 – emphasis mine.
6. *EP* II, p. 50.
7. Above, pp. 79-80.
8. Above, p. 127.
9. Confining the illusion to the house makes the example somewhat artificial. It can be suspected that if the existence of my house was an illusion, many other things, particularly events, were also illusions. Yet perhaps the illusion can be confined to significantly less than my whole life, even if not solely to the house. Thus we will take the house to represent the house plus whatever else would have to be included in a "plausible" story which attempts to establish the possibility of the non-existence of my house (if one could ever be plausible). We further suppose that the house is not my childhood house, in order not to get involved in the complication of undoing the primal institution of the sense "house."
10. See above, pp. 88-92.
11. Quoted above, p. 185.
12. See p. 96 above.
13. Husserl borrows the word "*Gewühl*" from Kant – see *EP* II, p. 48.
14. *Ideas,* section 49, p. 151 – translation modified, see *Ideen* I, pp. 114-15 and the "Textkritische Anmerkungen," pp. 473-74 to reconstruct the original text, or the Schuhmann edition, p. 103. Gibson's translation of "*ihre Dingsetzungen*" as "the things it puts together" is perhaps not correct ("thing-positings" would be technically correct), but it is insightful here, since Husserl is describing a process in which things "fall apart." One emandation of Husserl's which is included in the Biemel edition of the *Husserliana* text should be noted. Right after "adumbrations, apprehensions, and appearances," the clause "and that this actually remains so *in infinitum* is inserted. For a more extensive description of the constitution of the "rough unitary formations," see *Ding und Raum,* p. 289. For an analytic account of the dissolution process, see *Ding und Raum,* pp. 288-90; *APS,* pp. 106-108; *EP* II, pp. 48-49.
15. *EP*II, p. 49.

16. See also *APS*, p. 108: "For all people, the world is without question continuously there, and they mean [by that] that it will also continue to exist. They consciously live into a world-future."
17. *APS*, pp. 106-7; *EP* II, p. 46.
18. See *Ideas,* section 49 (*Ideen* I, pp. 114-19). See also *APS*, p. 215-16 and *EP* II, p. 50.
19. *Ideas,* section 49, p. 151.
20. *Ding und Raum,* p. 289.
21. Ibid., n.1 (to the previous statement above).
22. Above, pp. 47.
23. *Ideas,* section 49, p. 152—translation slightly modified, see *Ideen* I, p. 115.
24. Above, p. 47.
25. *Ideen* I, pp. 115-16—translation mine, cf. *Ideas,* section 49, p. 152. The reference to a consciousness which is "logically devised" is no doubt to Kantian or neo-Kantian philosophy.
26. Quoted more fully above, p. 184 – emphasis mine.
27. *EP* II, p. 49. See also p. 64 and *Ding und Raum,* pp. 288, 290.
28. This statement is contained in a supplement to sections 33-46 of *Ideen* I published in the second half-volume of Schuhmann's edition (Beilage 78, pp. 633-34).
29. See *Ding und Raum,* pp. 285-87; *Ideas,* section 49, pp. 150-51; *APS,* p. 107; *EP* II, pp. 46-48.
30. *EP* II, p. 46.
31. Ibid., p. 47. See also *Crisis,* p. 162-63.
32. See *Crisis,* p. 163.
33. Ibid., pp. 163-64.
34. See *APS,* pp. 212-14.
35. *EP* II, pp. 47-48.
36. Ibid. See also *CM,* section 28, pp. 61-62.
37. *EP* II, pp. 47, 52.
38. Ibid., p. 47. See also *Crisis,* p. 164: " 'The' thing itself is actually that which no one experiences as really seen, since it is always in motion, always, and for everyone, a unity for consciousness of the openly endless multiplicity of changing experiences and experienced things, one's own and those of others."
39. *EP* II, pp. 47-48, 51-52.
40. Ibid., pp. 386-88. On the possibility of natural science in this connection, see *Ideas,* section 47, p. 147. See *APS,* pp. 433-37 and *EP* II, p. 387 on the question of whether the world has the sense of being "definitely determinable" in a *mathematical* sense in all its aspects.
41. See *EP* II, pp. 48, 52. See also *Ideas,* section 47, pp. 147-49. It should not be thought that Husserl is saying that the "definitively true world" is posited within our world-perception *as* the "physical world" which is *constructed* by physical science.
42. For Husserl's rejection of the idea of an unperceivable reality, see *Ideas,* section 52, pp. 158-64.
43. See above p. 162.
44. *APS,* p. 21. An object's "individual essence" seems to be the same as what Husserl refers to as an object's "own essence" in *Ideen* I (pp. 12-13, 35) (see *Ideas,* section 2, pp. 52-54 and section 14, pp. 74-75). On this, see J. Mohanty, "Individual Fact and Essence in Edmund Husserl's Philosophy," *Philosophy and Phenomenological Research* 20 (1959): 226.
45. *APS,* pp. 21, 23-24. See also *EP* II, pp. 47-48.
46. *APS,* p. 21.
47. See above, pp. 36-45 and p. 130 for the distinction between the two correlates of the natural attitude, the being-on-hand of the world and the world's "actuality." See

pp. 42-44 for the concept of the "actual" as the "in itself."

48. Above, p. 191.
49. See *EP* II, p. 52.
50. *PP,* pp. 124, 126.
51. See above, pp. 124, 174.
52. *EP* II, p. 49. See also *Ideas,* section 2, p. 53.
53. See *EP* II, p. 53.
54. For the previous discussions of transcendental illusion, see above, pp. 78-80, 86-87, 128-30, 177. In the following exposition I will draw on various ideas presented and developed during the discussion of "constitution and constitutive analysis" above, pp. 159-77.
55. This is not the thing as the physicist conceives it, but physicality as encountered in everyday experience.
56. Above, pp. 185, 187-88.
57. Above, pp. 187-88.
58. *Ideas,* section 88, p. 259 — translation modified, see *Ideen* I, p. 220.
59. *Ideas,* section 53, p. 164. See also *EP* II, p. 71. Note that "real" here, as a translation of the German word *"real"* does not mean actual (*wirklich*).
60. *Ideas,* section 53, pp. 164-65.
61. Ibid., p. 164 and section 54, p. 167.
62. Above, pp. 127, 174.
63. *Ideas,* section 54, pp. 166-67 — translation modified, see *Ideen* I, pp. 132-33. See also *EP* II, pp. 56-57, 72-74.
64. *Ideas,* section 54, p. 167.
65. See *Ding und Raum,* p. 290.
66. See above, p. 83
67. *Ding und Raum,* p. 290.
68. *EP* II, p. 384.
69. Ibid., p. 404.
70. Ibid., p. 48.
71. Quoted above, p. 185.
72. *CM,* section 41, pp. 83-86; *Crisis,* pp. 182-183; *Ideas,* sections 53-54.
73. Above, pp. 170-71.
74. Ibid.
75. See p. 193 above. Such a life may be that of "lower" animals.
76. The alternatives would/should are provided to call attention to the fact that the issue here is not what might happen as a matter of psychological fact, but what would be epistemically justified. For stylistic reasons, "or should (not)" will be omitted in the rest of this paragraph.
77. For a review of the literature on this issue, see chapter 11 of Joseph Kockelmans' book *A First Introduction to Husserl's Phenomenology* (Pittsburgh: Duquesne University Press, 1967), pp. 315-55, or his essay "Husserl's Transcendental Idealism," which is a shorter version of this chapter, in his *Phenomenology: The Philosophy of Edmund Husserl and Its Interpretation* (Garden City, Doubleday, 1967), pp. 183-91.
78. See *CM,* section 41, and *Ideas,* pp. 18-22.
79. Our interpretation has already answered the question of the existence of a "perceived world" outside our "minds" in favor of an empirical realism.
80. See *EP* II, Beilage XIII, pp. 396-406.
81. *Ideas,* section 49, p. 152 — translation modified, see *Ideen* I, p. 116. See also *EP* II, pp. 64-65 where Husserl explains that the possibility of the non-existence of the world is not a "real" possibility.

82. *EP* II, p. 384.
83. See p. 199 above.
84. *Ideas,* section 49, p. 153 — translation modified, see *Ideen* I, p. 117 and chapter 4, n. 76 above.
85. Ibid., p. 21.
86. See ibid.
87. *Ideen* I, p. 117 (cf. p. 205 above). The words in brackets are those which supplement the text that Husserl published.
88. See *CM,* p. 86.
89. This is a viable position whose consequences will be discussed in the next chapter.
90. Above, pp. 39-40.
91. Above, p. 152.
92. Above, pp. 88-92.
93. Above, pp. 188 and 198.
94. *EP* II, p. 73.
95. See *EP*II, p. 52. See also *Ideas,* section 47, p. 148 and *APS,* pp. 108-109, 212-14.
96. See p. 129 above.
97. See pp. 11-14 above.
98. *EP* II, p. 73.
99. Ibid., p. 49.
100. For some of Husserl's thoughts relevant to this, see Iso Kern, *Husserl und Kant,* p. 294 and Eduard Marbach, *Das Problem des Ich in der Phänomenologie Husserls* (The Hague: Martinus Nijhoff, 1974), pp. 329-32.
101. *EP* II, p. 55.
102. Ibid.
103. Ibid., p. 56.
104. Ibid., pp. 55-56.
105. Ibid., p. 57.
106. Ibid., p. 64.
107. Ibid., Beilage XI, pp. 391-93.
108. Ibid., p. 391.
109. Ibid., p. 392.
110. Ibid.
111. Ibid., p. 391.
112. Ibid., p. 392.
113. Ibid., lines 2-6.
114. Ibid., p. 291.
115. See ibid., pp. 40-41, 44.
116. Kern, *Husserl und Kant,* p. 201.
117. Above, chapter 1, n.3.
118. Above, pp. 174-77.
119. Above, pp. 157-58.
120. See above, p. 179.
121. If Husserl's theory of the constitution of other subjects were incorrect, his story and its discussion could be criticized in another way. Although our subject cannot experience physical things, it is not completely evident that it could not have evidence of the existence of other subjects. Perhaps the subject could still be in communication with other subjects. Even if it be granted that this communication could not have the normal spatial dimension, as

proceeding from a subject who is *there* to a subject who is *here* in space, perhaps the subject could be aware of a voice speaking to it, much in the same way it "speaks" to itself in "thought," but being the voice of another. If we supplement the story so that our subject's experience disintegrates to the point that it cannot synthesize linguistic expressions into meaningful unities, might we have also distroyed the subject's capacity to think, and therefore to have beliefs of any sort?

122. See above, p. 211.
123. See *Ding und Raum,* pp. 291-92 on "real possibility."
124. *EP* II, p. 392.
125. See the previous discussion of these issues, pp. 177-79 above.

# 7. CONCLUSION: TOWARD A NEW INTRODUCTION TO PHENOMENLOGY

In the preceeding chapters I have tried to show that there is a certain inadequacy in Husserl's "introductions to phenomenology." The four books which Husserl wrote as introductions were seen to be based on a common schema composed of three main parts.[1] The first part, entitled "the motivating problem," explains what the problem is to which transcendental phenomenology is to provide the solution, namely, the problem of cognition. The second part, "acquiring the idea of pure transcendental consciousness," contains phenomenological analyses of a pre-transcendental character as well as a general argument, based on these analyses, which attempts to show that consciousness "constitutes" the world. It is in this part that I have located the inadequacy of the "introductions." In the third part of the schema, called "the entry into the transcendental realm," certain phenomenological methods for showing how consciousness constitutes the world are explained and applied.

Other commentators on Husserl's philosophy have also noted an inadequacy in the way Husserl introduces transcendental phenomenology, but they have focused on a different aspect than I have here. We recall that in the first section of the second part of the schema Husserl analyzes the natural attitude and discloses that it contains a thesis or positing. This positing is later identified as a doxic positing or belief. Husserl describes the analysis which discloses this thesis as one carried out in the natural attitude. Both Ricoeur and Fink have questioned whether such a thesis is discoverable from the standpoint of the natural attitude. They argue that the "radical" sense of the natural attitude cannot be discovered from within that attitude itself, so that Husserl, in sections 27 through 30 of *Ideas* for example, has already presupposed something which can only be revealed by the transcendental reduction. During his discussion Ricoeur asks: "Why call that attitude which consists in *finding there an existing world and accepting it as it gives itself, namely as existing,* a thesis or a positing? In short, for what reason is *finding there* equivalent to *posit*?"[2] The disclosure of a positing within the natural attitude, he adds, can only be achieved by the phenomenological reduction. According to Ricoeur, the natural attitude is a self-limitation on the part of the transcendental ego by which it conceals from itself its constitutive power.[3] This is what I have called the "self-forgetfulness" of the transcendental subject.[4] Ricoeur's discussion implies that to find a thesis within the natural attitude would involve revealing this constitutive power and hence leaving the natural attitude.

Ricoeur's criticism concerns the *radical* sense of the natural attitude. Only when understood radically is the natural attitude seen to contain a doxic positing of the actuality of the world. This belief is not a mundane belief; rather, it is a transcendental belief. The subject of this belief, Fink says, is not a human being, it is the transcendental ego.[5] Fink argues that a description of the natural attitude from within that attitude is necessarily inadequate, since it only isolates an attitude held by human beings, whereas, in truth, it is a transcendental function which is constitutive of our very apperception of ourselves as human beings.[6]

Both Ricoeur and Fink find that Husserl anticipates the transcendental reduction in some of his expressly non-transcendental analyses. My own view is that in portions of his texts like section 30 of *Ideas,* where the thesis of the natural attitude is discussed, Husserl is anticipating his *argument,* which occurs in a later section of the pre-transcendental part of the schema of his "introductions," that consciousness constitutes the world, for it is in this argument, especially the coherence-thesis, that Husserl attempts to establish that the natural attitude contains a transcendental belief. Both Ricoeur and Fink claim that the transcendental reduction "discloses" this transcendental belief. We have seen that the epoche, understood as a means for bringing about the reduction, is a method for gaining intuitive access to this constitutive belief.[7] The epoche embodies a certain conception of the problem of cognition and is a way of bringing the phenomenologist's interest in this problem into the concrete analysis of consciousness.[8] This conception of the problem depends upon the existence of the possibility of transcendental illusion, as does the determination that there is a transcendental *belief.*[9] However, as I have shown, the existence of the possibility of transcendental illusion has not been conclusively demonstrated by Husserl. In what sense, then, can the reduction or the epoche be said to "disclose" a constitutive transcendental belief? In an interpretation which I shall present shortly, I will propose that the epoche be understood as part of the way of structuring a task whose *aim* is to demonstrate that there is a constitutive transcendental belief.

If a general argument based on non-transcendental grounds could succeed in demonstrating *that* consciousness constitutes the world, the task of transcendental phenomenology would only need to be concerned with showing *how* consciousness achieves the being-on-hand of the world. In this case, the transcendental phenomenological reduction could be understood as the general idea of a method for gaining intuitive access to something or for "disclosing" something already known to be there, namely, the world-constituting function of consciousness. The method of constitutive intentional analysis could be thought to be the way of concretely elucidating how consciousness works to make a world present and available to us, and could be thought to be able to do this because it operates "under" the reduction, i.e., because the reduction, as a way of "seeing," has already brought that which is to be analyzed into view. The problem of cognition which motivates the task in its general sense and which gives rise to these two methods is, to put it simply, how we know the world as it is and how we know a world at all. This problem expresses a certain wonderment which takes hold of the philosopher who, concerned about certain foundational problems in the sciences, reflects naively and within the natural attitude on that to which all these sciences refer, the world, and on the most fundamental way in which the world is known, perceptual experience. The philosopher finds that the sciences, however "unnatural" they may be in so far as they challenge or go beyond the common sense notions of everyday life, share the epistemological realism of the natural attitude of everyday life. The philosopher, however, on the basis of an analysis of the foundational problems of the sciences, believes that this realism, no matter how appropriate it may be for the practice of science and how necessary for the scientists themselves in order for them to have "everyday lives," is unsuitable for the philosophical clarification of the foundational problems. It is here where the philosopher's own natural attitude and its view of perceptual cognition as a simple seeing of what is there ceases to be something matter of fact and becomes a mystery. Here the philosopher becomes a phenomenologist, one who, as Husserl expresses it, "lives in the paradox of having to look upon the obvious as questionable, as enigmatic, and of transforming the universal obviousness of the being of the world – for him the greatest of all enigmas – into something intelligible."[10]

We have seen that Husserl specifies the problem of cognition further than this. A thorough psychological phenomenological analysis of cognition ultimately discloses the problem of the actuality of the world which is on hand. Here, phenomenological analysis focuses on the issue of error in perception, at first in terms of such familiar phenomena as misperception and hallucination, but then more radically in terms of the possibility of transcendental illusion. It is here where Husserl, as part of his argument that consciousness is world-constitutive, asserts the coherence-thesis, the thesis that "the being-there [*Dasein*] of the world is the correlate of the unity of harmonious and continuously *verifying* experiences."[11]

If a general argument based on non-transcendental grounds could be successful in this regard (and "success" here basically means if the existence of the possibility of transcendental illusion could be demonstrated), then the argument would show that a belief which is a claim to cognition is the fundamental mode of the world-constituting function of consciousness, and that the world is a presumptive actuality. If this were a secure result, the method of the transcendental phenomenological epoche would be indicated as the proper method of bringing about the transcendental reduction. The epoche could be conceived of as a method of gaining intuitive access to the belief that the perceived world has a determinate whatness in itself, and the method of constitutive intentional analysis, operating under the epoche, could be specified as a method of revealing what I have called "verifying constitutions," i.e., how consciousness functions to generate and validate the belief in a world, and a world in which there are the sorts of things that there are.

Husserl's argument that consciousness is world-constitutive, as I believe I have shown, is not successful. Its chief deficiency is that it relies on, and would have to rely on, certain phenomenological analyses which, properly speaking, belong to the *transcendental* phenomenological task of showing *how* consciousness constitutes the world. But Husserl's argument had to fail, as would any argument which tried to do the same, because the "that" can only be shown by showing "how". Husserl's or anyone's concrete *transcendental* phenomenological analyses should be understood as the real demonstration of the "that." Husserl seems to have been aware of this, because in one place he remarks that the proof of his transcendental idealism is phenomenology itself, i.e., the actual work of uncovering the constituting intentionality itself.[12] But if this is so, how is one to understand the concepts and methods with which one is supposed to start, if an understanding of them that relies on Husserl's argument being successful is no longer available? I would like to suggest the following interpretation of the task of transcendental phenomenology as it relates to the issue of the world as an answer to these questions.

The interpretation is based on the idea that the thesis *that* consciousness is world-constitutive is: 1) a thesis which it is the task of transcendental phenomenology to prove, and to do so by means of concrete constitutive analyses which show *how,* through consciousness, the world is on hand, and 2) a thesis which conditions the sense of certain concepts and methods involved in the execution of the task and which is thus presupposed from the beginning. Rather than being regarded as having been demonstrated prior to the start of transcendental phenomenological analysis, the thesis is considered to be a sort of hypothesis. To express its character as the end or *telos* of an inquiry and as the assumption of that inquiry, I will call it a "telotic-assumption." Unlike the hypotheses of science, at least as they are usually considered, the thesis is not something which it is possible to either prove *or* disprove by methods which are independent of the thesis itself. Since the thesis conditions the sense of the methods, they cannot disprove the thesis. One can only fail to *prove* the thesis. Failure to prove the thesis is not to be taken to indicate that the thesis is wrong, but that the methods or concepts involved in conceiving and structuring the task of proving the thesis need to be examined, and then altered, deepened or refined. In this regard, the interpretation helps us to understand why Husserl wrote so many "introductions to phenomenology." Some of the significant differences between the "introductions" can be regarded as resulting from a rethinking of the key concepts and methods, a rethinking necessitated by difficulties encountered in working out the concrete constitutive analyses which contribute to the proof of the thesis. I will show how some of these key concepts and methods can be understood in terms of the thesis, conceptualized as a telotic-assumption, that consciousness is world-constitutive.

I have characterized the transcendental phenomenological reduction as the general idea of a method for bringing consciousness to intuitive givenness as world-constitutive. This "intuitive givenness" involves knowing, with insight, *that* consciousness constitutes the world. The intuitive givenness, however, is not available at the start of transcendental inquiry; it is something which is achieved through the inquiry itself, and is fully attained only at the end of the inquiry. Nevertheless, one can speak of "performing the reduction" and of "working under the reduction" from the beginning of the inquiry. To "perform" the reduction is just to adopt the thesis that consciousness is world-constitutive as something assumed to be true, and to aim to have its truth evidently given. It is to emptily intend the thesis and to aim for its fulfillment. To do phenomenological analysis "under" reduction is to work to fulfill this intention by doing constitutive intentional analyses which show how the world is "constituted" through consciousness. To see *how* the world is constituted is to fulfill the intention *that* consciousness is world-constitutive. It is to achieve the reduction and thus it is the "accomplishment of a reduction of 'the' world to the transcendental phenomenon 'world,' a reduction thus also to its correlate, transcendental subjectivity...."[13] The reduction is a process which is achieved in a step-wise manner by concretely showing how the various dimensions of the world are constituted. The relationship between the reduction and the method of constitutive intentional analysis is thus the reverse of what it would be if a general argument could show that consciousness constitutes the world. The reduction does not make the achievements of the analysis possible; rather, the analysis makes the achievement of the reduction possible.

As discussed earlier, the transcendental phenomenological epoche is *a* way for bringing the world-constituting function of consciousness into view intuitively. It is thus a way of performing and attaining the reduction. This way derives from a specific conception of the problem of cognition and a consequent specification of the thesis that consciousness is world-constitutive. In accordance with this specification, the epoche brings about an intuitive grasp of world-consciousness as containing a constitutive belief in the actuality or true being of the world. Through the epoche this doxic positing of the world as having a determinate whatness in itself is intuitively disclosed to be a cognitive claim which, although motivated and sustained by validating courses of experience, is essentially open to invalidation. The actuality of the world is intuitively revealed as a presumptive actuality. As in the case of the reduction in general, the intuition which the epoche is to bring about is not achieved as the start of transcendental inquiry. Rather, it is attained through concrete constitutive analyses which, by discovering the verifying-constitutions of the worldly object-senses and the norms of verification governing these constitutions, at the same time both prove that world-consciousness is a belief which is a cognitive claim and that the world is a presumptive actuality, *and* bring about an intuitive grasp of this belief and its correlate. Therefore the epoche is also a process, and here too one can speak of "performing the epoche" at the start of inquiry and of "working under the epoche." To "perform" the epoche would be to adopt the thesis that consciousness is world-constitutive with the specific meaning the coherence-thesis gives to it, and to aim to make the truth of the thesis so-specified evident. To perform phenomenological analysis "under" the epoche is to strive to fulfill this aim by showing how the world is constituted in consciousness as having a true being, and how the ongoing experience of the world conforms, yet could not conform, to certain norms of verification, norms through which the belief in the world is particularized into the belief in the actuality of this or that sort of object and which thus concretize the sense "true being" with respect to the world such as it is.

This interpretation of some of the methods and concepts appearing in Husserl's "introductions to phenomenology" could become part of a new "introduction to phenomenlogy." Let us consider what else might be included. The need for the above interpretation arose because the general argument which Husserl presents to prove that consciousness constitutes the world is inconclusive, specifically with regard to the demonstration of the existence of the possibility of transcendental illusion. This circumstance leads one to wonder whether the existence of the possibility of transcendental illusion is even a genuine issue. If it is, then the specification of the problem of cognition which is embodied in the coherence-thesis, in the epoche, and in the use of the method of constitutive intentional analysis to display verifying-constitutions does set out a meaningful task for phenomenology. But what if it is not a genuine issue? It seems to me that this problem must be dealt with in contemplating the content of a new introduction to phenomenology. If the issue is not genuine, there would have to be a reevaluation of the whole project of transcendental phenomenology. If the possibility of transcendental illusion simply does not exist, then it makes no sense to speak of a constitutive world-belief, or of pursuing phenomenological investigations into verifying-constitutions under an epoche. In this case a clarification of the general sense of the problem of cognition and of the methods of reduction and constitutive analysis would be part of the task of a new introduction.

There are indications in Husserl's later writings that he had misgivings about the way in which he had "introduced" phenomenology, and that these misgivings may have been occasioned by difficulties concerning the existence of the possibility of transcendental illusion. These indications come in the form of a criticism of his own previous "Cartesian way" into transcendental phenomenology.[14] In *Crisis* and elsewhere Husserl proposes another way into transcendental phenomenology by "inquiring back from the pregiven life-world."[15] He also remarks that the naturally first concept of being is the being-on-hand (*Vorhandenheit*) of the world.[16] I have tried to keep the issue of the being-on-hand of the world distinct from the issue of its actuality and to express the general sense of the thesis that consciousness is world-constitutive in terms of the former issue. I have also connected the transcendental reduction, which I have distinguished from the epoche, with this general sense of the thesis. If a new "introduction to phenomenology" were written, perhaps the actuality problem, as Husserl conceived it, could be dispensed with entirely, and along with it anything like the psychological phenomenological investigation of consciousness which appears in Husserl's "introductions," at least in so far as such an investigation would seek to pass beyond the concept of perceptual illusion in the sense of "empirical illusion" to present a prima facie case for a more radical concept of illusion and thus to formulate a more radical problem of actuality than the psychological one as *the* problem of cognition.

However, this is not to suggest that the "psychological problem of cognition" become *the* problem for phenomenology. The problem would be that of the being-on-hand of the world. In various places in this work I have tried to indicate the general sense of this problem. But more is needed than such indications. In this respect, a new introduction would have to contain a thorough, non-transcendental phenomenological analysis of the natural attitude, an intentional analysis which would aim especially to clarify what the "naive" reflection of the natural attitude intends as consciousness and world. The analysis would investigate the sense of the "pregivenness" of the life-world and would develop an ontology of the life-world to explicate the modes of pregivenness and determine the essential dimensions and content of "what" is pregiven. This analysis would provide the problem to which a *constitutive* intentional analysis of consciousness would provide the solution. Certainly many of Husserl writings, especially those of his later period, would be extremely helpful for this inquiry.

Originally, and I believe always, for Husserl, the thesis that consciousness constitutes the world is a response to "foundational problems" in the sciences. What really were these problems? Are they still problems? Or, if not, are there still similar problems? How do these problems motivate a *transcendental* phenomenology? These questions too would have to be considered in any new "introduction to phenomenology."

But, most important of all, a new introduction would seek to generate, and then to clarify, the sense of the wonderment which comes upon one when the "universal obviousness of the being of the world" becomes "the greatest of all enigmas."

## NOTES

1. For the titles of these books, see n.3, chapter 1.
2. Husserl, *Idées,* n.l, p. 95.
3. Ibid., and n. 5, p. 99.
4. Above, p. 200.
5. Eugen Fink, "The Phenomenological Philosophy of Edmund Husserl and Contemporary Criticism," in Elveton, *The Phenomenology of Husserl* (Chicago: Quadrangle Books, 1970), p. 110.
6. Ibid., pp. 107, 108.
7. Above, pp. 148, 179.
8. Above, pp. 155, 157.
9. Above, p. 179.
10. *Crisis,* p. 180.
11. *APS,* p. 215 – emphasis mine.
12. *CM,* p. 86.
13. Quoted more fully above, p. 148.
14. See *Crisis,* pp. 154-55 and *EP* II, pp. 257-68.
15. See *Crisis,* part IIIA, esp. section 38, pp. 143-47.
16. *EP* II, p. 263.

# BIBLIOGRAPHY

WORKS OF EDMUND HUSSERL

*Analysen zur passiven Synthesis. Husserliana* XI. Edited by Margot Fleischer. The Hague: Martinus Nijhoff, 1966.

*Cartesianische Meditationen und Pariser Vorträge. Husserliana* I. 2d ed. Edited by S. Strasser. The Hague: Martinus Nijhoff, 1963.

*Cartesian Meditations: An Introduction to Phenomenology.* Translated by Dorion Cairns. The Hague: Martinus Nijhoff, 1960.

*The Crisis of European Sciences and Transcendental Phenomenology: An Introduction to Phenomenological Philosophy.* Translated by David Carr. Evanston: Northwestern University Press, 1970.

*Ding und Raum. Husserliana* XVI. Edited by Ulrich Claesges. The Hague: Martinus Nijhoff, 1973.

*Erste Philosophie.* Second part. *Husserliana* VIII. Edited by Rudolf Boehm. The Hague: Martinus Nijhoff, 1959.

*Experience and Judgment: Investigations in a Genealogy of Logic.* Translated by James S. Churchill and Karl Ameriks. Evanston: Northwestern University Press, 1973.

*Formal and Transcendental Logic.* Translated by Dorion Cairns. The Hague: Martinus Nijhoff, 1969.

*The Idea of Phenomenology.* Translated by Willian P. Alston and George Nakhnikian. The Hague: Martinus Nijhoff, 1964.

*Ideas: A General Introduction to Pure Phenomenology.* Translated by W.R. Boyce Gibson. London: George Allen & Unwin, 1931.

*Die Idee der Phänomenologie. Husserliana* II. Edited by Walter Biemel. The Hague: Martinus Nijhoff, 1973.

*Ideen zu einer reinen Phänomenologie und phänomenologischen Philosophie.*

First book. *Husserliana* III. Edited by Walter Biemel. The Hague: Martinus Nijhoff, 1950.

*Ideen zu einer reinen Phänomenologie und phänomenologischen Philosophie.* First Book. 2 vols. *Husserliana* III, 1 and III, 2. Edited by Karl Schuhmann. The Hague: Martinus Nijhoff, 1976.

*Ideen zu einer reinen Phänomenologie und phänomenologischen Philosophie.* Second book. *Husserliana* IV. Edited by Marly Biemel. The Hague: Martinus Nijhoff, 1952.

*Ideen zu einer reinen Phänomenologie und phänomenologischen Philosophie.* Third book. *Husserliana* V. Edited by Marly Biemel. The Hague: Martinus Nijhoff, 1971.

*Idées directrices pour une phénoménologie.* Translated by Paul Ricoeur. Paris: Gallimard, 1950.

*Die Krisis der europäischen Wissenschaften und die transzendentale Phänomenologie. Husserliana* VI. Edited by Walter Biemel. The Hague: Martinus Nijhoff, 1962.

*Logical Investigations.* Translated by J.N. Findlay. 2 vols. New York: Humanities Press, 1970.

*Logische Untersuchungen.* 2 vols. Tübingen: Max Niemeyer, 1968.

"Persönliche Aufzeichnungen." Edited by Walter Biemel. *Philosophy and Phenomenological Research* 16 (1956): 293-302.

*Phänomenologische Psychologie. Husserliana* IX. Edited by Walter Biemel. The Hague: Martinus Nijhoff, 1962.

*Phantasie, Bildbewusstsein, Erinnerung: Zur Phänomenologie der anschaulichen Vergegenwärtigungen. Husserliana* XXIII. Edited by Eduard Marbach. The Hague: Martinus Nijhoff, 1980.

*Phenomenology and the Crisis of Philosophy.* Translated by Quentin Lauer. New York: Harper & Row, 1965.

*The Phenomenology of Internal Time-Consciousness.* Translated by James S. Churchill. Bloomington: Indiana University Press, 1964.

*Zur Phänomenologie der Intersubjektivität.* 3 vols. *Husserliana* XIII, XIV and XV. Edited by Iso Kern. The Hague: Martinus Nijhoff, 1973.

*Zur Phänomenologie des innern Zeitbewusstseins. Husserliana* X. Edited by Rudolf Boehm. The Hague: Martinus Nijhoff, 1966.

SECONDARY SOURCES

Bachelard, Suzanne. *A Study of Husserl's "Formal and Transcendental*

*Logic.''* Translated by Lester E. Embree. Evanston: Northwestern University Press, 1968.

Boehm, Rudolf. "Immanenz und Transzendenz." In Boehm, *Vom Gesichtspunkt der Phänomenologie,* pp. 141-216. The Hague: Martinus Nijhoff, 1963.

Bossert, Philip. "The Sense of 'Epochē' and 'Reduction' in Husserl's Philosophy." *Journal of the British Society for Phenomenology* 5 (1974): 243-55.

Brough, John B. "The Emergence of an Absolute Consciousness in Husserl's Early Writings on Time-Consciousness." *Man and World* 5 (1972): 298-326.

Cairns, Dorion. *Guide for Translating Husserl.* The Hague: Martinus Nijhoff, 1973.

———. "The Ideality of Verbal Expressions." In *Phenomenology: Continuation and Criticism,* edited by F. Kersten and R. Zaner, pp. 239-50. The Hague: Martinus Nijhoff, 1973.

———. "Perceiving, Remembering, Image-awareness, Feigning Awareness," In *Phenomenology: Continuation and Criticism,* edited by F. Kersten and R. Zaner, pp. 251-62. The Hague: Martinus Nijhoff, 1973.

———. "The Many Senses and Denotations of the Word *Bewusstsein* ('Consciousness') in Edmund Husserl's Writings." In *Life World and Consciousness,* edited by Lester E. Embree, listed below, pp. 19-31.

Carr, David. *Phenomenology and the Problem of History.* Evanston: Northwestern University Press, 1974.

Claesges, Ulrich. *Edmund Husserls Theorie der Raumkonstitution.* The Hague: Martinus Nijhoff, 1964.

Descartes, Rene. *Meditations on first Philosophy.* In *The Philosophical Works of Descartes,* translated by Elizabeth S. Haldane and G.T.R. Ross, vol. 1. Cambridge University Press, 1967.

Edwards, Paul. *The Encyclopedia of Philosophy.* Vol. I. New York: Macmillan, 1967.

Elveton, R.O., ed. *The Phenomenology of Husserl.* Chicago: Quadrangle Books, 1970.

Embree, Lester E., ed. *Life World and Consciousness.* Evanston: Northwestern University Press, 1972.

Fink, Eugen. "The Phenomenological Philosophy of Edmund Husserl and Contemporary Criticism." In Elveton, *The Phenomenology of Husserl,* listed above, pp. 73-147.

———. "Das Problem der Phänomenologie Edmund Husserls." *Revue internationale de Philosophie* 1 (1938-39): 226-270. An English translation of this article appears in McKenna, et. al., *Apriori and World,* listed below.

Gurwitsch, Aron. "Edmund Husserl's Conception of Phenomenological

Psychology." In Gurwitsch, *Phenomenology and the Theory of Science,* listed below, pp. 77-112.

——. *The Field of Consciousness.* Pittsburgh: Duquesne University Press, 1964.

——. "Husserl's Theory of the Internationality of Consciousness in Historical Perspective." In Gurwitsch, *Phenomenology and the Theory of Science,* listed below, pp. 210-40.

——. *Phenomenology and the Theory of Science.* Edited by Lester Embree. Evanston: Northwestern University Press, 1974.

——. "Problems of the Lift-World." In *Phenomenology and Social Reality,* edited by Maurice Natanson, pp. 35-61. The Hague: Martinus Nijhoff, 1970.

——. "Towards a Theory of Intentionality." *Philosophy and Phenomenological Research* 30 (1970): 354-67.

Held, Klaus. *Lebendige Gegenwart.* The Hague: Martinus Nijhoff, 1966.

Kant, Immanuel. *Critique of Pure Reason.* Translated by Norman Kemp Smith. London: Macmillan, 1929.

Kern, Iso. *Husserl und Kant.* The Hague: Martinus Nijhoff, 1964.

Kessler, Suzanne and Mckenna, Wendy. *Gender: An Ethnomethodological Approach.* New York: John Wiley & Sons, 1978.

Kockelmans, Joseph. *A First Introduction to Husserl's Phenomenology.* Pittsburgh: Duquesne University Press, 1967.

——. "Husserl's Transcendental Idealism." In Kockelmans, *Phenomenology: The Philosophy of Edmund Husserl and Its Interpretation,* pp. 183-91. Garden City: Doubleday, 1967.

——. "Phenomenologico-Psychological and Transcendental Reductions in Husserl's 'Crisis'." In *Analecta Husserliana* 2, edited by Anna-Teresa Tymieniecka , pp. 78-79. Dordrecht: D. Reidel, 1972.

Landgrebe, Ludwig. "Seinesregionen und regionale Ontologien in Husserls Phänomenologie." In Landgrebe, *Der Weg der Phänomenologie.* Gutersloh: Gerd Mohn, 1963. An English translation of this essay appears in McKenna, et al., *Apriori and World,* listed below.

Leibniz, Gottfried Wilhelm. *New Essays concerning the Human Understanding.* Translated by Alfred G. Langley. Chicago: Open Court, 1916.

Marbach, Eduard. *Das Problem des Ich in der Phänomenologie Husserls.* The Hague: Martinus Nijhoff, 1974.

Mates, Benson. *Elementary Logic.* New York: Oxford University Press, 1972.

McKenna, William; Harlan, Robert M.; and Winters, Laurance E., eds. *Apriori and World: European Contributions to Husserlian Phenomenology.* The Hague: Martinus Nijhoff, 1981.

Mohanty, Jitendra Nath. *The Concept of Intentionality. St Louis: Warren H. Green, 1972.*

——. *"Consciousness and Life-World." Social Research* 42 (1975): 147-56.

——. "Individual Fact and Essence in Edmund Husserl's Philosophy." *Philosophy and Phenomenological Research* 20 (1959): 222-30.

Paton, H.J. *Kant's Metaphysics of Experience.* 2 vols. London: George Allen & Unwin, 1936.

Poincaré, Henri. *Science and Hypothesis.* New York: Dover Publications, 1952.

Ricoeur, Paul. Husserl: *An Analysis of His Phenomenology.* Translated by Edward G. Ballard and Lester E. Embree. Evanston: Northwestern University Press, 1967.

Schmitt, Richard. "Husserl's Transcendental-Phenomenological Reduction." *Philosophy and Phenomenological Research* 20 (1959-60): 238-45.

Schutz, Alfred. "On Multiple Realities." In Schutz, *Collected Papers,* vol. 1, edited by Maurice Natanson, pp. 207-59. The Hague: Martinus Nijhoff, 1971.

——. "The Problem of Transcendental Intersubjectivity in Husserl." In Schutz, *Collected Papers,* vol. 3, edited by I. Schutz, pp. 51-91. The Hague: Martinus Nijhoff, 1966.

Smith, Norman Kemp. A *Commentary to Kant's "Critique of Pure Reason."* New York: Humanities Press, 1962.

Sokolowski, Robert. *The Formation of Husserl's Concept of Constitution.* The Hague: Martinus Nijhoff, 1964.

——. *Husserlian Meditations.* Evanston: Northwestern University Press, 1974.

Spiegelberg, Herbert. "Epochě' without Reduction: Some Replies to My Critics." *Journal of the British Society for Phenomenology* 5 (1974): 256-61.

——. "Is the Reduction Necessary for Phenomenology." Journal of The British Society for Phenomenology 5 (1973): 3-15.

Von Helmholtz, Hermann. *Popular Scientific Lectures.* New York: Dover Publications, 1962.

# INDEX